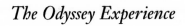

The Odyssey Experience

The Odyssey Experience

*Physical, Social, Psychological,
and Spiritual Journeys*

Neil J. Smelser

UNIVERSITY OF CALIFORNIA PRESS

Berkeley   Los Angeles   London

University of California Press, one of the most distinguished
university presses in the United States, enriches lives around
the world by advancing scholarship in the humanities,
social sciences, and natural sciences. Its activities are
supported by the UC Press Foundation and by philanthropic
contributions from individuals and institutions. For more
information, visit www.ucpress.edu.

University of California Press
Berkeley and Los Angeles, California

University of California Press, Ltd.
London, England

Library of Congress Cataloging-in-Publication Data
Smelser, Neil J.
    The odyssey experience : physical, social, psychological,
and spiritual journeys / Neil J. Smelser.
        p.   cm.
    Includes bibliographical references and index.
    ISBN 978-0-520-25897-6 (cloth : alk. paper)
    1. Insight   2. Introspection   3. Life change events
4. Vision quests   5. Pilgrims and pilgrimages   6. Voyages
and travels   I. Title.
BF449.5.S64   2009
155.9—dc22   2008040509

Manufactured in the United States of America

18   17   16   15   14   13   12   11   10   09
10   9   8   7   6   5   4   3   2   1

For Sharin

CONTENTS

ACKNOWLEDGMENTS

Writing this book has been mainly a solo odyssey, but I have received some help along the way. My research assistant, Michelle Williams, worked through the literature on the Peace Corps, finding and digesting the right sources. Lynne Withey, director of the University of California Press, supported the project from the first minute she heard about it and urged me immediately to sign up with the Press. Naomi Schneider, my sponsoring editor, orchestrated the review and preparation of the manuscript with her customary skill. I would also like to thank staff members of the Library of Congress, who supplied my every need efficiently and cheerfully during the fall of 2006, when I conducted much of the necessary research. Finally, I thank that wide range of unnamed people—students, colleagues, friends, even strangers on planes who asked me what kind of work I was doing—who showed enthusiasm for my ideas and from time to time offered insights that I pilfered, wholesale and shamelessly.

PREFACE

In these pages I present the results of my exploration of an idea
that germinated—vaguely—in my mind several decades ago and
has developed, irregularly, right up to the present time. I have
come to call this idea "the odyssey experience." Its essentials are
laid out in detail in chapter 1 and elaborated in the remainder
of the volume. A first approximate definition for that term is
a finite period of disengagement from the routines of life and
immersion into a simpler, transitory, often collective, and often
intense period of involvement that often culminates in some
kind of regeneration. All the substantive processes included in
this volume—rites of passage, pilgrimages, religious conversion,
travel, leaves of absence, absorption into a social movement, and
some ordeals—are subsumed under this general definition.

The origins of the idea are in my autobiography, but within
that I can distinguish between personal and intellectual origins,
if that distinction has any meaning. On the personal side, I have
experienced, throughout life, many such episodes, though at the

time I simply lived them; I did not begin thinking about them systematically until many years after they transpired. Accounts of many of these personal experiences are found in chapter 2.

With respect to intellectual origins, I do not know exactly when I began to think of the odyssey as a genre. If I stretch my imagination, I can see logical parallels reaching back to the early phases of my career. For example, the model of structural differentiation as a principle of social change employed in my first historical monograph (Smelser 1959) rests on a posited progression from less differentiated to de-differentiated to more differentiated social structures. Similarly, the model of value added that I employed in my theoretical work on collective behavior and social movements (Smelser 1962) relied on a logical progression from dissatisfaction with structure to generalized response and then to restructured behavior. Both schemes bear an imperfect logical parallel with Van Gennep's logic of separation to liminality to reaggregation, as well as with versions of that transition developed by Turner (see chapters 1 and 3). Yet in those early works I made no effort to extend the operative models beyond the range of the empirical subject matter I was attempting to interpret and explain. Only retrospection established the approximate logical parallels.

I suppose the explicit idea of an ideal-typical personal odyssey took shape dimly and not by that name in 1977–79, as I observed and reflected on the experiences of undergraduates in their education-abroad years. I noticed their uncertainties, fears, and anticipations in embarking on the experience, as well as the dynamics of their adaptation and personal growth.

Some years later, while writing a short book on academic committees during my 1992 residential stay in Bellagio (itself one of my most intense odyssey experiences), and before I had really formalized my thinking on odysseys, I gave the following rendition of the life course of an unlikely odyssey candidate, the academic committee:

> The committee is a creature with a temporally finite existence. It is born, it enjoys a life, and it dies. In that respect work on a committee may be said to resemble a kind of ocean voyage or odyssey, in which people are brought or thrown together for an experience, but with the full knowledge that the experience will end. So, in the expressive side of its existence, a committee excites—in a subterranean way, at least—all the feelings of union and dissolution that are associated with the human experience of life and death generally, as well as the accompanying feelings of separation and anxiety, loss and sadness, reminiscence and nostalgia, euphoria and despair. No life experience transpires without these deeper human feelings, and even the most superficial or boring experience in committee life excites them at least minimally. (Smelser 1993, 56)

Not long thereafter, as I began to think and talk about the idea more explicitly, Katherine Trow, a friend who was writing a book on the Experimental College Program at the University of California, Berkeley, in the 1960s, thought the idea of an odyssey captured the experiences of many students involved, and used the idea to interpret those experiences (Trow 1998, 257–62). In the course of her work, she interviewed me on the subject, forcing me to think more systematically about it.

Through the 1990s I continued to think about the odyssey idea. I noticed how inclusive it was of otherwise noncomparable kinds of events and episodes. I made periodic reference to the odyssey experience in my writings (Smelser 1998a; Smelser

2000a). Shortly after my retirement in 2001 as director of the Center for Advanced Studies in the Behavioral Sciences, I decided to write a book on the topic and began reading extensively. This effort was interrupted for several years, however, by my decision to write a general social-science book on terrorism, emanating from my work on the subject in the National Academies after September 11, 2001 (Smelser 2007). In 2005 I returned in earnest to the odyssey project.

Over these years of growing interest, I have spoken with scores of other people—both behavioral and social scientists and friends in general—either on my own initiative or in response to the eternal question "What are you working on now?" When I said what I was up to, the topic of the odyssey never failed to arouse interest. Moreover, almost everyone I have conversed with has, without prodding, recalled some episode of special significance in their own life—an initiation, service in the armed forces, a summer camp in their youth, a trip or a stay abroad, a religious experience. That is, they tell me about their own odysseys and, in that way, tell me I am onto something important. Very few conversations about one's research yield such impressive results.

Berkeley
June 2008

ONE

The Essentials of the Experience

This is a book both theoretical and empirical. It is about experiences that are widespread if not universal. These experiences are rooted in the necessities of the human condition—including movement in space and through time—and are found everywhere in mythology, religion, literary expression, the play of human imagination and experience, and cultural consciousness. They also make more informal appearances in private individual experiences, such as episodes of using drugs and alcohol, pursuing hobbies, watching movies and television, engaging in reverie, daydreaming and night dreaming. They pervade life from its most serious to its most frivolous aspects. I call them odyssey experiences.

In this chapter I introduce these phenomena by steps: first, I give an inkling of their omnipresence; second, I identify the names they go by; third, I remark the perils in naming them; fourth, I generate an ideal type of odyssey's essential characteristics; fifth, I record some intellectual debts; sixth, I identify the range of subject matter to be elucidated in the remainder of the book; and finally, I indicate the methods of inquiry employed.

THE GENERALITY OF
THE ODYSSEY EXPERIENCE

If one follows the lines of almost any mythical, religious, cultural, or literary tradition, one discovers the recurrent theme of the dramatic journey. An ancient myth of the Tohono O'odham Nation of American Indians in southern Arizona is a prototype of the odyssey experience. It survives in pictorial representations of the "man in the maze" (I'itoi), which appears on belt buckles, pendants, and coffee mugs sold to tourists (Figure 1). The explanatory cards that accompany these souvenirs describe the myth:

> The man at the top of the maze depicts birth. By following the white pattern, beginning at the top, the figure goes through the maze encountering many turns and changes, as in life. As the journey continues, one acquires knowledge, strength, and understanding. Nearing the end of the maze, one retreats to a small corner of the pattern before reaching the dark center of death and eternal life. Here one repents, cleanses, and reflects back on all the wisdom gained. Finally, pure and in harmony with the world, death and eternal life are accepted.

In the Melanesian island chains, myths and stories of beneficial journeys, replete with acts of daring, fateful encounters, and extraordinary innovations, circulated long before their incorporation and adaptation in the religious beliefs associated with the cargo cult movements during those islands' colonial period (Lacy 1990).

Figure 1. Man in the Maze on a coffee cup.

The world of Greek mythology is replete with dramatic adventures, the most famous of which is the Odyssey itself, which echoes throughout cultural history—right down to the recent motion picture *O Brother, Where Art Thou?* (2000). The Old and New Testaments of the Bible are full of journeys: Abraham's wanderings (Rosenberg 2006), Moses's flight from Egypt, the journey of the magi, Christ's wanderings, his ascent into heaven, and Paul's journey to Damascus, during which he dramatically converted to Christianity. The journey motif is conspicuous in Islamic religion as well, most notably in Muhammad's journey to heaven (Porter 1974; Waugh 1996).

The same theme appears in the enduring literatures of the world. Li (2002) has extracted relevant themes from Chinese literature (the best known is Wu Ch'êng-ên's *Journey to the West* [Yu 1983]), as has Zamiatin (2002) from Russian literature. Fathered by the Odyssey tradition, epic journeys are central to Dante's *Commedia* (Thompson 1974), Boccaccio's *Decameron*, Geoffrey Chaucer's *Canterbury Tales* (Utley 1974), John Bunyan's *Pilgrim's Progress*, Lewis Carroll's *Alice in Wonderland*, Jonathan Swift's *Gulliver's Travels*, Henry Fielding's *Tom Jones*, Daniel Defoe's *Robinson Crusoe* (Egan 1973), Robert Louis Stevenson's *Treasure Island*, and James Hilton's *Lost Horizon* (Hutt 1996). Shakespeare's dramas exhibit many glorious and tragic journeys, and his last major play, *The Tempest*, presents many variations of that motif as its dominant thread (Mowat 1994). The theme of "life as a journey" has been identified as central in eighteenth-century English literature (Paulson 1976). Woodward (1957) has traced the journey motif in Walt Whitman and Alfred Lord Tennyson. Mark Twain's *Huckleberry Finn*, *The Innocents Abroad*, *Roughing It*, and *Life on the Mississippi* are all journeys and adventures (Gleason 1999), as is Captain Ahab's quest for the white whale in Melville's most noted novel. More contemporary examples include the Joad family's fateful trek to California in John Steinbeck's *The Grapes of Wrath* and Jack Kerouac's *On the Road*. One must mention also that perennial favorite of young and old alike, *The Wizard of Oz*, in which Dorothy and her dog are whisked from flat Kansas farmland to a magical world where wishes come true. The genre of science fiction is mainly about adventures in space. In that genre, close encounters of the fourth kind involve the abduction of earthlings into space (Saliba 1995) (see chapter 5). The idea of a space odyssey is by now a familiar one. Several genres of more popular literature—postcatastrophic novels and flood stories, for example—are based on the theme of the "remade world," which includes violent death, a journey through the underworld or a wasteland, and rebirth (Yoke 1987).

Many historical journeys have been elevated to mythical status. Those that most readily come to mind are the medieval Crusades, Marco Polo's travels, the voyages of Columbus, Magellan, and Sir Francis Drake, the Lewis and Clark expedition, the gold rushes to California, Alaska, and Australia, the countless stories of the American western frontier ("Go west, young man"), the wandering cowboy as a symbol of freedom and movement ("Don't fence me in") (Fishwick 1952), Mao Zedong's long march, and the landing of men on the moon.

Movement as motif has been especially salient in the cultural lore of the United States. It is a nation discovered, settled, and peopled by colonial explorers, adventurers, waves of immigrants, and refugees, a nation that spread westward by those seeking fortunes and better lives on its expanding frontiers. Not long ago James Jasper wrote a book called *Restless Nation: Starting Over in America* (2000), in which he ranged far and wide through American history to document the themes of moving, starting over, regeneration, and rebirth. He found these themes in residential mobility and changing names, as well as historical, literary, and folkloric representations. In a kindred investigation, Kemp (1983) singles out the symbolic cultural significance of "the image of the road" in American culture, with its connotations of movement, freedom (the "open road," the "freeway"), speed, excitement, and escape (themes flogged to death in television commercials for automobiles). The freedom and wanderlust of the boxcar culture trump work and economic security in American hobo lore. Moving by trains and trucks is a conspicuous subgenre of country and western music; the theme is found in popular songs, such as "On the Road Again," "I'm Movin' On," "King of the Road," and "I've Been Everywhere, Man." Uninhibited movement is a constant theme in traditional Western movies, as well as darker contemporary films like *Easy Rider*, *Bonnie and Clyde*, *Kalifornia*, and *Thelma and Louise*.

WORDS THAT CAPTURE (PARTIALLY) THE EXPERIENCE

"Every story ever told," Dan Vogel asserts, "has movement by some character from one place to another" (1974, 185). Aided by his search for related meanings in the "journey" literature, I list the following terms to give a first approximation of the subject matter I have in mind. This book will be about all of them but about no single one exclusively:

Wandering is an apparently aimless set of adventures that have no apparent purpose but to which some larger meaning is subsequently attached, as in Mark Twain's *Adventures of Huckleberry Finn*.

Quest is a more deliberate kind of traveling, with some known or unknown goal on the part of the participant, as in J. D. Salinger's *Catcher in the Rye* or T. S. Eliot's *Love Song of J. Alfred Prufrock*.

Pilgrimage is a subtype of quest, in which the traveler knows the goal that is sought, as in Bunyan's *Pilgrim's Progress*.

Voyage or *trip* connotes a point-to-point movement through space, with a destination that may or may not have deeper meaning for the traveler.

Adventure is an episode with a beginning and an end, in which excitement and danger are salient.

Epic and *saga* refer to a complex set of adventures over longer periods of time.

Odyssey is a particular literary representation of a saga.

Ritual, especially its subset *rites of passage,* is movement in psychological and social space from one role or phase of life to another.

Transport in its psychological sense connotes a journey in psychological space, as in "transport of delight." In the psychedelic drug culture, transport became a *trip,* and the logic has been extended in words such as *ego trip* and *guilt trip.*

Regeneration is also a psychological journey—moving from one psychological status to a higher or better one. The process is often symbolized as death-rebirth.

Conversion is a religious subtype of regeneration.

Healing and *therapy* are also movements from a less desirable physical or mental condition to a better one.

Ordeal is a primarily painful movement, frequently imposed from outside, in which elements of hardship and suffering are salient, and from which some change, often for the good, is anticipated for the participant.

My aim is to work up a synthesis of these terms and thereby generate an ideal type of the core aspects of the variations but, in doing so, neither to claim that any is the one pure representative of the odyssey nor to posit an empirically unvarying universal.

WHY THE EXPERIENCE IS SO DIFFICULT TO NAME

As this plethora of overlapping representations indicates, any one label from the above catalogue (a) is incomplete, (b) carries with it baggage of specific denotations and connotations that cannot be generalized to the others, and for that reason (c) distorts the generic ideal type. Any selection of a single name from the list above is bound to be wrong.

Faced with these problems, one must become either paralyzed or arbitrary. I decided to take the latter route, and will stay with the term *the odyssey experience,* for the reasons that Homer's epic occupies such a conspicuous place in our own cultural tradition and that he represented the process in such a dramatic way. Thalmann's summary of the reasons for the universal appeal of the epic reveals its decisive elements:

> The poem tells a wonderful story. Here we have a wrong desperately in need of righting—chaos on Ithaka and within Odysseus's house, the suitors in possession, the wife's precarious position, the son chafing at his exclusion from his patrimony. The returned Odysseus wreaks satisfyingly gory revenge on the usurpers, and home and society are harmoniously reintegrated. One part of us, at least—our urge for clarity and order—responds deeply to the rhythm of this story. Another, contradictory impulse—the pleasure we take in adventure— opens to us the enjoyment of Odysseus's wanderings before he reaches Ithaka: his encounters with beings outside humanity's normal range, the excitement of the dangers he faces, and the ways he gets through them. Odysseus's adventures have the powerful appeal of folktale and fairy tale: from an early age children continue to be fascinated by them in prose paraphrases. . . . [W]e can see something else the *Odyssey* offers. . . . Throughout all his experiences in worlds known and unknown, Odysseus wants only one thing: to get home. (1992, 10–11)

There is a clear match between the main features of the epic and the generic features of the material I analyze in this volume.

Having thus defended my choice of words, however, I hasten to confess that I am aware that not all the specifics of Homer's *Odyssey* are literally generalizable, and I do not claim that all the diverse experiences I include contain all the ingredients of the story of Odysseus.

AN IDEAL TYPE OF THE ODYSSEY EXPERIENCE

The choice of the term *ideal type* is deliberate, and in employing the term I intend to be as true as possible to the intention of its inventor, Max Weber.

Weber's formulation of the term was his way of coming to terms with two contrary visions of the social sciences at the time he wrote: (1) the vision of science as a search for general laws, with formal economics, general psychology, and positivistic sociology as the main claimants; (2) the historicist vision, which insisted on the unique and nonreproducible context of specific cultural-historical moments. This latter approach, which defied generalization, is identified with the German historicist school.

Weber developed the ideal type as a way to generate descriptions of general (typical) social constellations and social processes. But it is not a simple inductive description of a "given" social reality, as positivists would have it. As the term *ideal* connotes, it involves a deliberate intervention—an act of imagination—on the part of the investigator to extract the essentials of historical situations. Or, in Weber's somewhat cumbersome formal definition, an ideal type is "formed by the one-sided *accentuation* of one or more points of view and by the synthesis of a great many diffuse, discrete, more or less present and occasionally absent *concrete individual* phenomena, which are arranged according to those one-sidedly emphasized viewpoints into a unified *analytical* construct" (Weber 1949, 90, italics in original). Weber typified most of his trademark categories, such as charisma, bureaucracy, rational-legal authority, rational bourgeois capitalism, and ascetic Protestantism, for purposes of comparative historical analysis.

The process of identifying ideal types involves an act of imaginative intervention into empirical reality on the part of the investigator, and therefore entails some arbitrariness. Other investigators might come up with different essential character-istics of a type or an entirely different set of types. Weber never formalized his rules of inference, with the result that any cre-ated type might be vulnerable to the criticism that the investi-gator artificially imposed it. Nevertheless, it is the mode I have employed in attempting to separate the core elements of the odyssey experience from the dizzying panorama of its concrete historical manifestations.

The Generic Social Features of the Odyssey Experience

The following is my selective account of the social features of the odyssey experience.

1. The experience is *finite*, a feature that is captured in the folk utterance "Every journey has an end." Sometimes the beginning and end points are explicit, as in the case of ritual religious experiences, pilgrimages, summer camps, ocean voyages, leaves of absence, initiation ritu-als, ordeals, and indeed, the journey from birth to death. Even in these explicit cases, the beginning and end are

often marked by defining events, not precise temporal moments. Other passages are more open-ended. Death has been described as an "unscheduled status passage" (Glaser and Strauss 1965), whose exact moment is not generally known but which is unequivocal once it happens. Psychotherapy, which I also treat as an odyssey experience, has a definite beginning but an indefinite end point; however, even in those heralded cases of psychoanalysis that last for twenty years or longer, there is some expectation of termination before death. Similarly, if we regard the intense experiences in the enthusiastic phases of social movements, onset and termination are not easily identified, but the general notion is that these experiences do not go on forever. Finiteness is one of the principles that endow the odyssey experience with uniqueness and specialness. It is demarcated "time away" from the routine and repetitive, or, in Tambiah's words, "an awareness that they [collective ceremonies] are different from 'ordinary,' everyday events" (1985, 126).

2. The experience involves a *social destructuring* of routine social roles, status, obligations, and rounds of activity that constitute the normal ebb and flow of life. This process goes by many names in accounts of odyssey experiences—separation, removal, liberation, freedom, disaggregation, stripping, and unfreezing. Sometimes destructuring is built into the social definition of the odyssey episode; for example, the normal institutional understanding of the sabbatical leave in the academic world is that the recipient is "relieved" of the normal duties of teaching, administration, and service activities at his or her home university,

with the corresponding expectation that he or she will thus disengage if the leave-taking experience is to be a successful one. More generally, one characteristic of leisure, which affords the occasion for many odyssey experiences, is that the person is removed from the routines of work, and perhaps community obligation, and is free to choose what he or she wants to do (Dumazedier 1974; Toner 1995; Tribe 2005). Turner (1974) goes so far as to define the consequences of destructuring as "antistructure," and therefore potentially radical. I do not regard this as a necessary ingredient, however, and will criticize that formulation later. Closely connected with the episodic character of the odyssey experience—as connoted by its finite essence—is the notion that after the episode is over, there will be a restructuring, or reincorporation into a more routine existence. This may be a simple return, but in many cases it is a qualitatively new kind of reincorporation, on the understanding that the experience will have created a regenerated person who rejoins routine life on new and altered terms. The latter is a feature of regeneration through pilgrimage and salvation through conversion, whereby the individual establishes a new set of relations with both the spiritual world and a new social milieu of souls who have undergone like experiences. Even in "milder" odyssey experiences, such as trips abroad or hiking vacations, it is commonly understood that the participant is renewed or refreshed in some way and returns to routine life the better for it.

3. Between destructuring and restructuring lies an intermediate phase, the core of the odyssey experience: the

journey, passage, or transformation itself. Van Gennep and others give the term *liminality* to this phase. It can be a solo experience, when the scholar on leave hides himself or herself in a library and deliberately shuns association with colleagues and students. This withdrawal is a special kind of nonstructure. When the experience is collective, the group is also unstructured with respect to previous involvements and subsequent reinvolvements with routine, but it reveals distinctive characteristics. There is a certain *homogenization* of social relationships, as contrasted with the multiply differentiated ones that people experience in the ordered worlds of specialization and status. This manifests itself, for example, in discarding or ignoring past differences on cruises, vacations, and informal ritual ceremonies (Colson 1977; Foster 1986; Lett 1983). A concomitant is *leveling*, the minimization of status differences among participants and a corresponding stress on their *commonality*, which sets them off from the profane, mundane, or routine world. In some cases the structure involves a leader and followers, all presumably equal in subordination to the leader, but this, too, is a relatively simplified structure. A consequence of these simplified structural relations is typically to create an atmosphere of *solidarity* and *mutual loyalty* among participants, a collective sense that the experience is *encompassing* and *personally involving*, a sense of *exclusiveness*, or being set off from those not privileged to participate, and often a sense of *group superiority* or even *hostility* to outsiders. Turner calls this complex of characteristics *communitas*, though he recognizes that not all groups are pure types and identifies the subtypes of spontaneous, ideological, and normative *communitas* (Turner 1979). Many characteristics of *communitas* are also those of total institutions (Goffman 1962), but the parallels are only approximate, and involvement in many odyssey experiences is voluntary, not coerced.

4. A less obvious but pervasive element of odyssey experiences is a negative one: such experiences are typically fraught with *uncertainty, danger, threat,* or *loss of security*. (It is worth noting that *travel* derives from *travail*, denoting the pain of childbirth [Mitford 1992, 3].) Danger is a constant in the vicissitudes of Odysseus's return to Ithaka, as Poseidon threatens to destroy him or thwart his plans, and Athena in turn thwarts Poseidon. But the issue is a more general one. The prospect of disengaging or destructuring is unsettling, because it involves leaving the routine and known and venturing into the uncertain. In some cases the dangers are physical ones. These are highlighted in many of the fictional adventure odysseys mentioned above and were real aspects of the medieval Crusades and earlier religious pilgrimages, in which pilgrims often fell prey to predators and thieves. Later we will also encounter a range of initiations and ordeals in which threats, physical abuse, and psychological harm are deliberately designed as part of the experience itself, which would be deemed incomplete without them.

5. One result of the combined characteristics of destructuring, liminality, and exposure to uncertainty and threat is that in many odyssey experiences it is thought that the

participants *leave this world* in some way and enter another. In many religious odysseys, participants typically leave the profane and make contact with the sacred. In weaker versions, the sense that participants are involved in the nonroutine or unusual makes for a similar feeling of remove or even transport, and this imparts another typical element—the *specialness* of the odyssey experience.

It is important to remind ourselves that what is being constructed is indeed a Weberian experiment in ideal-type analysis, and that many differences in the content and weighting of any given odyssey experience have been omitted. The search is for the essentials. Within these commonalities, evidence of historically diverse combinations will emerge as specific varieties of the odyssey experience are identified and explored.

The Generic Psychological Features of the Odyssey Experience

Before enumerating psychological features, I should make explicit the relations between the psychological and social levels. What follows is not ventured as a set of invariant, "natural" psychological universals. These psychological characteristics are advanced with the full understanding that all are mediated by social influences. This principle even applies to many physiological processes, such as rate of breathing and secretion of adrenaline, which vary according to the level of stress generated in social situations. With respect to emotional experiences, studies in the sociology of emotion (e.g., Hochschild 1979) have demonstrated that normative and other social influences affect the occasions on which emotions are supposed to be experienced (or not experienced), are actually experienced, or are to be revealed or not revealed to others. This principle applies to the psychological processes of the odyssey experience, with the full acknowledgment that they are socially mediated, particularly when the odyssey in which they are embedded is institutionalized (for example, in religious rituals and even "spontaneous" conversion experiences).

The following are the corresponding psychological processes associated with the odyssey experience:

1. Intimately associated with and occasioned by the process of social destructuring is a certain emotional *ambivalence* on the part of the participants. On the one hand, the odyssey creates a feeling of positive anticipation—as an adventure, a confirming ordeal, or a road to regeneration—and thus instills feelings of anticipation, hope, and perhaps euphoria. And, as indicated, along with the process of liberation from routine obligations comes a sense of unburdening and relief. At the same time, the necessary uncertainty associated with destructuring and freedom generates affects of apprehension and anxiety, for the fundamental reason that one is now called upon to find new psychological moorings in a more ambiguous environment. When initiation or ordeal is a conspicuous part of the experience, the feelings of dread are more explicit and salient.

2. When the odyssey experience involves a challenge to perform, another variation of the ambivalence appears. A single example will suffice. During my graduate years at Harvard, I was admitted to the Society of Fellows to

complete my doctoral dissertation. Seven others were appointed at the same time. This was a long odyssey, with three years of complete freedom to do one's research (other aspects of this experience are discussed in chapter 2). The society was an extremely prestigious group, with appointment to it regarded as a greater honor than receiving a junior faculty appointment at Harvard. (In its early years, the society restrained recipients from pursuing a Ph.D., on the theory that anybody admitted would surely land a faculty position at Harvard or anywhere else.) These circumstances generated a set of psychological consequences for the appointees that were so salient that we gave them a name—the "J.F. [junior fellow] crisis," typically experienced in the first year of the fellowship. This crisis resulted from living with extraordinarily high expectations for brilliant and original performance combined with a corresponding dread that one could not possibly live up to them. The typical consequences were anxiety, self-doubt, and procrastination, if not paralysis, in work. For most junior fellows, these reactions were temporary, but for some they persisted throughout the three years and adversely affected their productivity and possibly their future careers.

The processes manifested in such extreme form in the Society of Fellows stem from the sense in many odyssey experiences that the participants are some sort of *elect* who are privileged to participate and are privy to special experiences of new social membership, growth, transformation, or regeneration. This imparts a sense of being special, even "chosen." A common psychological consequence of this sense of privilege is a conscious or unconscious feeling of guilt about being special in relation to others not so chosen. Guilt, moreover, is an insistent and incessant affect and must be dealt with continuously.

3. The psychological concomitants of the intense solidarity in many odyssey experiences are feelings of *unique and special membership*, a sense of bonding and a belief that these relationships are not repeatable in routine life. These are the feelings of having been veterans of the same battle, alumni of the same institution, or survivors of a common adventure or calamity. Affects of pride, euphoria, and nostalgia often accompany the memories of participation in an odyssey experience.

4. The culmination—or better, the expected culmination—of psychological elements is a feeling of *personal betterment, growth, regeneration, or even rebirth*. This is the insistence on the happy ending of odyssey experiences. Kierkegaard captures the psychological process in the observation, "To venture causes anxiety, but not to venture is to lose one's self" (quoted in Stein 1988, 13). All the ingredients—uncertainty, fear, danger, and self-realization—are in that aphorism.

One remarkable feature of the psychological processes associated with the odyssey is that they constitute a template on which *all* human affects, both negative (anxiety, dread, hostility, regret) and positive (relief, hope, anticipation, elation), can play themselves out. In that respect, odyssey experiences resemble dramatic tales and performances in general, and the fact that they offer this affective combination is one of the keys to understanding their general appeal and durability. I develop this observation further in chapter 7.

Such are the prototypical social and psychological elements of the odyssey experience. To identify these elements, however, is not to claim that all odyssey experiences are identical. I note the following sources of variation:

- Participants experience variations in individual readiness or susceptibility to participating. These are subordinated when participation is mandatory (in some rites of passage, for example), but when voluntary, some individuals choose not to participate, others maintain a social and psychological distance from the process, and still others throw themselves into it.

- Closely related are variations in the ideal completion of the experience—the "success rate," if you will. When I was director of the University of California's Education Abroad Program for the United Kingdom and Ireland in 1977–79 (see chapters 2 and 4 for a general account), I observed (and on later reflection, concluded) that the experience of the participating students was that most of them underwent an odyssey experience of sorts, sharing feelings of specialness, a sense of accomplishment, new bonds and a solidarity with fellow participants and British students alike, a change in and consolidation of life plans, a major or minor alteration in their personal identity, and personal regeneration. Of course these experiences took on different forms and tones according to students' individual differences and circumstances. But at the same time, a minority—I estimated 10 percent—of the students were overwhelmed by the new experience, remained lonely and sometimes depressed, and experienced a desire to withdraw from the program. The experience simply did not "take" on them. This contingency should caution against psychological overgeneralization.

- One pervasive feature of odyssey experiences is the fact that they become the object of endless metaphoric play, in which participants compare them with other experiences, borrowing, enriching, and elaborating. Metaphors are the lifeblood of many cultural products, including folktales, adages, homilies, riddles, jokes, tricks, and puns (Fischer 1963; Beck 1978). As we will see, one master metaphor is that of death and rebirth, even for experiences that do not, on their face, seem to suggest that imagery. Turner (1977) vividly illustrates the pervasiveness of this metaphor in pilgrimage experiences. Lakoff and Johnson (1980) garner more than a dozen ways in which the experience of love is likened to a journey ("Look how far we've come," "We're at a crossroads," "We can't turn back now," "This relationship is a dead-end street," and others). Kerr and Mulder (1983) report on a variety of symbolic meanings associated with conversion to Christianity, to say nothing of other religions. This universality of metaphoric elaboration is the source of the richness and diversity of content of odyssey experiences. Yet it would be a mistake to argue that any experience *is* what the metaphor claims it to be, or that any experience is reducible to any one of its metaphorical expressions. One challenge in the analysis of generic experiences is simultaneously to make use of and to cut through their

metaphoric elaborations and thereby establish commonality of themes.

SOME THEORETICAL DEBTS

Though the exact scope of interest of this volume has not, to my
knowledge, been addressed in any earlier inquiry, a number of
seminal theoretical works—and traditions of research that have
followed them—have influenced my thinking. Among these are:

1. Émile Durkheim's sociology of religion, and within that
   his theory of ritual, especially his insightful discussion of the "collective effervescence" that accompanies
   rituals and other religious ceremonies (Durkheim 1954
   [1913]). More remotely, his discussion of the characteristics of simple societies governed by principles of
   mechanical solidarity (Durkheim (1969 [1891]) and
   his account of group solidarity in times of wartime
   and other crises (Durkheim 1951 [1895]) yield insights
   into the social homogeneity that characterizes groups
   involved in Odyssey experiences.

2. Akin to but not precisely in the Durkheimian tradition,
   the important work of Arnold van Gennep (1960 [1909]),
   the Belgian anthropologist who invented the term *rites of
   passage* and offered a systematic account that has persisted
   almost as an orthodoxy in the study of rituals and related
   phenomena. Regarding the regenerative process as a "law
   of life and of the universe" (Kimball 1960), van Gennep
   focused on the rites of pregnancy and childbirth, initiation, marriage, and funerals among "semi-civilized"
   peoples. He also established the well-known "stages" of

separation from routine life (preliminal), a transitional stage involving contact with the sacred (liminal), and reincorporation into a new world (postliminal). Van Gennep's account has influenced most anthropological and psychological accounts since, and was given imaginative extension to pilgrimages, rituals in general, and dramatic performances by Turner (1982).

3. The comparative anthropological research on ritual by Mircea Eliade (1994 [1958]), who established the pervasiveness of the imagery of death and rebirth in rituals.

4. The writings of Max Weber on the psychology of charisma and the nature of charismatic groups (1968).

5. Psychoanalytic and psychoanalytically informed writings. Freud's conception of regression, at both the psychological and group levels (Freud 1955 [1921]), is of special interest, not so much in its literal genetic rendition as a return to earlier childhood or an earlier stage of civilization, as in its reference to *structural changes* in personality and groups during intense collective processes. Philip Slater carried the analysis of regression at the social level to further lengths (1963), as did Thomas Cottle in his study of experimental small groups (1976). Freud's discussion of the "oceanic" feeling—"a feeling of an indissoluble bond, of being one with the external world as a whole" (1961 [1930], 65)—is relevant to understanding the mental states that appear in many situations of religious transport, including conversion. The psychology of elation (Lewin 1961) is also relevant. Finally, the literature on psychoanalytic and other forms of psychotherapy provide yet another variant of the odyssey experience.

CONTENT AND ORGANIZATION OF THE
CHAPTERS THAT FOLLOW

To convey a vivid sense of the odyssey experience to readers—
and perhaps to evoke their own personal memories—I devote
chapter 2 to a number of autobiographical experiences, each of
which shares many ingredients of the odyssey. I try to capture
in retrospect the psychological essentials of those experiences.
Chapter 3 is more formal, focusing on religious experiences and
their derivatives. This chapter begins at the beginning, I suppose, by looking at religiously based rites of passage in simple
societies, especially those for adolescent males, which anthropologists have discovered, detailed, and worried about for several hundred years. Without invoking any evolutionary theory,
I consider these rites to be the earliest prototypes of the odyssey experience. Then I turn to the manifestations of these rites
in more recent and more familiar religions, noting especially
birth, baptism, adolescent passages, marriage, and death. Both
commonalities and variations in emphasis are noted. Next I
turn to the pilgrimage, including the religious crusade, a significant ingredient of many religious traditions. The contribution of Turner is noted, as is his attempt to generalize the
essentials of the process. Special reference is given to the controversial topic of conversion to the "new religions" in the last
half of the twentieth century. I say a few things about the routinization and commercialization of the pilgrimage in modern
times, and this leads into an analysis of tourism. Next comes a
discussion of religious conversion (and a related phenomenon,
ritual possession), a complex and controversial topic that, however, merits inclusion under the odyssey heading. The chapter
concludes with two examples that are not religious at all—the

recent Peace Corps experience and the Freedom Summer of 1964—but which, in their moral essentials, resemble kindred religious experiences.

Chapter 4 deals with a number of secularized and commercialized phenomena that resemble the foregoing religious examples both socially and psychologically. I focus first on modern travel and tourism, which are well analyzed in the anthropological literature, tracing their historical development, their social and psychological significance, their massification, and their diversity, including the ocean voyage, the "weekend," and the search for the foreign and esoteric. The topic of tourism blends with leisure in general. In connection with tourism, I mention the modern honeymoon (an offshoot of the marital rite of passage), as well as the related rituals of the bridal and bachelor parties. Next I turn to four types of experience associated with the academic world—the undergraduate years, the education-abroad experience for college students, the sabbatical leave for faculty, and—a recent invention—centers for advanced study for faculty. To conclude the chapter, I turn to modern psychotherapy and related processes, including psychoanalysis, group therapy, encounter groups, and some religious cults that include psychotherapeutic processes as part of their repertoire.

Chapter 5 treats a miscellaneous collection of invented and improvised odyssey experiences, which inevitably overlap with those discussed in the foregoing chapters. Many of these have been regarded in the social-science literature as modern, contrived experiences meant to reactivate the human impulses expressed in dead or dying "genuine" historical rituals. Among them are more or less spontaneous but deliberate efforts to deal with the adolescent transition inside and outside schools;

modern ceremonies dealing with birth and death; and a spontaneous, collective, and quasi-religious movement, the flying saucer or UFO phenomenon. Some of these invented collective experiences pass from the scene, others move toward routinization and institutionalization.

Chapter 6 deals with coercive and quasi-coercive odyssey experiences. I include these with some hesitation because the line between voluntary and coercive is difficult to draw and because the social and psychological dynamics of coercive experiences are different from voluntary ones in some ways. I will look into the dynamics of several phenomena: military socialization (basic training, boot camps) and a number of cousins, such as resocialization in prisons, initiations into secret societies, fraternities, and sororities, and some aspects of training for professional roles. Finally, I turn to a topic that was very public and very controversial during the cold war: coercive thought control. This included "brainwashing," especially in the Soviet Union and China and of prisoners in the Korean War. The topic will include revisiting the brainwashing/deprogramming controversy as it applied to the "new" religious and other movements of the 1960s. As a sidebar to brainwashing, I also note the relevance of stimulus deprivation experiments and some of their offshoots.

Chapter 7 is a brief one, attempting to specify as carefully as possible the existential features of the human condition that account for the generality and even universality, the profundity, and the recurrence of odyssey experiences. In this connection I pinpoint existential features like cognitive and emotional exigencies, the cycle of life and death, growth and maturation, and space and time. All of these simultaneously constitute the human exigencies that odyssey experiences address and that contribute to their ultimate potency.

THE CHARACTER OF THIS WORK AS A SOCIAL-SCIENCE ENTERPRISE

Most work in the social sciences proceeds in a manner more or less consistent with a "normal science" model: a relationship or causal process is hypothesized within or consistent with some conceptual framework; relevant data are gathered and arrayed; and various "tests" or "demonstrations" of the relationship are attempted to establish its reliability, validity, viability, and causality. Issues of design and measurement are conspicuous and must be assessed as part of establishing the value of a particular piece of research.

The methods of inquiry in this book do not fit this model. This is an exploratory and theoretical work. I think of it more as an exercise in discovering a general pattern in human life (or better, the consolidation of many other discoveries in historical and comparative inquiry). As such it is consistent with another object of social-scientific inquiry, namely the search for, identification of, and articulation of general processes in social life. One is obliged to observe theoretical and methodological canons in locating and describing these patterns and avoid wildness in interpreting them. But because of the nature of the general enterprise—the effort to locate, identify, and describe commonalities—a certain methodological license is, I think, legitimate. One goes wherever one is led by the subject matter and by one's imagination.

In connection with this general characterization, I should indicate my sources of "data" for the exercise that unfolds in subsequent chapters.

First, I have tracked and voraciously read scholarly literature in history, anthropology, sociology, psychology, and folklore to locate the best accounts of the ranges of experience that I have identified as belonging to the odyssey genre.

Second, I have consulted my own experience as a director but also as an observing "anthropologist" in situations in which the odyssey experience is salient. In particular I have drawn on my experience as director of the above-mentioned Education Abroad Program (1977–79) and as director of the Center for Advanced Study in the Behavioral Sciences at Stanford (1994–2001).

Third, I have had the occasion in my eventful life to be a personal participant in a multiplicity of odyssey experiences, though I did not identify any of them as such in advance or at the time. I give an account of these biographical involvements in chapter 2 and mention a few others elsewhere in the volume.

I am the first to notice that none of the three sources is, by any stretch of reasoning, "representative" of any universe of experiences in the world. I hope this fact is balanced by whatever originality might be involved in casting the analytic net so widely and in bringing together phenomena not before gathered or compared under a common rubric.

TWO

Autobiographical Roots

Some Personal Odysseys

In the preface I indicated that the origins of this book are both autobiographical and scholarly. I do not know how to sort out these two origins, because they unfolded irregularly and built on one another. In this chapter I give an account of some of my life experiences. I have to say, however—and will elaborate later—that I did not, at the time they transpired, frame them in any way as odysseys or any other kind of generic experience, and did not regard them as directly comparable. My memories of these experiences are, I think, accurately and faithfully reproduced here, but their full significance was not available to me at the time. Reporting those memories now has involved reproducing them in the context of new ways of thinking and remembering. I suppose this is a sort of self-analysis. It is also a report, however, of how unique and idiosyncratic experiences are constantly re-experienced and re-remembered, not because they actually change but because their interpretative context changes. I add, finally, that these autobiographical events did

not directly determine the theory of odyssey experiences enunciated in this book, but they informed it and enriched my capacity to incorporate and interpret otherwise diverse phenomena.

EARLY YEARS

I was born on my maternal grandparents' farm outside Kahoka,
a small town in the northeast corner of Missouri, not far from
the Mississippi River. My parents were born and reared on
farms, but both went to college and became teachers. My date of
birth was July 22, 1930. (I once secured a copy of the front page
of the *New York Times* for that date and discovered that nothing much else of interest happened on it.) I was transported at
the age of six weeks to Phoenix, Arizona, where my father had
taken a job at Phoenix Junior College. He remained there during the rest of his career, initially teaching speech and drama
and later philosophy. My mother did substitute teaching during my childhood, taking up full-time teaching of Latin and
English at the high-school level only after her sons were older.
I lived in Phoenix and went to its public schools until I left for
college at age eighteen.

My childhood was by most standards devoid of odyssey experiences. As far as I can remember, I did not spend one night
out of the company of my parents until I was in high school.
The idea of any kind of summer camp was foreign to the family
culture. The exceptions to this homebound rule were, however,
significant. On alternate summers through the 1930s, and once
at the end of World War II, my family—my mother and father
and my two brothers (Bill, six years older, and Philip, three
and a half years younger)—piled into the car and drove back

to the Midwest on U.S. Highway 66 to pay brief visits to my maternal grandparents and other relatives in Kahoka and to my paternal grandparents and uncle in Vandalia and Farber, west of St. Louis. Also in those summers, my family would settle in some university community (Baton Rouge, Madison, Iowa City, Columbia, or Minneapolis), where my parents attended summer school. The drive from Phoenix to the Midwest was long and often boring, but my brothers and I were inventive in devising games and competitions to pass the time, including our favorite—shooting pebbles from homemade slingshots at highway signs and billboards, trying to set records for consecutive hits. The trips were times of great closeness for the family, and the destination of the Kahoka farm with its livestock, machinery, and open land was a true journey's end. I inherited a love of the open, movement, and the freedom of the road from these trips.

When I was a junior in high school, I traveled to California with the Phoenix Union High School debate team and a teacher chaperone. We debated (and lost) in Bakersfield and Compton, and spent a long weekend in Los Angeles. This seems a pale episode to qualify as any kind of odyssey, but I was short on them, and going to see *Rigoletto* featuring Lily Pons at the Los Angeles Opera was a grand experience for a parochial youth who had introduced himself to opera and other classical music through radio and 78-rpm records with the encouragement of his mother.

GOING TO HARVARD

In chapter 3 I will say something about the college years as an imperfect type of odyssey experience—a genuine one, to be sure, but tempered by its length, its complexity, and its own structure. My own college experience, however, was a special one. I applied to Harvard mainly because my older brother had been stationed there for training during World War II and had told me about the place. When I was admitted and granted a National Scholarship, I couldn't believe it. My high school advisors were happy for me but warned me that I was going to be swimming in a big pond and could expect to be a "B" student at best. I was a yokel venturing three thousand miles from home, disengaging from my parents, my friends, and the Phoenix life remote from Harvard. Two little incidents remind me of this. When I first arrived in Boston's South Station I made my way to the subway stop to proceed to Harvard Square. When the train came and the doors opened, I just stood there with my bags, not knowing what to do, until the train's doors shut and it moved on. A little later on, at my first lobster meal ever in a Boston restaurant, I drank the contents of the finger bowl, wondering about the kinds of cups they used in New England.

Yet after a period of confusion and loneliness, I adapted, performing at the top level academically, making friends, and throwing myself fully into the wonderful cosmopolitanism of Harvard's world, while, in deference to my family's egalitarian values, always remaining aloof from that university's elitist culture. What made Harvard so important was that it completely reshaped me, an unsophisticated local, into a young man prepared and bound for a career and level of life accomplishment of which I could never have dreamed as an isolated Phoenix boy. My college years were a memorable movement upward, and I have never forgotten my obligation to Harvard for that journey.

THE SALZBURG SEMINAR IN
AMERICAN STUDIES

In 1946 three Harvard undergraduates, immersed in the idealism that seems destined to follow wartime grimness, ventured on an improbable enterprise of forming an American institution in Europe dedicated to fostering international understanding through education and, in particular, to teaching American culture and society to the best of Europe's cadres of scholars emerging in the postwar reconstruction period.

These young men named their fledgling institution the Salzburg Seminar in American Studies and found a place for it in Schloss Leopoldskron, a romantic eighteenth-century castle just outside Salzburg, with a rich history, both cultural (the home of Max Reinhardt of Salzburg Festival fame) and military (the home of Nazi Gauleiter officials during World War II). They scraped together funds from sympathetic contributors on American's East Coast and held the first seminar in the summer of 1947. It was an enormous success, drawing on American faculty to teach young West European scholars as participants. In its early years the faculty included such notables as F.O. Matthessen, Margaret Mead, Henry Steele Commager, Talcott Parsons, Daniel Bell, and Alfred Kazin. The seminar, now sixty years old, still thrives, though its instructional program is more directed and practical than at the beginning.

The seminar's summer format in the early years included six to eight faculty, fifty or sixty European scholars, and four graduate students and four undergraduates from Harvard. The courses offered were multidisciplinary, mainly in American history, society, and literature. They were conducted in one or another of the sumptuous baroque rooms of the castle. All participants resided in the Schloss, the majority sleeping on cots in a huge room on the top floor. Meals were taken collectively in a dining hall. So, while participants could frequent a *gasthaus* around the lake or walk into Salzburg, the six-week summer program was mainly an isolated and intense experience.

As a junior at Harvard in 1951, I applied for one of the four undergraduate slots in that summer's session. I did so partly at the suggestion of a couple of Harvard faculty members, but to a young man who had only dreamed about going to Europe, it seemed like a romantic adventure. I was selected after several interviews, and as part of my socialization for the coming experience, I went to New York—as a clean-cut young Harvard student, I suppose—and raised some money for the needy seminar. I was excited about the coming experience but could only imagine what it would be like.

I went to London early in the summer, five weeks before the seminar began, bought a bicycle, and took off on my own. I cycled to Oxford, knowing I wanted to apply for a Rhodes scholarship there the following year. Then I took off for Newhaven and a channel crossing to Dieppe, and cycled across France to Strasbourg, stopping for several days in Paris. I was completely on my own for that month, conversing only with occasional farmers and people in country inns and bistros. I slept in open fields and under bridges (and in a new, not-yet-inhabited housing project in Saint Denis outside Paris). If the experience at Salzburg was to be an odyssey within a larger odyssey (my Harvard undergraduate years), then that bicycle trip was a solo subodyssey within that. I remember that month of cycling with the unalloyed nostalgia that one feels after a glorious experience surely never to be repeated.

The seminar itself lasted from early July to mid-August 1951. I was apprehensive at the beginning. Though I had completed three successful years at Harvard, I was among the youngest participants (I turned twenty-one that summer) and still regarded myself as a young man with only limited experience and horizons. I felt sure I would be completely overwhelmed by the Europeans, whom I expected to be far more sophisticated intellectually and culturally. One of the things that gave those weeks their magic was my discovery that I could more than hold my own in intellectual, political, and cultural discourse. I felt myself growing in confidence where I had expected to be deflated.

More generally, I became caught up on a daily basis in the excitement of that intellectual voyage, made up of peaceful, civilized people from nations that had been destroying one another only a few years earlier. I found myself experiencing confidence, happiness, and personal closeness, sentiments foreign to my earlier experience and inconsistent with my self-image of sensibility, self-sufficiency, and cool passions. This excitement was not mine alone. New but fast relationships were cemented, as on a voyage, and the good-bye celebration at the end provoked tears and vows to reunite in the future. I emerged from that summer feeling—realistically or unrealistically, I do not know—like a new, better, and more mature person. This was my first full and my most important odyssey, a prolegomena for many other large and small ones to follow. What still fascinates me most is that I did not understand or articulate the experience, only felt it. But that is to the good, I suppose. It seems a general principle that self-conscious reflection and critical analysis are enemies of the romantic, consuming journey.

In subsequent years I visited Schloss Leopoldskron every time I was near Salzburg, the last time in 2004 on a side trip from Vienna, where I was teaching. The most notable visit was in 1974, when I was abroad for the year on sabbatical with my family. I was especially proud to show the Schloss to my five-year-old son and three-year-old daughter. When we were standing before the edifice, I told them that this was "Daddy's castle," and so it has been called in the family ever since. This was a little narcissistic jest on my part, but somehow the naming symbolized the special affection I have for the place that nourished such a memorable journey.

GOING TO OXFORD

In the fall of 1951—my senior year at Harvard—I applied for a Rhodes scholarship, which grants those who attain it two (sometimes three) years of study at Oxford University. Most who receive the scholarship make the experience into a second undergraduate experience, since the undergraduate program, with its legendary tutorial system, is regarded as the best that Oxford has to offer. In a way I was psychologically primed for this to be an odyssey. In the seventh or eighth grade I had come across the Rhodes scholarship and Oxford in some reference work. In the early stages of developing a consuming academic ambition, I promised myself I was going to win one of those and go to England. At the time I even announced this to my mother, who, I believe, was skeptical but supportive (for more background, see Smelser 2000b). The dream never weakened, and it was what motivated me to bicycle there from London in the summer of 1951. This was my romance-in-advance with Oxford.

Applying for the scholarship was itself a kind of mini-odyssey. I had to undergo an interview at Harvard to be "cleared" to apply. I drove nonstop from Boston to Denver with three other applicants and then hopped a Greyhound bus for Phoenix. I had to journey to Tucson for the state interviews, and then to Pasadena for the regional finals. The whole process was fraught with uncertainty, and given my ambition, I was very uneasy from beginning to end.

The arrangements at Oxford were conducive to making the scholarship experience an odyssey. Scholars were required to live in a residential college for at least one year. At that time the Rhodes regulations forbade marriage, further encouraging immersion in the collegiate society. And above all, the experience was defined—and we all defined it—as a "time away" from our major career path, though we all believed that being a Rhodes scholar would help us greatly along that path. It was also a time away for me academically, for I had decided that I wanted to pursue an academic career in sociology and Oxford had no program in sociology. So instead I read philosophy, politics, and economics—all valuable in my subsequent career but also an interlude away from it.

In many respects the Oxford experience "took" on me. I became fully engaged and confident in the academic life and participated successfully as an oarsman on the Magdalen College crew in my first year. I still retain my romance with Oxford and have returned to visit with my family on subsequent European trips. Yet there were three elements that detracted from full involvement in an odyssey experience. The first was the fact that the young woman who was to become my first wife accompanied me to England. We could marry only on pain of forfeiting the scholarship. She lived and worked in London, so I visited London on many weekends and spent the vacations with her. Though this pattern was my choice, it pulled me away from involvement in college life. The second was also personal. I was twenty-two years old when I arrived in Oxford and had already completed my college years. Most of my Oxford colleagues were English eighteen-year-old boys (Magdalen College was all male at that time), and given the slow maturation of English adolescents, my psychological distance from them was great. Most of the time I felt neither common interest nor community with them. Third, and most intangibly, this was my *second* undergraduate experience, which in many subtle ways subtracted from its magic; I had been there before. These personal circumstances diluted my engagement in the collective Oxford collegiate experience.

BEING A JUNIOR FELLOW

The Society of Fellows at Harvard is a remarkable institution, providing an elite group of young scholars with three years of complete freedom to pursue their own research. During my term (1955–58), junior fellows were all male, and during the three years they could work on a doctoral dissertation but could not fulfill other requirements for the doctorate (for example, course work or qualifying examinations) or teach. The annual stipend was generous and the prestige was high. The only formal obligation for the fellows was to attend one elegant dinner with the senior fellows (mainly eminent Harvard faculty) and guests every Monday night and lunches every Tuesday and Friday with the other junior fellows. At that time fellows completed the entire three-year term before taking on a faculty appointment. Since then, women have been admitted to the fellowship, and many junior fellows now leave before the end of their terms to take faculty positions as a result of the increasingly tight job market.

My main faculty sponsor, Talcott Parsons, recommended me to the society during my second year at Oxford. I was interviewed in Queen's College by the philosopher and senior fellow Willard van Orman Quine, a visiting professor at Oxford that year. I was not accepted and was of course disappointed. As an alternative, I enrolled in the graduate program in Social Relations at Harvard in the fall of 1954. During that year I was recommended again, both by Parsons and by Barrington Moore, Jr., and was interviewed by all the senior fellows. This time I made it. My initial failure followed by success proved to be something of a blessing, for I was able to complete all my predissertation requirements in Social Relations during that first year so as to dedicate the entire tenure of the junior fellowship to my dissertation, a sociological interpretation of industrial development and changes in family life in Great Britain during its Industrial Revolution. I completed the dissertation in my third year, and it was published as my first single-authored work (Smelser 1959). I moved directly from the Society of Fellows to an assistant professorship at the University of California, Berkeley, in the fall of 1958.

The years at the Society of Fellows were an odyssey experience in many respects. They had that "time away" quality—in this case from the routines of graduate school in the Department of Social Relations. By the same token, it was a " destructured" and completely free experience. The senior fellows assiduously avoided asking any of their junior charges about what they were working on or how they were progressing (for some of the psychological burdens of that freedom, see chapter 1). There was a communal element as well (the lunches and dinners with the others), and we all believed ourselves to be special in our own ways. And the fellowship had a known beginning and end, the latter symbolized by the ritual presentation of an engraved silver candleholder to each departing junior fellow.

Yet at the same time the junior fellowship fell short of the idealized odyssey experience for several reasons.

- In the nature of the case, three years is a long time to sustain the special feelings associated with a special journey. Odysseys cannot last forever, and the longer they are scheduled to last, the more their essentials fade.

- I arranged an "odyssey within an odyssey" by spending the second year of the fellowship in London and elsewhere in Britain, conducting the massive amount of historical research necessary for my dissertation. My work was mainly in the British Museum Library, and that was a romance in itself, but that year was mainly a solo journey.

- I was the only sociologist among all the junior and senior fellows, and though I made a number of enduring friends, there was a deficit of intellectual camaraderie.

- More generally, I experienced a certain lack of fit with the atmosphere of the Society of Fellows. As I mentioned, I was reared in the American West and my father was an ardent New Deal democrat and something of an agrarian radical. He held a prejudice against all privilege

and vilified the financial institutions and cultural preten-
sions of the East. I picked up enough of that background
to be mildly alienated from Harvard's elitism, and, of
course, the Society of Fellows was the elite of the elite.
In a way it was my fault that I could consider myself
only a half-member of the society, but that is the way it
worked out.

In my three years in the society, it was actually an "odyssey
within an odyssey within an odyssey" that moved me most. During the spring of my second year—spent mainly in London—I
applied for and received a fellowship at a small, remote institution in France at which I spent about six weeks. This was at a villa
in the hills above La Ciotat (a maritime town midway between
Marseilles and Toulon on the Mediterranean coast). The villa
was called Rustique Olivette. The little center was established
by Daniel Guérin, a wealthy, left-leaning French intellectual,
for scholars to come and spend a season of completely free time.
My stay there was timed to coincide with the writing phase of
my dissertation, and I completed most of the first draft in the
benign environment of sun and sea. Daily life, including meals
with several French and other scholars, enhanced it all, and the
feelings of isolation, freedom, self-fulfillment, and community
remain with me.

PSYCHOANALYSIS AS ODYSSEY

There are two reasons why I must make reference to my personal psychoanalysis, which lasted four and a half years, from
early 1963 through late 1967. The first reason is that it is in my

mind the most important journey I have taken. Second and less important, it would be unpardonable not to say something about it in a chapter on personal experiences in a book in which psychotherapy is considered to be, from an analytic point of view, a type of odyssey (see chapter 4). At the same time, it is extremely difficult to include it, both because I regard it as unnecessary and tasteless to reproduce the intimacies of my personal life and because I (as the patient) am probably the least likely to remember the experiences without distortion. Nevertheless, I will reproduce a few relevant threads.

Certainly the idea of a personal psychoanalysis had been in my consciousness for a long time. My older brother earned his doctorate in clinical psychology at the University of California at Berkeley. The dominant worldview of the Harvard Department of Social Relations, in which I was an undergraduate major (1948–52) and a graduate student (1954–58), was predominantly psychoanalytic, and as it turned out, almost all of those who were to become my mentors had undertaken research training in psychoanalysis at the Boston Psychoanalytic Institute. By the time I left Harvard for Berkeley, I assumed, more or less consciously, that one day I would do the same.

The timing of my decision to enter analysis was completely personal. My first marriage had come to a turbulent and miserable end in 1962, and I was consumed with unhappiness and a sense of personal failure. About that time, I decided to undergo treatment as part of the Research Training Candidacy program of the San Francisco Psychoanalytic Institute, which included not only a personal analysis but also a long and rigorous period of intellectual work and the analysis of a requisite number of patients under supervision. I chose this route partly because

I was interested in the intellectual side of psychoanalysis, but also, as I reconstruct it, because I wanted (and deserved) a special experience above and beyond being "just another patient."

My analysis, probably like all others, did not proceed in a recognizably orderly fashion. An explicit incident, dream, memory, problem, or idea would begin each hour of the analysis, and I would move off in unanticipated and unknown directions. Sometimes my analyst would utter only a few words over several sessions. I would forever move back and forth from feeling a sense of discovery or progress to one of backsliding and hopelessness. Certainly the analysis met the test of liminality, because this was my (or better, our) little world into which I retreated while meeting all the "normal" routines and rounds of life outside. That circumstance imparted a sense of both comfort and unreality to the process.

The analysis also met the test of being an ordeal, another trademark of many odysseys. I was afraid to begin it, mainly out of fear of the unknown. I was right to be afraid, moreover, because the process uncovered dozens of loves, hates, ambivalences, fantasies, and hang-ups, to many of which I had been more or less blind and the discovery of which was deeply disturbing. The work of facing up to these psychic demons was always painful, sometimes traumatic. I was also afraid of ending the analysis; when I suggested it and my analyst asked "when?" I panicked.

One element of the analysis was both enlightening and disturbing. No matter where I started with a problem (remembering a dream, reporting an incident that disturbed me or a thought about my analyst), my subsequent associations invariably led me to the same place: a core neurosis, or core neurotic conflicts, if you will. Furthermore, these turned out to be the standard ones found in the textbooks of psychoanalysis and abnormal psychology. This was an important and positive source of insight, to be sure, but at the same time I was repeatedly humbled and enraged by the recurrent and boring discovery of my ordinariness. This was especially painful because I had cultivated a protective image of myself as a complicated, psychically rich, and above all, very special person.

There was, finally, the element of *communitas*. This was mainly the steady companionship of my analyst. Rail and rant against him as I often did, for his silence, his imagined coldness, and his unreasonableness, I always maintained a deep respect for his forbearance, his style, and his intelligence. After my analysis was over, the supervisor of courses at the institute asked if I wanted to take a seminar given by my analyst. (Such an arrangement required both our consent.) I jumped at the chance. I found it to be a very gratifying experience. A community of lesser import also developed with my cohort of trainees, though we almost never traded information about our personal analyses.

I regard my analysis as a successful one. This does not mean that personal problems, sometimes serious, have not resurfaced from time to time. But as a relative matter, the analysis dramatically improved my capacity to experience positively and not to wreck intimate relationships, not to compete destructively with authorities, colleagues, and students, and to bear criticism with greater equanimity. In addition, the psychoanalytic framework has continued to find its way selectively into my academic research (see Smelser 1998b), including this work on odysseys. I suppose all this counts as a sort of regeneration.

Some years after I ended my analysis, a number of researchers at the San Francisco Psychoanalytic Institute asked me to participate in a "follow-up" of my analysis after some time had passed. The procedure was for me to meet for an unspecified number of hours with a senior psychoanalyst (not my own), presumably to reflect on my memories of the analysis and the intervening years.

The dynamics of the six or seven meetings with the follow-up analyst took me completely by surprise. We did not use a couch, but he was as uncommunicative as if free association were expected. He asked no direct questions, in fact no questions at all. And there was no indication of how long the meetings were to go on or where we were going. I was surprised to find that, in this context and after a completed analysis several years before, I experienced a flood of the anxieties, turbulence, even symptoms that I had struggled with during my analysis years earlier. It was deeply troubling, and in a very important way I reentered the analytic situation fully, beyond my intention and control. A second surprise came when, after approximately five meetings, the follow-up analyst said that there would be only two more meetings. From that moment the anguish and the symptoms seemed to salt themselves away again. Great relief set in, and I experienced some of the same euphoria I had felt at the end of my earlier analysis.

In a word, the follow-up turned out to be a recapitulation, in miniature, of the prolonged odyssey of my original analysis. In later interviews with the researchers, I was told that my experience was typical of follow-ups. That knowledge comforted me, but I also felt the familiar irritation at the fact that I was not all that special. Above all, the follow-up confirmed the principle—developed in chapter 5—that psychotherapy, no matter how deep or how "successful," does not "cure" and certainly does not eradicate conflict, but rather involves a reordering of our capacity to cope with the psychic ghosts that haunt us all.

THE IDEAL SABBATICAL LEAVE

In chapter 3 I take up the sabbatical leave as a special but often incomplete odyssey experience. In this account of personal odysseys, I want to mention a special year in Europe. By 1972 I had resided in Berkeley for nearly fifteen years. There were several reasons for this immobility. First, I was in the early stages of my academic career, and I was living on the half-articulated assumption that the best way to make the most of my career nationally and locally was to stick to the hard work of research and teaching on the spot. Second, my first marriage had ended in 1963, and I was constrained to remain in the area as a parent responsible for my son and daughter, who were very young when we separated. A second, happier and permanent marriage began in 1967, and another son and daughter were born in 1968 and 1971. Finally, much of my geographical constancy was enforced by years of psychoanalytic training, which calls for a period of physical immobility if one is to take one's own analysis and that of others responsibly. In all events, after being in residency all these years, I was ready for the leave I had accumulated. I graduated from the San Francisco Institute in the spring of 1973. A Guggenheim fellowship for 1973–74 supplemented my sabbatical salary and permitted a year away.

Though I had not conceived of a grand plan for this sabbatical, it turned out to have been well designed. I knew what

I wanted to accomplish intellectually. I was under contract to prepare a second edition of my earlier book on economic sociology (Smelser 1963; Smelser 1976a), and I set my sights on completing a general book on comparative methods in the social sciences (ultimately Smelser 1976b). I took a small library of important books along for the second project and, to complete the library work for both projects, decided to spend the first months in the libraries of the British Museum and the London School of Economics, followed by several months on the continent, after which we would return to London so that I could finish the remaining research and complete the writing.

The only other commitment I had made was to live for six weeks in the spring in a villa in Moderno on the Lago di Garda. I had arranged to trade our Berkeley house for the country home of Alberto Martinelli, a colleague and friend from Milan. Otherwise we had our choice of where to spend the winter months. We bought a Bedford camper in London and set out in November to find the best place. We camped in the environs of Paris, then headed southward, looking around in Aix-en-Provence and then driving to explore possibilities along the Spanish coast. Spain became the "danger" side of that year's odyssey, because our camper was burglarized twice, and in the second robbery the thieves made off with most of my notes and books on the theoretical part of the comparative methods volume. We fled Spain after those events, and ultimately, in an adaptive frenzy, I asked some Berkeley graduate students to send me notes from lectures I had given and took a one-day trip to London to replace the stolen books. We ended up finding a beautifully located villa named Ma Vie in Cagnes-sur-Mer (a coastal town situated between Cannes and Nice on the Riviera), where we lived for four months. Then we moved on to the Lago di Garda, thence back to London after spending a couple of weeks camping outside Vienna (with that side visit to Salzburg).

Everything fell together that year. I was able to complete the books, and we had the excitement of living in and exploring at leisure areas of Europe we came to love. But what gave the year its collective magic—and made the odyssey—was the family experience. We were a small, intimate troupe moving freely as if in a boat or a spaceship, going and stopping where we wanted for as long as we wanted. The year was given more life—though not always pleasure—because we lived through the OPEC oil crisis of that year, with its fuel shortages, spiraling prices, and economic and political alarm. During the same period, Watergate was tearing apart the country back home. The year became a kind of signature experience for the family, providing stories and memories that stayed with us in future years, and establishing travel and camping as permanent motifs in our family life.

AN ODYSSEY-OBSERVING ODYSSEY:
THE EDUCATION ABROAD DIRECTORSHIP

Anticipating a continuation of the pleasures of living in Europe, in the winter of 1976, I applied for a position as director of the Education Abroad Program for the United Kingdom and Ireland, for a term that would extend from the summer of 1977 through the summer of 1979. I was ready to leave Berkeley again, having spent two tough years as department chair—a job sufficiently alienating to ready one for a break. The directorship meant supervising, each year, the academic work of about 135 University of California undergraduates who were scattered in a dozen universities, and playing the role of dean and kindly uncle to them.

In chapter 4 I look at the odyssey experiences of students on leave from their collegiate years. For us the experience as a family was another prolonged adventure. Our children, then aged eight and six, were enrolled in St. Michael's School in Highgate, where we lived. Those years, punctuated with travel around the British Isles and to the continent during holidays, made an even deeper impact on their development than the earlier sabbatical. I confess that at first I regarded the period mainly as an opportunity to work on my second major monograph on British social history. I did that, but I was also able to bond with students as I visited them on their campuses and as they stopped in London on the way to their own travels. Much of the positive value of odyssey experiences comes from what one does not expect to happen.

From 1994, the year of my retirement from Berkeley, until 2001 I held another position where I supervised odyssey experiences: the directorship of the Center for Advanced Study in the Behavioral Sciences at Stanford, where forty-five to fifty scholars gather for one-year residency fellowships away from their home institutions. The experiences of these fellows were remarkably similar to one another and remarkably reflective of the odyssey experience. I give an account of life at such centers in chapter 4.

AN URBAN ADVENTURE: A YEAR AT THE RUSSELL SAGE FOUNDATION IN NEW YORK

The 1980s were active years for me, but not especially active from the standpoint of original scholarship. I became heavily involved in the governance of the Academic Senate of the University of California, serving a one-year term as chair of the Berkeley Division's Committee on Educational Policy (1980–81), a two-year term as chair of the Berkeley Division (1982–84), and a two-year term as vice-chair and then chair of the system-wide Academic Assembly (1986–88). I also spent two years as director of the Center for Studies in Higher Education on the Berkeley campus (1987–89). In addition, I served as an active member and chair of an eight-year National Research Council committee on Basic Research in the Behavioral and Social Sciences (1981–88), which produced three major reports on the present, past, and future of the behavioral and social sciences. This involved frequent travel to Washington, D.C. These years of institution management and service to the profession were not without their gratifications, but as time passed I became progressively more impatient with the slowdown in my research. In particular, I was very anxious about my lack of progress on a major monograph on the history of working-class education in Great Britain, on which I had begun work in 1977. I lived in silent dread of never finishing that work.

In that context of career dissatisfaction, I was granted a fellowship year at the Russell Sage Foundation to supplement a sabbatical leave. This leave freed me from most obligations, and to add to that effect, I resigned from most national committees and other involvements. The foundation had designed a perfect year away, welcoming the scholars, supplying them with unlimited books and articles, and providing secretarial help, research assistance, and computer advice in abundance. In addition, my wife and I, originally apprehensive of the noise, anonymity, and crime of New York City, found that the city yielded none of these; on the contrary, it provided a cultural richness we had experienced only in London. There was a collection of other scholars at the foundation with whom now familiar feelings of solidarity and good fellowship developed. I resumed my research and writing on British primary education and was able to complete the book (Smelser 1991), thus experiencing a sense of scholarly rebirth. I had not thought that such a year of combined isolation and involvement could happen in a mighty metropolis, but once again I was proven wrong. In my years as director of the Center at Stanford, I often regretted that I had never taken an academic year in residence there—it didn't seem very grand to move only forty miles down the peninsula when more exotic places beckoned—but the year in New York amply compensated for that void.

A DREAM IN BELLAGIO

In 1991 I was selected as a visiting scholar at the Bellagio Study and Conference Center, managed by the Rockefeller Foundation, on the Lago di Como north of Milan. The period of residence was five weeks in May and June of 1992, providing a welcome respite from a difficult year as chair of the Sociology Department at Berkeley.

The setting at Bellagio almost guarantees an uplifting personal experience. The institution is situated in the Villa Serbelloni, at the end of the peninsula that splits the southern arms of the lake. Its grounds are preserved in classical style and beautifully maintained. A spectacular view to the north includes the Italian Alps. Scholars and their spouses reside in or near the villa. The setting is self-contained, though it is possible to walk across the properties to the lakeside town of Bellagio, with its charm and its array of gelato shops. The center houses about fifteen scholars at any given time. All meals are taken together in a somewhat ceremonial fashion (ties required), and each week there is an evening seminar at which a scholar gives a presentation on his or her work. Late afternoon games of bocce ball attract almost all visitors and partners, because no particular level of skill is required to participate.

A prospective visiting scholar describes his or her intended work during the application process. Once at the center, however, the keynotes are complete freedom and no supervision. I had a work plan: to advance my research on certain themes in the history of American sociology. This plan was aborted, however, by the pace of the Italian mail, which failed to deliver my books and notes—mailed from Berkeley well in advance of leaving for Italy—until *after* my visiting term ended in early June. (All the boxes of books had to be mailed back to Berkeley unopened.) By good fortune, however, I had a second project. It was to write a short scholarly-cum-practical book on committees in academia, to be based explicitly on my own extensive committee experience and requiring no bookish research (see Smelser 1993). I threw myself into this project and, to my surprise, completed the entire book during the five weeks of residence.

The arrangements at the study and conference center conspire against a full, collective odyssey experience in two ways. First, the term of residence for scholars—five weeks at the time I was there, subsequently reduced to one month—is on the short side. Second, the center's policy is to stagger the arrival and departure of what might otherwise be a single cohort of scholars. Every Wednesday two or three scholars arrived and two or three others departed. This meant that one shared the full five weeks with very few others, and in some cases the overlap was as little as one week. This arrangement runs counter to the principle of concurrent collective involvement.

Neither of these features, however, could inhibit the dynamics of the odyssey. Strong personal bonds began to develop immediately, and we made lasting friendships with people with whom we had only two weeks in common at the villa. The visiting scholars regarded themselves as a band of chosen people, engaging in self-admiration and self-congratulation, and despising those "inferiors" who were "down the hill" for conferences that lasted only three days and who invaded our collective meals like so many unwelcome aliens. Afterward, too, the feelings of self-realization and joy remained strong. In 2002 I applied for a return term to Bellagio—this time, with completely appropriate symbolism, to have another odyssey to work on this odyssey project—but I was not successful. That left me ambivalent: disappointed and resentful that I could not repeat the experience but comforted by the subconscious knowledge that you can't go home again and that my nostalgia for the place and the experience would never be sullied by a less dramatic return.

NEVER TOO OLD? A SOJOURN AT THE LIBRARY OF CONGRESS

In 2004, three years after my retirement from the directorship at the Center for Advanced Study at Stanford, I received an e-mail from the Librarian of Congress. It was an invitation to spend a period from three months to a year as a Kluge fellow at the library, at a time of my choosing, during which I could work on anything I pleased (no advance description of project required). He also mentioned a handsome monthly stipend. The invitation was made possible by a large gift from John Kluge, entrepreneur and philanthropist. All scholars dream of such an invitation. I accepted immediately and said I would like to come for three months in the fall and winter of 2006.

I did not expect this visit to be an odyssey. After all, I was retired, not young (age seventy-six at the time of the visit), perhaps too old for that sort of thing. For various reasons, Washington, D.C., did not hold out the romantic promise that I had experienced in Salzburg, Oxford, La Ciotat, New York City, and Bellagio. My wife and I even drove across the country in a camper, so we could spend weekends *away* from Washington on the Maryland beaches and in Virginia's beautiful places. Furthermore, I defined the visit in mainly instrumental terms—to read freely, voraciously, and in isolation (after all, that is what the Library of Congress is equipped to provide) so I could more or less complete the research required for this book on the odyssey. Finally, as I discovered, the Kluge program was not designed to be a collective experience. As a senior visitor, I was assigned an elegant, wood-paneled office all to myself in the Jefferson building, not in the company of other senior scholars, who had their own offices, and not in the company of the troupe of junior scholars who labored in carrels one floor above. There was only one communal experience per week, a voluntary Thursday lunch that was somewhat sparsely attended.

Despite my advance expectations and intentions and despite the arrangements, I could not prevent an odyssey experience from happening. The staff of the Kluge Center were welcoming and hospitable. The availability of books and my pace of work surpassed even my advance ambitions. Washington, D.C., possessed so many cultural attractions that our camping plans eroded. And quite by accident, my term overlapped with a respected friend, Gerhardt Casper, the legal scholar and former president of Stanford University. We made immediate contact, discovered dozens of overlapping intellectual and political interests, and bonded into a kind of two-person odyssey during those months, which included the dramatic congressional elections of 2006. This stay in Washington and at the Library of Congress convinced me, on a personal level, that the lure of the odyssey is more or less universal, compelling, and incapable of being wished away.

As I indicated at the beginning, all these events and episodes in my life were experienced in and of themselves, and without too much reflection on my part. It was almost as though I were not an agent but as if the experiences were "happening" to me. That feeling is wrong, as I will explain, but that was in large measure how things felt. All of my systematizing—identifying common elements, comparing them with one another, and above all, comparing them with different ranges of phenomena that I have never experienced but only read about—has come only later.

The problem of agency is a complicated one. Most of the experiences I have reported happened because there were opportunities supplied by some organization—a college, a university, or another body—for the recipient to advance in his or her educational or academic career. Without such opportunities, those experiences would not have transpired, and I frequently call to mind how fortunate I have been to live at a time in American and human history when such experiences for self-advancement and self-realization are available. At the same time, I remind myself that I sought out and strove for all these opportunities and had talents that were recognized by those responsible for selecting winners in the competition. That is agency, of course, and a necessary part of becoming privy to these special experiences and making the most of them when the opportunities are made available.

All the experiences seemed to have something in common. They were preceded by a general dissatisfaction and a wish to disengage. My own ambition was the common source—ambition is a kind of perpetual dissatisfaction. But in addition, on some occasions I was fed up with or discouraged about some aspect of my ongoing life and desired to set it straight by being away. A second feature is that, with one or two exceptions, I did not plan out or give detailed design to these odyssey experiences in advance. They grew upon me and developed logics of their own, also seemingly beyond my control.

As part of this unfolding process, all the odyssey experiences turned out to be more than advertised. Most educational experiences and leaves of absence for academics are defined in instrumental, career terms—an opportunity to do research, write it up, have it recognized, and likely gain a measure of advancement, prestige, and salary. The great complex of uncertainties, dreads, hopes, mood fluctuations, disappointments, and euphoria is not on the program. These feelings happen to those who live them. As often as not, I actively discounted the possibility of a complex journey, but it became a journey anyway. Sometimes, too, the experience ran counter to my self-image. For whatever reasons, I grew up considering myself a down-to-earth, rational, and not very sentimental or nostalgic person. The odyssey experiences invariably surprised me and gave the lie to these expectations, but that did not seem to prevent me from reinventing them and being surprised the next time around.

More particularly, I was not brought up with religious training and have never been a religious person. All the odyssey experiences I have related in this chapter were secular ones. Yet every one of them had an emotional, spiritual, even "oceanic" element at one point or another, and these feelings, also often surprises, were most important in guiding me to and helping me appreciate the ultimate roots of the odyssey experience, which are religious.

THREE

Religious Foundations and Their Derivatives

We begin with religion-based rites of passage because they are such an early, enduring, and well-analyzed form. Within that genre, the initiations into adolescence of traditional societies have provided the most fascination for anthropologists and for that reason have produced a flood of interpretations. After tracing a number of different historical manifestations of these rites, I will then turn to two other religion-based phenomena—pilgrimage and conversion—examining both their essences and variations. The chapter concludes with an account of two modern, secularized, but moral crusades, the Peace Corps and the 1964 Freedom Summer in Mississippi.

THE ANTHROPOLOGY AND HISTORY OF RITES OF PASSAGE

Preliterate societies developed highly elaborated and institutionalized systems of noticing and ritualizing the major transitions of life—childhood to adulthood, marriage, childbirth (including the couvade), and death.

One bit of conceptual brush clearing is necessary. Rites of passage are only one of subset of rituals, many of which do not share its characteristics. Wallace (1966) classified rituals as technological (e.g., the rain dance), misfortune-avoiding, therapeutic, ideological (to exert control over groups), social-intensifying (to enhance solidarity), ensuring salvation, or revitalizing (see also Chapple and Coon 1978 [1942]). In a related classification, Grimes (1985) listed a dozen types of rituals in addition to rites of passage. He (Grimes 2000) also mentioned more than two dozen subactivities associated with birth alone that have become ritualized. All this means that what follows is not a general account of rituals, even though I acknowledge that rites of passage are a subgenre of rituals and that many kinds of odyssey experiences may become ritualized.

What are the ideal-typical features of the initiation of males into adolescence? The following is a distillation from studies accumulated from Australia, Africa, North America, and island peoples by Webster (1968 [1908]), La Fontaine (1986), van Gennep (1960 [1909]), Eliade (1994 [1958]), and Turner (1969, 1974). I focus on the process itself rather than on the kinds of functional significance that have been attributed to such rites (social integration, reducing uncertainty, management of tensions, expressive action, meaning creation, etc.) (Englehart 1998).

- The ceremony is mandatory, not elective ("institutionalized and pre-ordained" [Turner 1974, 248]).
- The ceremony is a transition from one status (youth) to a more advanced state (adulthood). More generally, Freud

observed that "detachment from the family has become a task that awaits every adolescent, and often society helps him through it with pubertal and initiatory rites" (1961 [1930], 103). Such a transition is implied in the very term *passage* (van Gennep 1960 [1909], 3).

- The ceremony is carefully controlled by tribal elders and leaders, who supervise all its aspects in detail (La Fontaine 1986; Turner 1987). These elders are thought to possess special knowledge of the ritual, its religious foundations, and its traditional significance (Beckwith and Fisher 1999).

- The transition strips the characteristics of childhood, in particular the initiate's relations with women, and entails the acquisition of the knowledge, lore, and responsibilities of an adult male. "Failure to undergo the rites means deprivation of all tribal privileges and disgrace for life. The uninitiated are the 'barbarians' of primitive society. They belong with the women and children. Those who would remain with the women after having reached manhood are subjects of ridicule and abuse" (Webster 1968 [1908], 23–24).

- To symbolize the stripping, the ceremony is carried out in isolation from women, who are excluded from the process. More recent research (Bonnemère 2004) has offered a corrective, stressing a more active presence of women in the ceremonial activities.

- The isolation often involves sending the initiate into a sacred place, perhaps into a forest or a ritual house. This is the time for the initiate to "turn inward and connect with the spirit of his culture, and the ancestors that will guide him throughout his life" (Beckwith and Fisher 1999, 16).

- Activities conducted during the ceremony are scrupu-lously kept secret. The secrecy is intended, among other things, to separate the sacred from mundane elements of tribal life. "The special genius of ritual secrecy . . . is to provide a means of living in two cultural realities simul-taneously—a perfect or utopian one, that of formulas and deities, with often hidden hierarchies, which elide all the messy difficulties that trouble an ideology of intimate, vulnerable bodies, situated in imperfect earthly exis-tence, full of the human emotions of conflicted desires, demands, and impossible loyalties" (Herdt 2003, 62). The secrecy connects the ceremony with remote and sacred knowledge. This feature has survived, with similar func-tions, as a generic characteristic of secret societies (La Fontaine 1986).

- Many rites of passage also have an element of temporary license. Webster refers, no doubt with exaggeration, to "a period of almost indiscriminate cohabitation" accorded to novices after the ceremony (1968 [1908], 43).

- Of special significance is the almost universal presence of an ordeal—the instillation of fear at the least, and more typically some kind of physical assault: knocking out a tooth, scarification, circumcision, or in milder cases, a tattoo. These "leave permanent records upon the body of the novice" (ibid.). They serve as a test for the initiate, to be endured stoically, and as "evidence" that he is ready to be a man and endure pain and suffering. We will see that the transformational significance of the ordeal survives in many modern initiations. The infliction of wounds during the rite has been the subject of intense scrutiny by interpreters, especially those with a psychoanalytic bent. In a controversial formulation, Bettelheim argued that both male and female circumcision have a universal significance in demonstrating that "one sex feels envy in relation to the sexual organs and functions of the other" (1962, 18). Reik interpreted the physical assault on the initiates as an expression of fathers' hostility toward the neophytes (1976 [1931], 104). Eliade asserted that circumcision introduces the initiated to the "mysteries of blood" that still bind him to his mother, and separate him from her by a transformative process (1994 [1958], 27–28). These "universal" symbols, to my mind, are not very helpful because they are posited as universal. Nonetheless they reflect an abiding preoccupation with the riddle of why punishment and pain are so conspicuous in ritual transitions (see chapter 6).

- The metaphorical representation of death and rebirth is pervasive (Engelhart 1998). It "indicate[s] that the novice has attained to another mode of existence, inaccessible to those who have not undergone the initiatory ordeals, who have not tasted death" (Eliade 1994 [1958], xiii). The child must die before he can be reborn (on rebirth in general, see Jung 1971).

- Above all, the initiations are infused with the religious worldview of the people. Again, Eliade: "The puberty

initiation represents above all the revelation of the
sacred—and, for the primitive world, the sacred means
not only everything that we now understand by religion,
but also the whole body of the tribe's mythological and
cultural traditions" (1994 [1958], 3).

- It is evident that these ceremonies, profound as they are
for the societies in which they are embedded, are bathed
in rich symbolism. Turner (1969) identified symbolism
not only of death but also of the womb, invisibility, darkness, and eclipse of the sun or moon. Beidelman (1997)
traced the multiple meanings and layers of meaning of
the "cool knife" in male and female initiation ceremonies
and in the organization of cultural beliefs generally.

To concentrate on male initiation rites does not imply that
these are the most important rituals in those societies. Female
initiation rites are also typical and share fundamental characteristics. In some cultures, initiation rites may be overshadowed by
other rites, such as the funeral (Engelhart 1998). I have singled
out male initiation rites because they are so highly elaborated
and because they have attracted the most scholarly attention.

JUDEO-CHRISTIAN RITES OF PASSAGE

Adolescent rites of passage have occupied a significant place in
the Judaic and Christian traditions, though the weight given
to their several ingredients is variable. The traditional Jewish
bar mitzvah is explicitly a transition to adulthood ("Today I am
a man"), accompanied by acquisition of religious knowledge
under the supervision of a religious authority and by assuming a

new religious status. The elements of ordeal are by now muted, though the preparation may be experienced as arduous. Like other rituals, moreover, the bar mitzvah has changed according to historical circumstances, though it is represented as eternal in significance. Marcus (1996) has argued that much of the symbolism of the bar mitzvah can be regarded as a limited acculturation to Christian rituals in the eleventh through the fourteenth centuries, and that in their subsequent history, both the bar mitzvah and confirmation moved from an emphasis on the passive child toward consensual choice. During the same period, the belief in miracles and authority receded. In recent times Christian confirmation remains a vital institution in the Roman Catholic Church but is of diminished importance in Protestant denominations. The modern bar mitzvah has been modified to include initiation of adolescent girls, and the ritual has evolved in the direction of a community celebration, with emphasis on socializing and gift-giving. More generally, the secularization of both religions has rendered adolescent rituals less universal, though, as we will see in chapter 4, many scattered secular counterparts have appeared.

Baptism, as both an infant and an adult rite of passage into the Christian community, has been a central and highly controversial theological issue in the history of Christianity. It was a core element in the Rite of Christian Initiation for Adults (RCIA). As described in the fourth century A.D., this rite involved three phases—a preparatory, cleansing period characterized by a ritual dosage of salt and various exorcisms (a ceremony that stripped the individual of past sins); a second, enrollment period; and a third period of six weeks that involved further exorcism of sins, self-scrutiny, study and acquisition of liturgical knowledge, presentation and recitations of the creed, recitation of the Lord's Prayer, a prebaptismal bath, and finally baptism itself, which symbolized the final cleansing and symbolic rebirth as a believing Christian (Yarnold 1994).

Muir has interpreted Christian baptism in the late Middle Ages in a framework explicitly taken from van Gennep's three phases of rites of passage. The first phase of separation "involved a striking exorcism carried out at the door of the church, the threshold that separated the realm of the devil from the blessings of God. The infant, far from innocent, had been brought into the suffering world because of Adam and Eve's primal sin of disobedience induced by the arch-deceiver, Satan. The sexual congress of the infant's parents compounded the sin, and the shivering little boy or girl brought to the font was, in fact, a corrupted piece of flesh. To expel the evil and make salvation possible, the priest had to act quickly after birth" (2005, 23). In many ceremonies, the devil was represented as being actually present at the ceremony, and the infant was scrutinized to make certain that it had been freed from the devil's influence (Kelly 1985).

In the second phase, the child was separated from his or her parents. The prescribed ritual demanded that the baby be dipped facedown in the water (a ritual cleansing combined with an ordeal of mock drowning). On many occasions this practice was abandoned in favor of sprinkling water on the infant's forehead, and salt and oil were often administered to counter the effects of cold water. Muir interprets this as the liminal period of isolation.

The third period was one of reincorporation. The priest returned the infant to the parents, who raised it from the font, thus incorporating the child into the Christian community. The godparents responded on the child's behalf, recited the Credo, said a paternoster, and promised to educate the child in the faith of Christ (ibid.).

The last great passage is death, a universal religious concern. Hagglund has argued persuasively that its representation is typically that of a journey:

> In imagination, death is experienced as a trip, punishment, liberator, satisfier of sexual desires, or a condition uniting people. The most usual attitude toward death is acceptance of its inevitability, yet in such a way that its absoluteness as the end is simultaneously denied. From time immemorial man has cherished various fantasies of life in the beyond. In any cultures life on earth is believed to be only part of human existence. . . . Prehistoric man provided the deceased with food, necessary clothing, and weapons. The ancient Egyptians embalmed the bodies to prepare them for life hereafter. Death meant merely a journey or moving from one physical sphere to another. In the religions of primitive cultures death was often described as a voyage across a river or large body of water. (1978, 14)

Reincarnation as death and rebirth is another instance. In traditional Christian cosmology the soul leaves the body and makes its journey to heaven or hell, with a "liminal" period in purgatory. Death is also typically surrounded by preparatory rituals (extreme unction) and followed by a social ceremony for the survivors, the functional objective of which is to incorporate the deceased into the community of the dead and reestablish the community of kin and friends absent the deceased (Muir 2005). Modern times have seen the weakening of rituals as a monopoly of organized religion in the ritual management of death, as well as the invention of alternative forms of observance, such as scattering the ashes in a remote spot symbolically important for the deceased. I note some of these changes in chapter 5.

THE RELIGIOUS PILGRIMAGE

Like rites of passage, the memorializing religious expedition stretches into the remote past of human history: "Upper Paleolithic cave paintings of probable religious significance suggest that prehistoric Europeans may have made pilgrimages of thanks or supplication for successful hunts. Megalithic monuments, thought to date from as early as 4000 B.C., probably were places of religious gatherings that drew people from considerable distances. In historic times, pagan Mediterranean, Celtic, and Germanic peoples practiced various forms of pilgrimage. A few of Europe's contemporary sites of Christian pilgrimage are found at places once sacred to pagan peoples" (Nolan and Nolan 1989, 3). In more recent times pilgrimages have been an integral part of the world's great religions. The idea of a journey to a sacred place for religious reasons is found in the old Semitic culture (Waugh 1996). Christian pilgrimages began as early as the first century A.D., when the veneration of relics of the saints became common practice. As with most cultural inventions, they incorporated many practices and symbols from the surrounding cultural environment.

A simple definition of the pilgrimage was ventured by Baumer: "The basic structure of the pilgrimage is the same: an individual or, more often, a group sets forth on a journey to a chosen place to ask God and the saints—at that particular place—for aid in a variety of concerns. Afterward, one returns to one's everyday world" (1978, 22). Notwithstanding this common core, pilgrimages have shown great variation in content and style. Furthermore, they melt into a variety of kindred practices, such as healing, taking of the sacraments, ceremonials in general, and in the case of the medieval Crusades, war. They have become fully ritualized and institutionalized, and sometimes they have appeared in more secularized though structurally similar garb.

We owe much to Victor Turner (1974, 1979) for his explicit comparison of pilgrimages to initiations and other rites of passage, as well as to dramatic representations and literary myths. We are also obliged to him for providing such a thorough, extended, and rich identification and elaboration of its ingredients, though, as we will see, like many intellectual pioneers, he overshot the mark in several ways. I will follow Turner's analysis in laying out the essentials of the pilgrimage and will supplement this by referring to other empirical studies.

The pilgrimage lies midway between the coercive and the voluntary. It contrasts with the initiations described above: "[In] tribal societies men and women *have* to go through rites of passage transferring them from one state and status to another." The same is true of many rites of passage in religious communities (Turner 1979, 131). To join a Christian religious pilgrimage is voluntary, a matter of individual conscience. Participation is, however, a sacred obligation coerced by the weight of church authority and the threat of damnation without penitence, though escape clauses have always been available (ibid.). In modern times, with the institutionalization and quasi-secularization of many pilgrimages, the voluntary element is stronger.

The first essential element of the pilgrimage is that participants disengage from the routines of daily life. This is implied by the definition of pilgrimage: removing oneself from one's place of residence and traveling, usually a long distance, to a sacred spot. Yet more is involved. Pilgrims undergo "a separation from a relatively fixed state of life and social status and [pass] into a liminal or threshold phase and condition for which none of the rules and few of the experiences of their previous existence had prepared them" (Turner 1979, 122). They are "free of the encumbrances of . . . role, status, reputation, class, caste, sex, or other structural niche" (ibid., 46). Traditionally, pilgrims to Santiago de Compostela (a site of pilgrimage for the past eight hundred years) formalized this disengagement by requesting permission from the feudal lord for the journey (Hoolihan 2000).

Corresponding to this destructuring is the appearance of a homogenous, simplified group structure for the journey itself. Coleman identified one of the characteristics of the pilgrimage as "crossing conventional cultural, social, and religious boundaries" (2001, 1445). The pilgrims all share the same circumstances, seeking spiritual relief through penitence and contact with the holy. The ultimate focus—to reach the sacred spot, to pray, to repent, and to be absolved—is identical for all. The sameness is sometimes symbolized concretely. Pilgrims to Santiago de Compostela traditionally don simple and identical garb signifying their pilgrim status; this distinctive uniform is still available for purchase by participants (Hoolihan 2000). With sameness comes equality. Of the many defining characteristics of the liminal period of the pilgrimage, Turner identified "equality," "anonymity," " absence of property," "absence of status," "nakedness or uniform clothing," "minimization of sex distinctions," "absence of rank," "disregard of personal appear-ance," "no distinctions of wealth," "suspension of kinship rights and obligations," and "simplicity" (Turner 1969). All this is part of the *communitas* that includes oneness, solidarity, and an out-of-time quality.

One suspects that Turner has gone too far toward typifica-tion and reification in his dichotomous contrast between the pilgrimage and the routine world. In principle, it is difficult to believe that all distinctions cease to matter, particularly when the participants come from societies dominated by rank and orders. In his ethnographic study of pilgrimages in the Andes, Sallnow (1987), while stressing the common hope that the shrine holds out to all comers, also notes that participating peasants from the same communities travel together and form separate groups within the larger movement. In a more extreme case, Messerschmidt and Sharma (1981) remark the internal divisions, avoidance, and hostility among castes in a Hindu pil-grimage. They even suggest that this pilgrimage constituted a "structure-confirming" event, in contrast to the "brotherly love" motif in Christian pilgrimages.

A second point of contention is Turner's treatment of the liminal period and *communitas* as not simply nonstructure but antistructure. For him, this element is an ingredient of rituals in general, including pilgrimages. He suggests that, in releasing people from their status and roles and creating a simpler, more diffuse set of relationships, the ceremony involves a "liberation from conformity to general norms" (Turner 1974, 274). The term *antistructure* suggests subversion, and Turner argues that such episodes of liberation must be transient "if society is to continue in an orderly fashion" (ibid.). He draws some parallels between religious phenomena and contemporary manifestations of *communitas* in protest movements:

> In modern Western society, the values of *communitas* are
> strikingly present in the literature and behavior of what
> came to be known as the "beat generation," who were suc-
> ceeded by the "hippies," who, in turn, have a junior divi-
> sion known as the "teeny-boppers." These are the "cool"
> members of the adolescent and young-adult categories . . .
> who "opt out" of the status-bound social order and acquire
> the stigmata of the lowly, dressing like "bums," itinerant in
> their habits, "folk" in their musical tastes, and menial in the
> casual employment they undertake. They stress personal
> relationships rather than social obligations, and regard sexu-
> ality as a polymorphic instrument of immediate *communitas*
> rather than as the basis for an enduring structural social
> tie. . . . [T]he "sacred" properties often assigned to *communi-
> tas* are not lacking here. (Turner 1969, 112–13)

The quarrel one might have with Turner is that, while he is correct in capturing the *non*structure of the communities that form in rituals, pilgrimages, and some protest movements, it is a an exaggeration to suggest that this feature generally implies an antagonism to structured life. This family of phenomena reveals a range of functional properties, only some of which are opposed to the existing order. While rejection might be the signature of most bohemian and communal movements, the primary significance of religious rituals, including pilgrimages, appears to be acceptance and reinforcement of the religious world in which they occur.

Several additional features establish the religious pilgrimage as a prototypical odyssey experience. The first is the presence of uncertainty and danger. The most dramatic case was the medieval Crusades, which were sometimes marked by several years of extreme hardship and disease, to say nothing of assaults by brigands and religious enemies. Mortality rates were apparently very high (Riley-Smith 1986). The elements of hardship and danger were also present in less warlike pilgrimages (Melczer 1993), though that element has receded in its more protected modern manifestations.

A second is the pervasive symbolism of death and rebirth. "Pilgrimages in the salvation religions . . . are full of metaphors for death, and also are directly concerned with the dead. The dead may include the founder of a religion, his kin, disciples, or companions; saints and martyrs of the faith, and souls of the ordinary faithful" (Turner 1992, 29). Turner also treats the destructuring of social life—"extrusion from system"—as a symbolic death (1979, 122). The journey itself is a kind of limbo, and the forgiveness for sins and the promise of salvation at the end is clearly a kind of rebirth, as in conversion. The healing motif is an ingredient of many Christian pilgrimages. The eleventh- and twelfth-century journeys to Compostela and Canterbury were thought to offer "a potential escape from famine, pestilences, war, and fear of death (and hell) which, together with infertility, poverty and persecution, created a misery that lay beyond mortal control" (Smith 1992, 7). Rebirth symbolism is evident in these promises, and in this respect the pilgrim's journey shades into many practices of shamanism and ethno-medicine.

Many traditional pilgrimages survive today in Christian and other religious worlds. Many remain culturally powerful— for example, Muslim pilgrimages to Mecca and other holy places. Many have adapted over time and have taken on mixed religious and secular significance. Two examples of this have been described by Bremer (2000). The first is Mission San Juan Capistrano, a Franciscan mission located in Orange County, California, which draws a half-million visitors annually. The mission is a religious place but "retains only a trace of its religious character" (ibid., 423). The management of the mission describes its purpose as primarily educational, stressing the cultural heritage of California. Only the chapel of Father Junipero Serra sets off specific Catholic practices from other points of historical interest. The management's main activity is to collect money for restoration and preservation. Though the historical connection with Father Serra is not denied (he is represented publicly by a statue), a certain "political correctness" has found its way into the mission's publicity. The father is represented as a benign sympathizer with and helper of Native American peoples, and no reference to "the terrifying and genocidal consequences of that encounter" is to be found (ibid., 431). While vestiges of the pilgrimage remain in visitors' experiences, the place has evolved into a self-sustaining, generally religious but ecumenical tourist attraction. As if to underscore its touristic as well as religious significance, it is located very close to Disneyland and Knott's Berry Farm.

Bremer also explores the significance of visits to the Church of Jesus Christ of Latter-day Saints (Mormons) in Temple Square, Salt Lake City. The religious significance of the site is more visible than at Mission San Juan Capistrano. The temple is the mecca for believing Mormons, and visitors are continuously reminded that they are "experiencing a religious place" (ibid., 423). It was designed to replicate "the Mormon view of the universe and the journey of human life through that universe" (ibid.). But in addition to serving as a gathering place for the faithful, the temple offers attractions for non-Mormons as well, especially musical events featuring the Tabernacle Choir, the Mormon Youth Chorus, and the Mormon Youth Symphony. Publicity describes the site as "the friendliest place on earth," and one of the temple's former mission presidents described it as "the Disneyland of Mormonism" (ibid., 422). The temple is a site for attempting to convert non-Mormons to the faith, but it is also expected that there will be frequent encounters with anti-Mormons, and professional guides at Temple Square are trained to deal with antagonists and hecklers in nonconfrontational ways. The leaders explicitly regard the square as "a place of prayerful beauty and meditation," and the intention is to make all comers, both devout and nondevout, feel welcome (ibid., 433).

Other secular echoes of the pilgrimage can be noted: Gandhi's marches through India in protest of British rule and civil rights protests such as the March on Washington (1963) and the Million Man March (1995). One interesting adaptation is French president François Mitterrand's annual pilgrimage to Solutré beginning in 1981. Prior to that time he had gone there annually to relive memories of the war years, when he hid in that community after his escape from Germany. During his presidency, he converted this ceremony into a sacred political event, which symbolized the transcendent history of France and gave him the opportunity to reflect on his presidency and the political issues of the day (Abeles 1988).

In chapter 4, I explore general relations between pilgrimages and tourism, but I cannot resist the temptation to describe one firsthand encounter with an apparently spontaneous and completely secular pilgrimage, which, however, bears many similarities to visits to holy sites. The decisive event occurred one summer day in Arches National Park, located not far from Moab, Utah. The entire park is beautiful beyond description. Its most famous feature is called Delicate Arch (its likeness is reproduced on Utah welcome signs and automobile license plates). This magnificent structure is located on the edge of a natural amphitheater, so people can gather in groups at some distance or even at its base. It is also brilliantly illuminated when the sun sets. The climax of a visit to the park is to be present at sunset. The site can be reached only by a fairly arduous uphill walk of about one mile across slick rock surfaces. A couple of hours before sunset, crowds of people begin making their way up the slope, resembling a marching army, or better, a pilgrimage. Many languages are heard among the visitors, but all those who could talk with one another were doing so, excitedly and warmly. All, including myself, seemed to be submerged in an atmosphere of warm collective sentimentality and were made equal and close by the anticipation of the natural wonder. When we gathered in and around the amphitheater and the sun began its light show, the arena was filled with sounds of wonder and awe. The people seemed to be elevated aesthetically and spiritually. They had made it to the holy place in time for the holy experience. After the sunlight on the arch subsided, the multitude began making its way down the slopes in time to return to their cars and their touristic routines before darkness fell. This pilgrimage to Delicate Arch repeats itself daily, and without doubt there are hundreds of beautiful places in the world where similar, if less intense, experiences transpire.

THE CONVERSION EXPERIENCE

We turn now from the pilgrimage—a physical movement, usually collective, to a sacred place for purposes of regeneration—to religious conversion, a psychological voyage, usually but not always individual, involving movement from one psychic state to another. It is also regenerative. Their commonality as journeys does not escape notice. The language of journeys is pervasive in the imagery of conversion. The prototypical conversion of Paul to Christianity took place on a physical journey to Damascus. Conversion narratives in some cults make explicit reference to conversion as a journey (Glazier 2003). A conspicuous modern convert, the Reverend Jerry Falwell, described the Christian life as "a journey that began at my second birth. That journey or Christian walk took a lifetime and ended only upon my physical death, when I would stand before the Lord to be rewarded for my faithfulness. The lifelong journey was fraught with danger. I had to make my way through two different and competing worlds simultaneously: the world of God and the world of man" (quoted in Holte 1992, 94). In addition to the metaphorical connection, structural and dynamic parallels justify comparing the two genres as odyssey experiences.

Essence, Variations, and Controversies

In dealing with conversion, we must ask ourselves whether it is a generic thing or a name given to many different historical and psychological processes. Actually, it is both. The word itself implies a "turning around" (Kerr and Mulder 1983, ix), or more specifically, a personal change that involves "a deliberate turning which implies that a great change [is] involved, that the old [is] wrong and the new [is] right" (Frederickson 1986, 5). William James's classic rendition is more dramatic but consistent with these definitions: "It is natural that those who personally have traversed [a conversion experience] should carry away a feeling of its being a miracle rather than a natural process. Voices are often heard, lights seen, or visions witnessed, automatic motor phenomena occur; and it always seems, after the surrender of the personal will, as if an extraneous higher power had flooded in and taken possession. Moreover, the sense of conversion, safety, cleanness, rightness, can be marvelous and jubilant as well to warrant belief in a radically new substantial nature" (James 1963 [1902], 228), Even Nock, who challenged the historical universality of James's definition, arguing that it could not be found historically outside countries with a Christian tradition, conceded that by definition conversion "implies turning from something to something else and you put earlier loyalties behind you" (1998 [1933], 34).

These classic definitions have persisted. However, it is characteristic of the scholarly literature that once a generic characterization of a phenomenon is put forward, small armies of historians and anthropologists subsequently march in to demonstrate that it is not generic but variable. That is the essence of Nock's criticism of James. A sample of such qualifications follows:

Even the New Testament, which has many accounts of conversion experiences, is rich in different figures of speech, referring to it as a movement out of darkness into light, a spiritual rebirth or being born again, a restoration from impurity, a return from death to life, a turning away from Satan to God, a totally new creation, getting rid of the old and acquiring a new humanity, or dying but rising again in Christ (Kerr and Mulder 1983, xi). Medieval Christian accounts stressed "a movement from death to life, from strife to love, from pollution to purity, from ignorance to truth, from human weakness to cosmic power and glory" (Morrison 1992, 22). It can be sudden or gradual (Austin-Broos, 2003). Kerr and Mulder (1983) have suggested many different emphases in the conversion process—emotional, intellectual, moral, and aesthetic.

A sample of case studies also demonstrates that what might be called conversion does not necessarily involve inspired individual commitment and change. A classic pattern of conversion among Germanic peoples occurred when a ruler or governing body agreed to be baptized and then encouraged or coerced followers to do the same (Cusack 1998). Luria (1996) interprets conversions of Protestants to Catholicism in seventeenth-century France as opportunistic in the sense that they were political accommodations to the French Catholic Church and the monarchy. Meyer (1996) makes a similar suggestion that conversion to Christianity in many African colonies appeared to be accommodation to colonial and missionary pressures, as contrasted with the generic "change of heart" model. Oddie (1997) interpreted South Asian "conversion" not so much as "change in faith" as a change of communal affiliation accompanied by some kind of ritual (for a general account of conversion in Hinduism, Buddhism, Islam, and other non-Christian religions, see Underwood [1925] and Bryant and Lamb [1999]). In the Christian West, versions of conversion as an emotional personal transformation shade into less dramatic forms: movement from one Christian denomination to another, becoming generally more religious or less religious, and what Taylor (1999) calls "awkward" or "weak" conversions, in which individuals join a religion to marry within it or marry without converting with the understanding that children will be brought up in the religion. These and other variations led Merrill to conclude "that no single universally applicable definition of conversion is possible or even desirable" (1993, 154).

All these considerations dictate caution in venturing generalizations about the nature, causes, and consequences of religious conversion. Nevertheless, something can be said about typical but scarcely universal social settings in which conversionist groups arise, the psychological background of converts to these groups or more established religious denominations and sects, and the social and psychological processes involved in conversion. I include a special reference to the "new religions" of the 1960s and 1970s, which commanded much attention and evoked controversy among scholars, in the media, and in public discourse.

Social Settings for Conversionist Activity

No single set of social circumstances is exclusively productive of religious conversion, but some settings stand out. The first, long familiar to anthropologists, is cultural domination, of which colonialism is a prime example (Meyer 1996; Lanternari 1963). Three features of colonialism can be pinpointed: first, the economic, social, and political dislocations occasioned by economic exploitation and political domination; second, the importation of cultural values of the colonizers; and third, as a subclass of the second, special efforts on the part of missionaries, educators, and colonial administrators actively to convert—to change the religious beliefs, loyalties, and practices of the "natives." When successful, this conversionist activity works toward the "globalization of Christianity" (van der Veer 1996).

In addition to encouraging conversion to Christianity, colonial domination is also notable for the rise of millenarian groups that often become conversionist. Two classic studies focus on the "cargo cult" movements in Melanesia (Worsley 1957) and messianic groups among Native Americans (Mooney 1896; Slotkin 1956). Similarly, messianic cults appear among extremely oppressed peoples within a society. A classic study of these is Fauset's (1971 [1944]) account of cults among poor urban blacks. Periods of cultural confusion and disappointment also seem to produce cult activity; it has been argued, persuasively in my estimation, that the rise of the "new religions" in the 1960s and 1970s in the United States was in part a response to dashed political hopes and disillusionment with drug-taking among a subclass of young people (Robbins 1988).

The limitation of identifying these kinds of social conditions is that they can be regarded as predisposing or facilitative only—increasing the probability of but neither necessary nor sufficient for the appearance of cults and sects. These are not generated by all situations of deprivation, dispossession, and confusion; furthermore, many arise from other combinations of circumstances.

Psychological Preconditions for Conversion

If the religious narratives of converts to Christian denominations and sects are consulted, they usually reveal that the convert believes the psychological condition that precipitated his or her journey into religion was a state of sin and that conversion saved them from sin. As a self-reported psychological account, these have to be honored if for no other reason than that they are reported, but for several reasons they are not satisfactory accounts of psychological preconditions. First, the narratives are often nonspecific; second, they may be stylized accounts that express conformity to norms voiced by religious leaders and other converts as to what the conversion experience ought to be.

Psychologists and other social scientists have tried to be more specific about preconversion psychology, but these efforts have not proven satisfactory. Early twentieth-century psychological literature (for example, Starbuck 1900) argued that the psychological problems of adolescents made them ready candidates for religious conversion. Downton summarizes the argument: "Adolescence is the prime time for conversion. Spiritual search begins at this time, and young people reach out for universal truths. New ideals emerge to compete with the old self and its bad habits. The teenager is full of sin. . . . Conversion is experienced in giving in to [the highest powers] and allowing the new ideal to be realized. The deep sense of sin gives way to harmony, joy, and peace, often spoken of as 'rebirth'" (1979, 78). As a general explanation, this theory has not endured, though a thread of continuing relevance appears in some research results—for example, the strong representation of the young in the new religions of the 1960s (Snow and Machalek 1984).

Many versions of the psychological conditions facilitating conversion have appeared in the literature, all suggesting some kind of psychic void or disequilibrium. Lofland, whose work on conversion stresses social and interpersonal factors, nevertheless lists an experience of "enduring, acutely felt tension" as the first step toward conversion (1977, 7). Often, after some cognitive structuring of this suffering, the candidate comes to identify himself or herself as a "seeker," a category that has found some general currency in the literature on conversion (Galanter 1999). Words like *deprivation* (Stark and Bainbridge 1985) and *neurotic distress* (Galanter 1999) also appear. Some students of psychotherapy point out the parallels between the unhappiness of those who convert and those who seek therapy: "The conversion narrative is a response to contradictions in the common-sense understanding of volition, intention, etc., contradictions that are felt by subjects in confusion, guilt, and fear in the face of their own behavior. Of course, these sorts of feelings may be addressed in other ways than by having a conversion. The most culturally prominent means of addressing such feelings are the various forms of psychotherapy. . . . [O]ne should be able to observe parallels between these two social forms" (Stromberg 1993, 126). Other continuities between religious transformation and the psychotherapeutic process will be explored later.

Two additional psychological factors have also been ventured. The first, identified by Stark and Bainbridge (1985), refers to the preexisting tightness of religious ties: the tighter they are the less available the person is for a conversion experience. Following this logic, poll results of those drawn into various new religions reveal, for example, that Baptists are more reluctant to convert than Episcopalians, Jews who go to synagogue are more resistant than those who do not, and the secularized are more likely candidates than those with strong religious ties (415–17). The second factor, similar in nature, is the availability of potential candidates among people who are dissatisfied with their parental faith, finding it too exclusive or dogmatic, full of contradictions, or unable to answer their spiritual and personal questions (Harper 1972).

In the end, the search for specific psychological causes or predispositions suffers the same limitations as the search for the social. It seems clear that the common underlying factor is some combination of experienced psychological pain, a sense of loss, and an inability to frame this suffering cognitively. The explanatory power of such a formulation must remain at a general level, however; the invoked factors are so pervasive in the human condition that they cannot be linked specifically and causally to the conversion experience. It appears prudent to accept Stark and Bainbridge's conclusion that "deprivation [seems] unable to serve as more than [a] very general contributory condition . . . in any satisfactory theory of recruitment. Although [it does] limit the pool of persons available for recruitment, [it] does not limit it very much in comparison to the very small number of . . . persons . . . who actually join" (1985, 323).

The Psychological Process of Conversion

The nature of convertees' psychological experience is not entirely clear. It is described in many different languages. Almost all accounts of the "turning" involved in conversion emphasize the generic process of destructuring-unstructuring-restructuring that is characteristic of odyssey experiences in general. Leone (2004) organizes his empirical studies of famous Christian conversions by identifying three phases: the destabilization of the self, the crisis of the self, and the restabilization of the self. Underlying the variations of the term *conversion* reviewed by Heirich is the rejection or reformulation of a previous self, a dramatic episode, and a subsequent shift in understanding, commitment, and behavior (1977, 654). More particularly,

- The destructuring phase involves a dismantling of the past, an active abandonment of undesirable behaviors and outlooks (drifting, drinking, or sinning generally). The key is renunciation. Sometimes this process is closely monitored and stylized, as in a conventionalized revival meeting. Some conversionist religious groups actively engage in identifying and reforming undesirables. The practice of auditing—"guided fantasy and introspection"—by cult leaders in the Scientology movement is a case where active intervention "bring[s] about a disruption of the subject's ordinary reality" (Whitehead 1987, 26). As we will see, this aggressive involvement in destructuring on the part of many new religious groups in the 1960s contributed to accusations that joining was not voluntary conversion but the result of coercion or even brainwashing.

- The middle, unstructured, or "liminal" phase is typically experienced as a personal crisis. This is the conversion itself. In her search for continuities, Whitehead argues that this phase shares commonalities with the psychoanalytic process of regression and "deautomization" in recent cognitive psychological studies of mediation (ibid., 25). In extreme cases the individual experiences a loss of control, for example in seizures. Behaviors such as public displays of emotion, sobbing, shouting, jerking, speaking nonsense, and experiencing visions are tolerated and expected, even though they are unacceptable in most social situations (Clements 1976). This phase, too, is usually socially monitored in a church, cult, or revival setting, and as such it involves an ingredient of *communitas* as well, sharing the experience in an extremely emotional way with the other faithful (ibid.).

- The result of conversion is a new or reconstituted self, a positive mirror image of the frailties, failures, and sins of preconversion life. The convert has "seen the light," has found God or Christ, is sober, and is able to lead a "clean" life. The result is often characterized as "total," involving a fusion of cognitive, emotional, and moral change. Snow and Machalak (1984) have suggested that the conversion experience amounts to a " change in one's universe of discourse," which includes all these cognitive, emotional, and moral elements but lays stress on the dimension of meaning and framing. This formulation is a fruitful one, and establishes a continuity between religious conversion and related forms of psychotherapeutic change and rehabilitation to be taken up in chapter 4. Conversion frequently involves changes in group membership and new patterns of interaction, as converts join established churches, sects, or cults. This altered pattern of social life generally operates to solidify the conversion experience, though, as we will see, it can also prove alienating.

The literature on religious conversion is characterized by running controversies about the genuineness of religious conversion (i.e., "whether these displays are attributable to authentic and enduring inner change or merely to compliance with the demands of intense normative pressure" [ibid., 1984]); to what extent conversions "last"; to what extent they are voluntary or coerced; and whether the primary driving causes are individually motivational or rooted in group processes (or in some combination of these). Such questions reflect genuine ambiguities about the process. However, I also believe that there is something deeper at work in these recurrent expressions of skepticism. By and large, contemporary scholars are products of the world trend of secular rationality bred by the eighteenth-century Enlightenment and its historical unfolding, and whether they acknowledge it or not, they are indifferent or hostile to religion and tend to treat religious rituals as nonrational (Muir 2005; Rieff 2007). The question of genuineness and lastingness can be asked of all odyssey experiences, but religious conversion appears to have been especially selected out for skeptical attention in the scholarly world.

Recent Developments in Thinking about Conversion

Writing in the mid-1980s, Snow and Machalek noted and documented that the preceding decade had produced "a burst of scholarship on conversion" (1984, 167). Two special developments spurred this burst, one in the religious world itself and one in the way that conversion was conceived by those who studied it.

NEW RELIGIONS

A striking feature of American—and, indeed, world—religious history in the 1960s and 1970s was the appearance and flourishing of large numbers of unconventional sects, which came to be known as the "new religions" (Glock and Bellah 1976) or "alternative religions" (Kyle 1993). Not that these were entirely new. Jenkins asserts that there have been so many cults based on "extreme and bizarre" religious ideas that it is a mistake to call them "fringe" at all (2000, 7). He identifies many instances in the nineteenth century, including the communitarian experiments, as well as waves of cults and anticult movements in the first half of the twentieth century. Around 1980 Melton and Moore (1982) counted some nine hundred religious denominations in the United States, of which six hundred did not share the Western Christian heritage. In particular, Melton and Moore treat the flourishing of new religions as a further extension of pluralism, the identifying feature of American religious history. In all events, the period witnessed an efflorescence of cults with a dizzying variety of names—Divine Light Mission, Hare Krishna, the Health, Happy, Holy Organization, Transcendental Meditation, Scientology, and the Christian World Liberation Front. All were syncretic, and many were adaptations of Far Eastern and Middle Eastern religions.

The stir created in the public mind and the attention given by scholars to these new movements were striking. Much of the excitement was generated by the appearance of the movements themselves, but its intensity also depended on the context of the times. It is possible to identify several interrelated sources of this fascination and concern, even alarm:

- The movements arose in a general period of social turmoil, especially among the young, a period that encompassed an aggressive civil rights movement followed by black militancy, student activism in the universities, protest against the Vietnam War, countercultural movements, and a resurgence of the women's rights movement. The new religious movements seemed to add to the chaos.

- Many of the movements appeared to engage in "weird" practices: the chanting and dancing of the saffron-clad Hare Krishnas and the rituals of the satanic cults were extreme and conspicuous instances. More generally, the non-Christian characteristics of the new religions—whether originating from non-Western religions or from secular or therapeutic syntheses (e.g., Scientology)—tended to consign them to "outsider" status (Melton 2004).

- Some of the new movements showed evidence of strong-arm strategies in recruiting members and enforcing discipline—notably the Unification Church (Moonies) and Synanon (Janzen 2001).

- In that connection, public memories of sensory-deprivation experiments and the "brainwashing" strategies practiced on prisoners by the Chinese during the Korean War and by Soviet Communists were reactivated (see chapter 6).

- The period produced a number of electrifying and gruesome episodes of murder and suicide that dominated the media and excited public attention and outrage—notably the Manson family murders in 1969 (Gilmore 2000), the massacre at Jonestown in 1976 (Chidester 1988), the assault on the Branch Davidians in Waco, Texas, in 1993 (Newport 2006), and the sirin gas attack in the Tokyo subways perpetrated by the messianic cult Aum Shinrikyo in 1995 (Reader 2000). All these accentuated the bizarre and the destructive in cults, as well as the passionate reactions to them.

The fascination with new religious cults was thus overdetermined by their own characteristics and by the social context in which they occurred. Moreover, since most of these cults were conversionist, both public and scholarly interest was similarly skewed toward that aspect.

Some of the research on the new religions echoed conventional issues in research on conversion, namely the backgrounds of those who joined and what the new religions provided psychologically to those people. Dawson (1998) drew up a composite list of background characteristics of the joiners, finding that they were youthful, well educated, and middle-class. The concept of "seekership" was invoked as well, though this concept involved a certain circularity of explanation. Saliba (2003a) argued that the cults held out particular appeal to people who had become "stuck" in some developmental stage; the transformative experiences in the new religious movements constituted a dramatic rite of passage. Some authors suggested that the new movements provided a new identity, an ordering of life, and therapeutic relief, all implying a deficit or life disorder that attracted potential converts. By far the most salient preoccupation of interpreters, however, was with coerciveness, brainwashing, and manipulation of cult recruits by cult leaders. I will return to this controversy in chapter 6.

SOCIAL TIES AND CONVERSION

Coinciding more or less with the rise of the new religious movements was the rise in salience of a range of social factors among the determinants of conversion: the role of acquaintance, friendship, and networks. This marked a departure from the emphasis on spiritual, psychological, and social-background factors. Developed by Lofland and Stark (1965), the approach was extended and systematized in dozens of case studies and subsequent formulations (e.g., Stark and Bainbridge 1985; Rambo 1993). The basic idea is that, in addition to whatever social preconditions and psychological predispositions may be at work, the process of conversion is greatly facilitated by interpersonal persuasion and emulation. Furthermore, many conversionist religious organizations realize the importance of this factor and capitalize on it. In a way this development should not be surprising, since a consistent theme in twentieth-century sociology was the "discovery" of the importance and even omnipresence of the primary group in work settings, the military, voting, consumer behavior, disaster responses, and elsewhere. Nevertheless, the emphasis is salutary, if for no other reason than to remind us that the most intense psychological experiences— which many odyssey experiences are—are firmly rooted in and partially determined by their social and normative contexts.

THE PEACE CORPS: AN ORGANIZED, SECULAR, BUT HOLY ODYSSEY

The Peace Corps (1960s and 1970s) is notable as a national effort to aid less-developed countries of the world by sending young people on missions to provide technical assistance and leadership (Hoffman 1998; Rice 1985). Conceived during John F. Kennedy's campaign for the presidency in 1960, the corps was founded early in his administration. Its legitimizing context was a liberal political vision of America's role in the world. From the outset it was advertised to Congress and the American people as a realistic yet moral, worthy, and idealistic project in which citizens might play a role in making the world a better place (Redmon 1986). According to an ad posted in 1963, the "Peace Corps brings idealists down to earth" (quoted in Hoffman 1998, 124). The entire effort, moreover, was intimately linked to Kennedy's presidency and his charismatic presence (Redmon 1986; Rice 1985). In the 1990s the corps distanced itself from the idealistic phases of the Kennedy and Johnson administrations, and became more technically oriented (Reeves 1988). I will concentrate on the earlier years.

The Peace Corps held out the promise of an exciting and valued period abroad for participants, in the context of a national mission of helping others. As such, it resembled but fell short of being a religious mission—it was more moral than religious in emphasis—and it also fell short of the subsequent exportation of human rights (the Carter administration) and American democracy (the second Bush administration), both of which tended to be more coercive and less popular with the receiving nations. It was a mission based on understanding, caring, and help, not power or guns, and thus represented to some a high-road alternative to the uglier sides of the Vietnam War.

The Peace Corps was designed, consciously or unconsciously, to be an odyssey experience for the volunteers. As such, it frequently involved the following experiences for those who participated:

- It had the earmarks of a rite of passage, beginning with the training period and ending with the completion of service (Shea 1966). Christopher (1996) makes explicit the analogy to an odyssey, describing the Peace Corps (as well as VISTA and Conservation Corps) as characterized by a call to adventure; location in a separate place isolated from previous life; a role with new responsibilities and obligations; new interpersonal roles; a sense of expanded autonomy; gaining of new skills, knowledge, and experience; display of a new status; and acquisition of a new sense of self.

- As a rite of passage, it often generated feelings of personal regeneration—a transformation of the self through giving to and acceptance of others vastly different from oneself (Boyer 1966). One comment: "The Peace Corps experience is equivalent to having successful psychotherapy" (Carolyn Payton, quoted in Redmon 1986, 371). Because the experience was embedded in idealism, altruism, nobility, and asceticism, it constituted a way of doing something with and giving meaning to one's life— renouncing personal advancement and materialism and embracing morality (Hoffman 1998). Many volunteers were influenced to go into international work, for example the Agency for International Development, other ameliorative activity, or public service (Redmon 1986).

- Many volunteers, while alone in the field, came to experience a strong sense of group and moral community with other volunteers (Peace Corps 1995; Rice 1985)—*communitas* and the feeling of specialness that attends it. One comment: "I've never been a team player and have always been very much a solitary individual; this was one time in my life when I have felt solidly and warmly part of a group" (quoted in Redmon 1986, 381). The drive for nonbureaucratic, "people-to-people" contact extended to relations with citizens of other countries in which the volunteers worked (Textor 1966).

- As part of the immersion, there was a certain amount of stripping of one's past evident in rigorous training, internal discipline, strict regulation of volunteers' personal behavior, internal discipline, and shedding of many prior beliefs (Hoffman 1998). Heath (1966) describes the emergence of a distinctive culture with the ingredients of energetic activity, egoistic altruism, proud humility, local identification, realistic idealism, planned expedience, situational austerity, and organizational loyalty.

The experience had its threatening sides as well. Many volunteers came from the middle class but spent their tour in the midst of abject poverty, disease, and sometimes personal danger (Rice 1985). Many of the "natives" with whom they worked resented their presence. They experienced anti-Americanism among those to whom they thought they were bringing the best America had to offer (Boyer 1966). These negative aspects contributed to the solidarity among those who had "made it," and in that sense former volunteers represent a group similar to military veterans.

Though the Peace Corps seems an unequivocal instance of an odyssey experience at both individual and social levels, three qualifications of this conclusion must be ventured:

(a) there was a great deal of individual variation among participants; (b) much of the experience was not spontaneous or individual, but subject to a semiofficial "Peace Corps culture" that influenced and gave meaning to the enterprise; and (c) like many heroic episodes in history, the Peace Corps experience has undergone routinization, with a corresponding reduction in the social and psychological consequences experienced in its days of moral enthusiasm.

FREEDOM SUMMER:
A SECULAR/POLITICAL BUT HOLY CRUSADE

Freedom Summer was one of the most dramatic and important moments in racial and political history of the twentieth century. It was short in duration, lasting only three months in the summer of 1964. It was a project—initially referred to simply as the Summer Project—initiated and organized by the Student Non-Violent Coordinating Committee, a visible and active civil rights organization in the 1960s. Its purpose was simple: to send a large number of young people into Mississippi to register blacks for upcoming presidential elections and to educate prospective voters in so-called Freedom Schools. The project involved more than a thousand people—mostly white, middle-class, northern college students—converging on Mississippi to do their work.

The project was politically significant in a number of ways. It marked an apex of the political strategy of nonviolence, which was the trademark of the civil rights movement under the leadership of Martin Luther King, Jr., in the late 1950s and 1960s. In some respects the apex was also the end, because interracial cooperation immediately diminished with the rise of the more radical black power and black separatist movements, and nonviolence ended with the urban racial disturbances symbolized vividly by the Watts riots in 1965. As a brief but dramatic episode, it supplied the inspiration, language, strategy, and tactics—and in notable degree, the manpower and leadership—for the student activism that already had some momentum but which broke into the open in a spectacular way with the free speech movement at Berkeley in the fall of 1964 (McAdam 1988). The civil rights movement and the flurry of student activism, moreover, fed into the anti–Vietnam War protests, spun off into numerous countercultural movements, and served as the backdrop for the rise of a more militant feminism and greater consciousness and political activity among other minority groups in the 1970s.

Aside from its broader political significance, the episode of Freedom Summer stands out in its significance for the participants—and in its collective aspects—as an odyssey experience. The following ingredients establish it as such:

- In terms of physical movement, Freedom Summer had the earmarks of a pilgrimage, however secular. Those who participated in it took temporary leave from their home locations and moved to a site—Mississippi—that, while not holy or sacred in a religious sense, marked the most visible and symbolic place of evil in the form of extreme racial segregation and oppression. The flip side of the evil was the moral work to be done in fighting it. This geographical convergence was also symbolically consistent with the march motif, a significant feature of the civil rights movement.

- The brief movement resembled the medieval Crusades in one important particular—as a fusion of pilgrimage and moral war against an immoral force. The event also echoed in microcosm the American Civil War and its enduring collective memories.

- The participants were, to a number, young idealists emanating from an idealistic phase of American history, inspired by the recent accomplishments of the civil rights movements, as well as the optimism of Kennedy's New Frontier (including its idealistic Peace Corps) and the stirrings of the Great Society (including VISTA and Job Corps) (ibid.).

- The venture into Mississippi was fraught with danger. In the early weeks of the summer, three participants were kidnapped and murdered by segregationists led by Mississippi law enforcement officials, and the whole period was marked by arrests, assaults, beatings, and intimidation of the volunteers. Blacks who dared to mobilize and attempted to register to vote were similarly exposed to danger and violence.

- The element of *communitas* was evident. All were in a crusade together. Those who were not housed in black households lived together in Freedom Houses. The solidarity was made vivid by the participants' articulated sense of the "beloved community" (ibid., 108), despite the fact that that community was so short-lived and fraught with racial tensions and sexual inequalities.

- The impact on many participants was profound. Many felt liberated, many felt radicalized, many felt increasingly alienated from the larger society, and all experienced some type of regeneration through their participation. The end of the heroic period of activism meant, almost by definition, that the participants had to return to a more routine way of life, but the political and personal effects of the experience remained with many of them (ibid., ch. 4).

This chapter has *religious* in its title, and most of the proto-typical illustrations brought forward have been religious. Yet in noting in a preliminary way the continuities between the pilgrimage and tourism (to be elaborated in the next chapter), and by including two completely secular illustrations at the end, the continuities between the religious and the secular emerge. Though the religious and the secular are manifestly different in many regards, I would like to argue that the odyssey experience in its social and psychological essentials minimizes the differences and constitutes a common dynamic that bridges them.

FOUR

Secularized and Commercialized Odysseys

The title of chapter 3, on religion-based transitions and journeys, and of this one, on secularized and commercialized ones, suggest an either-or contrast. As I noted at the end of the last chapter, that suggestion is misleading. The types fuse together. In chapter 3, I found myself compelled for reasons of continuity to include a number of secular episodes that had the ingredients of their religious cousins. In this chapter, the same overlap appears. For example, I will say some words about shamanism and religious healing by way of introducing the therapeutic process. This principle of fusion underlies a larger assumption on which this book is based: the odyssey experience is a pervasive human phenomenon that cuts across many received conceptual distinctions.

TRAVEL AND TOURISM

Like most modern odyssey experiences, tourism as a search for the unfamiliar and desirable reaches back into premodern history (for historical analogues, see MacCannell (1976). Its massification, however, is very recent. The reason for this is that its two major preconditions are themselves by-products of changes emanating from the commercialization and industrialization of the world. These are:

- The spread of leisure from the ranks of the elite to most of the population. Scholars of leisure generally define it as time aside from the routines of work and related community obligations, with the implication that the individual's control over that time is discretionary (Dumazedier 1974). The sources of leisure are the shortening of working hours and the provision of variable periods for vacation. That precondition provides *time* for tourism, though tourism is not the only use made of leisure.

- The rise in disposable income for most people in developed societies, associated with their increased economic productivity. This precondition provides *resources*, or the capacity to fill leisure time with travel, which is never without cost.

Two additional features should be mentioned. First, the term *discretionary* implies that travel is among the most voluntary of odyssey experiences. It contrasts both with coerced, ordeal experiences, such as initiations in rites of passage and other forms (chapters 3 and 6), and with the religious pilgrimage, voluntary in the sense that pilgrims can choose not to join but nested in an often compelling set of religious obligations.

Second, to say that modern tourism is voluntary is not to say that it is not normatively regulated. Smith (1989) defined tourism as leisure time + discretionary income + "positive local sanctions." There are prescriptions—obligatory rites—for the traveler-to-be: "If one goes to Europe, one 'must see' Paris; if one goes to Paris, one 'must see' Notre Dame, the Eiffel Tower, the Louvre; if one goes to the Louvre, one 'must see' the Venus de Milo and, of course, the Mona Lisa. There are quite literally millions of tourists who have spent their savings to make the pilgrimage to these sights" (MacCannell 1976, 3). Tourists are expected to display appropriate wonder and appropriate behavior (gasps, admiration, raves) at their objects of interest. As a somewhat ludicrous example of this, while my wife and I were gazing at Edinburgh Castle, another American tourist leaned toward us and said, without humor, "This castle does for you what a castle is supposed to do for you." More generally, "the tourist 'has to' enjoy himself. If he does not join in, he is a spoilsport" (Brown 1996, 36).

The growth of mass tourism has taken different national and cultural paths. In contemporary France, it evolved in large part as stylized month-long holidays defined in the context of social justice for working people (Furlough 1998). The Grand Tour, originally a prerogative of the European elite classes, subsequently spread to the middle classes in forms such as the Cook's Tour (Graburn 1995). In Britain the "vacation by the sea," long a prerogative of the wealthy classes, also evolved to the working classes, as costs dropped with the advent of the railroad and holidays caught their interest (Walton 1981). A special American emphasis is the European tour (sometimes a college graduation gift for a child when parents can afford it), often tinged with a sense of "return to roots." In cold-war Eastern Europe, organized two-week mass holidays at sites such as Varna on the Black Sea became the norm, dictated largely by government policies, prohibitions on travel outside Iron Curtain countries, and unavailability of hard Western currencies. My treatment of tourism will emphasize the dimensions that cut across such differences.

One further initial clarification: Modern tourism has become above all a market phenomenon, a giant industry. Associated with this fact is a dilemma that repeats itself in the scholarly literature. Is the impulse to tourism an expression of psychological attractions to experiences regarded as gratifying to travelers (the "genuine" approach) or an expression of influence and manipulation on the part of those who profit financially from these experiences (the "artificial" approach)? I do not regard this as an either-or issue but see tourism (and other commercialized odysseys) as a coming together of personal and commercial interests. It is impossible to understand the phenomenon without reference both to its psychology and to its embeddedness in economic and social contexts.

Though mass tourism is both secular and mainly commercialized, scholars have not failed to compare it with religious odyssey experiences. Explains Brown, "The structure of tourism is basically identical to that of ritual behaviour: it first translates the tourist into a sacred world, then transforms/renews him, and finally returns him to normality. What [the tourist] has experienced . . . is a classic rite of re-creation and renewal" (1996, 35–36). Hitchcock makes the comparison to the pilgrimage explicit: "Tourism functions outside ordinary time as the secular equivalent of religion. Leaving behind the mundane, the tourist passes through a series of rites of passage, crossing the threshold of the sacred, eventually returning home anew. The journey may be likened to the spiritual death and rebirth that characterizes baptism and pilgrimage" (2000, 3). Nash (1995) makes an explicit effort to apply van Gennep's and Turner's stages of separation-liminality-reintegration to tourism as a form akin to both initiation and pilgrimage Pilgrimage and tourism blend substantively in the phenomenon described as "religious tourism" (Rinschede 1992), touring to religious sites as inspirational experiences without actually taking on the role of pilgrim.

Tourism has been written about for as long as it has existed, mainly in the form of travelogues. Scholarly interest in the topic is barely a half-century old, and that interest crystallized in large part as an expression of the great growth in tourism after World War II. The work has been carried out largely by anthropologists. The most important conceptual innovation is the structural approach of Victor Turner, and the two most notable theorists are Dean MacCannell (1976) and Nelson Graburn (1989). In 1973 a journal, *Annals of Tourism Research*, appeared as a tangible expression of the growing interest and a testimony that tourism was crystallizing into a definite, albeit somewhat marginalized subfield of anthropology, sociology, psychology, and semiotics.

Essentials of the Tourism Experience

I turn now to an ideal-typical account of tourism, which establishes it in the family of odyssey experiences. In undertaking this analysis, I make no claim that the psychological motives and experiences of all who travel are identical. The different types of tourists suggest a diversity of motives and interests; Yiannakis and Gibson (1992), for example, identified the sun-lover, action-seeker, anthropologist, archaeologist, organized mass tourist, thrill-seeker, explorer, jet-setter, seeker, independent mass tourist, high-class tourist, drifter, escapist, and sports-lover. Investigations of the psychology of individual travelers reveal the greatest range of individual motives and interests (Pearce 1982; Kohn 1997). The analysis that follows attempts to cut across the psychological sources of variation.

SEPARATION

Of all odyssey experiences, tourism is the most obvious candidate for this ingredient. To travel means, by definition, to leave and separate. It is commonly defined as "getting away from it all" (Dann 1977). Many who write about tourism regard it as an expression of alienation from routines, especially work routines. This is certainly the symbolism of the "weekend away" (Rybc-zynski 1991). Graburn (1989) stresses the departure as a move-ment from the profane to the sacred and finds analogies between leaving home for a trip and dying symbolically (with the return home a changed person as the counterpart of rebirth).

An autobiographical account of an experience of "getting away" is in order. In September 2001 my wife and I were sched-uled to take a ten-day trip to Norway, where I would first lecture at the University of Oslo and then we would travel around the country for a week or so. We were scheduled to fly from San Francisco on September 12. But 9/11 happened, the airport closed for four days, and the trip had to be postponed. We were as shocked and disoriented as the rest by the September 11 disaster. And we had ten empty days before us. In an impulsive moment, we decided to take to the camper and go to the Pacific North-west—to get away from the self-torture of gluing ourselves to CNN for all the bits of new news and non-news, commentaries, and tedious replays. It was a spontaneous odyssey experience to escape from the pain. To be sure, we kept the camper radio on continuously—reflecting the ambivalence of it all—and, quite unconsciously, I developed a compulsion to include Mount St. Helens in our wanderings, which I interpret retrospectively as a symbolic reminder to myself of the violent side of life.

DANGER AND THE UNKNOWN

Tourism, especially international tourism, has a number of often unspoken sources of danger and uncertainty. By definition, a person leaving on a trip travels in several different vehicles, each with greater or less probability for accidents, and over which he or she has little or no control. In addition to this residue of physical danger, the traveler often ventures into unknown lands, populated by people speaking foreign languages and following foreign ways of life. There also may be encounters with frustration and hostility (Furnham 1984). The traveler does not know exactly what to expect. This uneasiness is, of course, part of the excitement of travel. The danger and uncertainty vary according to the choices of travelers themselves. They may take a tour that is completely scheduled and organized. If not that, they may themselves schedule every hotel and every sight. Or they may choose to drift. They may choose to try or avoid dangerous activities, such as rock climbing, rapids shooting, and bungee jumping. But as a general rule, leaving the routines of life involves some anxiety and its accompanying psychic discomfort.

IDEALIZATION OF THE EXPERIENCE: MYTHOLOGY

A common feature of travel is the elaboration of "myths of place"—images of what a destination is like and what it offers:

the culture of London, the gaiety of Paris, the grandeur of Rome, the antiquities of Egypt and Turkey, the shrines of Kyoto, the moral latitude of Sweden, and the romance and wealth of Hollywood. The myths have a basis in historical reality, but they are simplified and frozen into stereotypes. Other, general motifs appear as part of the idealization process. Dann (1996) extracted the following types of paradise portrayed in tourist brochures:

> *Paradise contrived:* no people; natives as scenery; natives as cultural markers.
>
> *Paradise confined:* tourists only—tourist ghetto; *communitas;* tourists enjoying one another.
>
> *Paradise controlled:* limited contact with locals; natives as servants, entertainers, and vendors.
>
> *Paradise confused:* further contact with locals; attempting to enter locals-only zones; tourists as natives.

These types of idealization have commercial value, and for that reason become the object of commercial cultivation. Tombstone, Arizona, more or less makes its living from the memory of Wyatt Earp and the OK Corral. Movies like *City Slickers* and *Deliverance* help preserve the frontier myth (Butler 2002). Bryson records a classic distortion:

> [A Ladybird Book in the 1950s and 1960s] contained meticulously drafted, richly coloured illustrations of a prosperous, contented, litter-free Britain in which the sun always shone. . . . My favourite . . . portrayed an island of rocky coves and long views that was recognizably British, but with a Mediterranean climate and a tidy absence of pay-and-display car parks, bingo parlours, and the tackier sort

of amusement arcades. . . . I was strongly influenced by this book and for some years agreed to take our family holidays at the British seaside on the assumption that one day we would find this magic place with summer days, forever sunny, the water as warm as a sitz-bath, and commercial blight unknown. (1995, 124–25)

The paradox of contemporary travel is that it involves a search for some type of unique simplicity in a world that is becoming both more homogeneous and more complex (Lanfant 1995).

AUTHENTICITY

Another common theme of contemporary tourism is the search for the authentic: "There is a cachet connected with international travel, exploration, multiculturalism, etc., that [foreign exotic arts] symbolize; at the same time there is the nostalgic input of the *handmade* in a plastic world" (Graburn 1976, 2–3; see also Stuart 1984). The search for authenticity often reflects an explicit or implicit alienation from contemporary life in the developed world. To be authentic, an object must be unique, have proper workmanship, historical integrity, and genuineness (Litrell, Anderson, and Brown 1993). One consequence of the demand for authenticity, reflecting "native" adaptive rationality, is the cultivation of "staged authenticity" (MacCannell 1976) and "genuine fakes" (Brown 1996) for tourist viewing and purchase.

THE SOUVENIR

The souvenir is a concrete way of symbolizing, remembering, reliving, and making permanent the mythical and authentic qualities of the tourist experience. It is simultaneously a way of sharing the magical quality of a journey with others and impressing them by claiming special status. It is often also proof of the authenticity of the experience and evidence that the tourist has "touched the real" in his or her travels. More profoundly, like the relic from the pilgrimage, the souvenir may serve as a denial of the temporariness and nonreproducibility of a journey and even keep alive what has died in its transience (see Graburn 1989; Hitchcock 2000). In a word, the souvenir touches closely the yearning for immortality. Souvenirs are also fair game for genuine faking, as testified, for example, by the great lines of tourist shops hawking thousands and thousands of "genuine" Eskimo dolls for the thousands of tourists who pour out of cruise ships into the streets of Juneau, Alaska.

COMMUNITAS

Two case studies—both of people who are "in the same boat"—illustrate the power of community, leveling, and regressive identification that frequently accompany collective touristic adventures. Foster describes the culture of conviviality that developed on a South Seas cruise ship: "First names were in, and titles out. . . . There was little evidence of attempts to establish status. . . . [P]olitics, especially, was a near-taboo topic," as was religion (1986, 227–33). Observing a very different kind of cruise experience—young people on a carnivalesque group tour to the British Virgin Islands—Lett (1983) described the same leveling characteristics, giving special attention to the intimacy, equality, homogeneous informal dress, and shedding of items of status distinction. Also to be brought to mind are the occasions—familiar to most of us—when strangers seated together on a plane exchange intimacies for that period, confident in the expectation that the revelations will never get beyond that place and time. Sometimes the basis for group solidarity is very specialized, as when groups of campers owning the same model or same year of recreational vehicle gather in a campground and deem themselves a group through common ownership (Green 1978). In general, tourists, especially those living the "confined paradise," form little communities, though there is also a class of tourists who, in their search for genuineness and the native or natural life, set themselves off from and above "typical" tourists, though often in the warm company of other superior seekers.

My wife and I experienced an extreme of the *communitas* effect in May 2002, when we took a fifteen-day rafting trip on the Colorado River through the entire Grand Canyon. About twenty others were on the trip, including guides. There was an undertone of threat to the adventure, symbolized by the isolation and desolation of the trip (despite its beauty), as well as the thrilling but frightening daily rides over sometimes savage rapids. The group became a tightly knit band, everybody convivial and friendly in a world apart. In comparing notes later, my wife and I agreed that if we had met fully half of the adventurers in ordinary life, we would have found them disagreeable and offensive, certainly not to be befriended. But that impulse was overwhelmed by the community and camaraderie of that little band.

The *communitas* of travelers evidently has its limits, however. Writing in 1840, Alexis de Tocqueville (1968) cited differences in the behavior of Americans and Englishmen traveling abroad. Americans, he said, are at once friends because they conceive of themselves as equal. Englishmen, however, are quiet and remote from other Englishmen, unless they happen to be of the same social rank. The point is the same as that made with reference to caste and pilgrimages in chapter 3: sometimes social differences are so fundamental and pervasive that they override the power of *communitas* generated by the odyssey. Eade (1992) has also pointed out the persistent tension and even conflict observed in modern pilgrimages, between "genuine," believing pilgrims and tourists who come for the spectacle.

NOSTALGIA

Nostalgia is a complex affect that combines the happiness associated with the odyssey of touring with the sad recognition that it cannot be repeated as it was originally experienced. Nostalgia is the void that souvenirs excite and attempt unsuccessfully to fill. It is the reproduction, in memory, of "life as it was," something discovered in experiencing the authentic. Similarly it can be the preservation, also in memory, of the world we are losing (Jules-Rosette 1984; Graburn 1995). Nostalgia is also a basis for *communitas*-after-the-fact, as tourists who have visited the same places and done the same things are brought together by comparing experiences, material objects, photographs, and postcards.

THE END OF THE JOURNEY

Graburn (1989) has identified reentry as an integral part of the experience of tourism. It is an ambivalent element, combining happiness in returning with sadness and relief at ending the emotion-charged experience of being away. It is routinely marked by a special "last night in Europe" restaurant meal or ritual exchanges of addresses and phone numbers, with vows to see one another, all parties knowing secretly that this will never happen or, if it does, will not be the same. Sometimes the journey ends with a blast. I remember crossing the Atlantic on the *Ile de France* in the late 1950s. On the last night before docking, a special meal was served. At the end—and evidently tightly orchestrated by crew and attendants—the party turned into a kind of frenzy, involving food fights and other regressive behavior, such as forcing grown adults to don giant diapers and suckle from oversized baby bottles.

Above all, the end of the journey is an occasion for most travelers to remind themselves, with true conviction or not, that they have profited from the experience, are rested, improved, fulfilled, or renewed. Such self-vows are made with the knowledge that the transformation is not permanent and begs to be repeated on another trip at another time. A small minority acknowledge to themselves that the trip was a disappointment or a waste of time (also evidence for and a commentary on the high expectations that travel engenders).

Offshoots of Mass Tourism

Anthropologists and others who write about tourism raise issues other than the quality of the experience expected or lived. Travel and tourism have become a signature of globalization, and scholars have focused on the following offshoots:

- From an economic point of view, tourism has become a massive industry with a turnover of billions of dollars per annum. It has stimulated allied industries such as airline companies, spawned numerous organizations such as travel agencies and tour organizers, new roles such as travel agent, guide, and new practices of image organizing and public relations about destinations to be visited

and how to get to them (Reimer 1991). The tourism
industry is the largest single enterprise sustained by the
human attraction to odysseys.

- Also from the economic point of view, mass tourism
  transforms local economies by generating tourist craft
  enterprises, restaurants, hotels, and guide services. Since
  travel involves the expenditure of discretionary consumer income, it is especially responsive to economic ups
  and downs and subjects these local enterprises to a high
  level of economic instability.

- From the cultural point of view, the presence of foreign
  visitors and the consequent exposure to foreign values
  means that the "natives" are placed in a situation of
  economic dependence, as well as having their traditional
  ways challenged. Tourism generates ambivalence toward
  both foreign and native cultures (Sadler and Archer
  1975). Societies that receive tourists have also proven
  adaptive in herding them to certain spots, generating
  specialized roles to deal with them, and otherwise insulating them from local life, but these are only partially
  successful in minimizing the impact (MacCannell 1977).
  Anthropologists have been especially sensitive to the
  impact on populations that are targets of tourism (Nash
  and Smith 1991).

- From the environmental point of view, the costs of mass
  tourism, also mainly for the target communities, have
  been identified as price increases, loss of resources, pollution, traffic, vandalism, litter, and low-paid seasonal
  employment. Some scholars and interest groups have

promoted the idea of "alternative tourism" (Butler 1992), which, broadly defined, refers to practices that respect local environments, communities, and values (Smith and Eadington 1992).

- From the social point of view, tourism constitutes an ingredient of social stratification. To travel abroad itself is a sign, albeit often weak, of status. For centuries, elite and wealthy travelers, when witnessing their preferred form of travel becoming massified, have sought out more distant, more expensive, more exotic, and less available destinations and modes of tourism. Some tourists regard themselves as "above" the rest in seeking less contrived, more "natural" locations. And "alternative tourists" may regard themselves as morally superior to those who supposedly respect local peoples, cultures, and environments less than they do. However, a special dynamic may develop: insofar as alternative tourism "catches on," it too may develop in the direction of massification and routinization—in the form of a "more subtle, covert and insidious form of staging" (Cohen 1989, 57), thus setting up a new cycle of seeking even more remote, authentic, "alternative" experiences, thus perpetuating the eternal chasing game for the truly authentic and superior.

THE MARRIAGE, THE HONEYMOON, AND SURROUNDING RITUALS

Marriage as the formal establishment of reproductive kinship units is for all intents and purposes a universal phenomenon. Furthermore, it is the focus of formal rites of passage involving the marrying couple as the primary participants, but also including extended kin and generally a public proclamation of the event. Marriage is a standard rite of passage in religions, though its exclusively religious status has been compromised by the institutionalization of alternate forms, mainly civil marriages by the state authority and in other circumstances (for example, performance of a legal marriage ceremony by a ship captain at sea), and in all kinds of novel settings—in a university faculty club, in the wilderness, or in a hot air balloon. In recent decades, the marriage ceremony has been further diluted in its exclusiveness by serial marriages (ceremonies move toward the informal for second, third, and further marriages), temporary or permanent cohabitation without marrying, same-sex unions, communal alternatives, and efforts on the part of participants to make the event more personally meaningful, for example, by writing one's own wedding vows (Chesser 1980).

Marriage ceremonies are causes for celebration, but the somber side is always present. The couple is reminded of the their heavy permanent responsibilities to love and care for one another ("from this day forward, until death do us part") and warned of the perils and rough times that mingle with happiness in the journey of life. Public notice of some sort is sometimes but not always given (in the form of marriage banns or invitations sent out for the ceremony), and the community is given a ritualized opportunity for involvement ("Speak now, or forever hold your peace"). The passage, of course, is from the freer, less responsible single state to the many obligations implied by permanent intimacy and any children issuing from the union.

Of recent vintage are a number of secular adjuncts to marriage, mainly the honeymoon and attendant celebrations. The honeymoon is a rite of passage fused with tourism. It stands in contrast to both the marriage ceremony and the state of marriage itself, in that it is intended as a delimited period of isolation and indulgence, free from care and responsibility. Reaching a high point of institutionalization and romanticization in the late nineteenth and early twentieth centuries (Dubinsky 1999), the honeymoon has been diluted in more recent times, for the same reasons as marriage ceremonies: more informal marriages, serial marriages, and alternative forms of intimate arrangements. Nevertheless it remains a fully secular and more or less completely commercialized ritual, and it reveals the features of an odyssey experience.

It was Slater (1963) who developed the most sensitive psychological and sociological interpretation of the modern honeymoon. Writing in the psychoanalytic tradition, he elaborated the idea of "social regression" to account for its characteristics. By that term he meant the transition from structured involvements in community and society to a brief period of simpler structure and minimal involvement, with a subsequent return to a new set of obligations. While not citing van Gennep, Slater's interpretation is completely consistent with the conceptual framework of disaggregation-liminality-reaggregation that van Gennep applied to rites of passage in general.

The following features of the honeymoon are the most salient:

- A period of more or less complete *withdrawal* of the couple, both geographically to a remote location and socially, so that during the honeymoon they have one another to themselves. This is the liminal period.

- Closely associated with the withdrawal is the couple's *isolation* from others. At one time, though not so common nowadays, the destination of the honeymoon was

kept secret, except for a few intimates of the couple.
Once at the destination, the themes of isolation and
secrecy become more informal, more self-imposed.
Non-honeymooners staying at the same resort or hotel
observe an almost ritualized inhibition when they meet a
honeymooning couple: they express delight and congrat-
ulations, perhaps ask the couple when and where they
were married, and where they will "settle"—a word that
itself reveals the "unsettledness" of the honeymoon and
the transition back to routine—but generally observe
a taboo on further inquiry or involvement. In many
cases the isolation from the mundane is accomplished by
package deals, theme parks, and cruises, "where money
does not change hands and daily details are taken care
of in advance" (Rapoport and Rapoport 1964). Many
ads from resorts and travel agencies stress the theme of
isolation—away from people, on walks in the wilderness.
Some resorts have fashioned their services exclusively for
honeymooners (ibid.), providing a kind of "company of
equals" of honeymooners. This creates a kind of *communitas* as well, in which the only status that matters
is being honeymooners, and "outside" markers of the
honeymooners, such as differences in occupation and
income, are diminished.

- *Finiteness* of the period. Honeymoons vary in duration
  and elaborateness, but all end with the return of the couple to the routines of married life—a new home, a new
  level of commitment to one another, and new social and
  financial obligations. The episode of carefree and bliss-
  ful existence must come to an end, since by definition

a honeymoon cannot last forever; its temporariness is symbolized in the adage "The honeymoon is over."

- An emphasis on *license*. This refers above all to the couple's sexual experiences on the honeymoon. Fantasies on this theme abound, and it is also a source of ribald humor ("I wonder if they eat like rabbits, too") and envy. License is part of the package of secrecy and taboo as well, seldom talked about *to* honeymooners but thought *about* all the time. Once again, this thread has become diluted in recent times, largely because of relaxed mores calling for virginity until marriage and the general acceptance of premarital sex and cohabitation, which compromise the specialness of sex on the honeymoon. Nevertheless, commercial advertisements play up the symbols of freedom, passion, sexuality, and loss of control in exotic settings such as waterfalls, rivers, oceans, and the tropics—all symbolizing wildness or heat (Rapoport and Rapoport 1964).

- A subterranean emphasis on *perils* and *dangers* in the experience. Marriage itself is frequently described not only as "tying the knot," which means losing freedom, but also as "taking the plunge," which connotes the tension between indulgence and trepidation (Bulcroft, Smeins, and Bulcroft 1999). The special significance of Niagara Falls, which was *the* symbol of the honeymoon in the late nineteenth and early twentieth centuries, rested on its connotations not only of remove, unreality, and excitement, but also of danger, wildness, and lack of control. It was the place not only for honeymooners but also for daredevils who plunged over the falls in barrels (Dubinsky 1999). At the moment of the couple's departure for the honeymoon, friends paint slogans and hang signs and tin cans on their getaway cars—making public what is supposed to be private and intimate—and subject them to practical jokes, such as tying the couple's clothes in knots (for a vivid vignette, see Thompson and Bridges 1971). These stunts no doubt have many meanings, mainly envy on the part of perpetrators, but they also serve as symbolic reminders that all is not bliss, even on honeymoons (Slater 1963).

So much for the classic ingredients of the odyssey experience in the honeymoon. One effect of its widespread commercialization is that some elements are highlighted and others downplayed. In a content analysis, Gersuny found that advertisers lay stress "on a vocabulary of romantic love, on evocation of exotic places, on sensuous imagery, and on eulogies for the beds and bathtubs available for guests" (1970, 260). Bliss and isolation are front and center, and the themes of uncertainty, danger, letdown, and sexual failure are avoided or buried in remote symbolism. The reason for this distortion seems simple enough: negatives do not sell. This principle is a generic feature of commercialization and, as we have seen, is conspicuous in the promotion of travel and tourism in general.

Other rituals surround marriage. One of the most significant is the traditional bridal shower, a way of celebrating and seeing the bride into marriage (mainly but no longer exclusively by other women) through the offering of ceremonial gifts. In recent times this form has occasionally been extended to the "groomal shower" (Berardo and Vera 1981), not differing in essentials from the bridal shower but centered on the bride-groom and symbolizing his "equality" with the bride. Both are benign and largely positive ceremonies, despite hostile joking and some hostile gifts (ibid.).

The traditional bachelor party, or "stag party," for the groom-to-be is a more complex illustration. Williams (1994), using ethnographic observation, has described the full array of ingredients of this mini-odyssey. They include isolation of the males from female company, "stripping" of the future groom's masculinity and "feminizing" and otherwise humiliating him by "pantsing" and sexual teasing by a hired stripper, regret-ting his loss ("another one bites the dust"), and commemorat-ing his last night of freedom—all in the context of "buddiness" and solidarity among male friends. Williams interprets the stag party as a rite of passage, characterized by an "expulsion from manhood by peers," denial of the groom's feminine side, and commemorating his "loss" in a passage to the new, less free state of marriage. It is a process of honoring by humiliating, and symbols of death and rebirth are often in evidence. Like other ceremonies associated with weddings, the classic bachelor party has weakened, largely because of the weakening of the entire passage into the married state, but nonetheless it reflects the essentials of the transitional odyssey experience.

FOUR TYPES OF ACADEMIC ODYSSEY

I turn now to several arrangements found in college and univer-sities and allied research institutions. My methods rely in part on consultation of published sources and in part on anthropo-logical or biographical experience, based on my years as faculty member and as director of an Education Abroad Program in the United Kingdom and Ireland and director of the Center for Advanced Study in the Behavioral Sciences in Stanford.

The Collegiate Years

Going away to and being at college—at least in the United Sates—is an experience about which there is a kind of national mythology and romance. This is perpetuated in part by alumni of colleges and universities who remember (selectively) their years of freedom, the growth they experienced, their fellowship with other students, their favorite Mr. Chips professors, the athletic contests and fight songs, partying, and days of courtship. They are supposed to be years of happiness and happy memories—happier than the turbulence of adolescence and happier than the later, more responsible years of job, family, and community. The collegiate myth has also been reinforced in novels and films and by college and university fundraisers who try to capitalize on the remembered happiness and institutional loyalty of their graduates. This idea of college as an isolated and serene refuge is often latent but comes into the open from time to time. It made an odd, somewhat tragic appearance in the wake of the slaughter of students at Virginia Tech on April 16, 2007, when commentators from the president on down proclaimed that this sort of tragedy ought not to happen at colleges, which are supposed to be serene, peaceful, isolated, positive settings.

In many respects the college years, especially as ideally portrayed, do constitute an odyssey experience. They are a rite of passage, a moratorium period between adolescence and the years of adult responsibilities. They have a distinct beginning (starting in the freshman year) and a distinct end (the graduation ceremony). Many traditional colleges are isolated from their surrounding communities. College is clearly a disengagement from family life and authority. It is less structured than the work and family life to follow. In those senses it is a liminal period. It has a certain *communitas* centering on one's class and on special groups and friendships. Students develop feelings about the specialness of their institution and about themselves as its members (for example, "Reedies"). The collegiate experience also involves maturation, increased confidence, and identity development—in a word, a generative process.

Despite this general conformity to the odyssey experience, the collegiate years qualify only partially as a pure type for several reasons:

- Four years presses the upper limit for an odyssey experience; it is difficult to sustain the special sense of remove and exceptionality.

- The collegiate years, while unstructured, also have their own structure, largely in the form of a curriculum of courses to be completed, the administration-faculty-student roles (still important, even though the principle of *in loco parentis* has decayed) and less formal structures in the form of memberships in clubs, societies, bands, athletic teams, and residential groups.

- The massification of higher education has also changed the character of the collegiate experience. Many more students, especially those in community colleges, reside at home, thus lessening the break from it. Many more

students come from working-class and immigrant families; these students tend to have a more instrumental,
self-advancing approach to college and, for that reason,
are less likely to be attracted to the collegiate myth.
Many of these students must work, and this makes for
less full-time and inclusive involvement in college life. A
much higher proportion of students stop out, drop out,
or transfer from college to college; this also dilutes the
myth. Many of these "swirlers" do not partake of the
ceremonial aspects of college life, including attending
graduation.

• Closely related, there has been an upward drift in the age
of undergraduates, making the idealized years of eighteen to twenty-two less the norm. Older students, moreover, are more mature, know more about where they are
going, as a rule, and are not so attracted to the youthful
diversions and hijinks of traditional collegiate life.

By virtue of these trends and modifications, the undergraduate years deserve inclusion in that large family of experiences
described as the odyssey, but in reality they are only a partial
manifestation of it.

Education Abroad

The institution of a year in a foreign country during the collegiate years is of relatively recent vintage. It is a designed odyssey
(a year away) within a longer odyssey (the collegiate moratorium). At one time stereotyped as a somewhat fashionable thing
for young women to do (and associated with the Smith College

program), it has now become an experience for growing minorities of students at many colleges and universities. Like most odysseys, its beginning, duration, and end are fixed and known in advance. The year abroad typically carries as its justification the expectation that such an experience is educationally and culturally broadening and personally maturing, and this appears to be a significant element in students' motivation to seek it out (Carlson et al. 1990). One can also point to kindred experiences—for example, high-school years abroad with the Friends Service Committee and graduate experience abroad to conduct research or undertake fieldwork—but the most visible institutionalized type is the undergraduate year in another country.

The year abroad is simultaneously an exciting adventure, a challenge, and a threat. It is an adventure in the same sense that leaving home for college is an adventure, a journey into a wider world with many open possibilities. It is a challenge because it often calls for demanding communication in a language other than one's own. It is a threat largely because it means that the student of necessity becomes unmoored and is forced to adapt to the unknown. I observed this in dramatic fashion when students participating in the program I directed arrived in London for an orientation session. Whereas I as director was interested in giving them a broad and informative orientation to British universities and British society, most of them expressed an immediate and obsessive hunger for small adaptive details like where to change dollars into sterling at the best rate, where to find a vegetarian restaurant, how to convert 220-volt electricity for use in 110-volt hair dryers—all questions involving a search for the familiar. Research by Deutsch revealed that the adaptation process was facilitated according to the "level of information [and familiarity they have] about the new culture" (1970, 68). In my own reading of several hundred "statements of purpose" of students coming to the United Kingdom and Ireland, I was struck by how many of them had spent previous time abroad (for example, "army brats" or those with parents who had lived or traveled abroad extensively). This also seemed to be a "readying" factor that both motivated the students to go abroad and diminished their apprehension about the uncertainty of the experience.

Education-abroad programs vary in the degree to which the students are "destructured" from their home institutions. Many programs last for one year, others for a briefer period. Some universities establish their own centers abroad, where faculty members from the home institution do the teaching. Other institutions have institution-specific agreements with foreign universities and place a supervisor from the home institution on the scene. Still others ask that the students enroll in a foreign university largely on its terms. In all events, their situations abroad become somewhat restructured in short order, as they find housing, enroll in courses, and begin to meet others.

The degree of destructuring is in part in the hands of the students themselves. Because the experience typically involves a group of students from home institutions in the United States, any given student has the option of interacting mainly with fellow nationals or with foreigners, and any given group is likely to break down along these lines. The issue is a general one, but more pressing when students are in a language setting other than their own. In general, the interaction with fellow nationals is likely to constitute "a carryover of peer-group pressure from the home . . . culture" and possibly to mean "a retreat from growth-producing experiences in the new environment" (Kauffmann et al. 1992, 107). The research by Carlson et al. on students from several groups found that "a low level of interaction with fellow American students correlated positively with international learning, lack of problems experienced abroad, integration into the host culture, and strong academic performance" (1990, xii)—that is to say, whichever the causal direction in such a correlation, the odyssey experience "took" more deeply on students who immersed themselves in it.

Most research on the experiences of students abroad has focused on two issues: changes in attitudes toward both home and host countries, and level of personal growth—both asking how effective the period abroad has been. Two conditions that appear to generate more positive feelings toward the host culture are the depth of personal interaction with "natives" and the length of stay in the host country—the longer the stay the more profound the change (Kauffmann et al. 1992). Studies also indicate that students abroad generally develop a more "international perspective," and many express a wish to utilize their international experience in later life (ibid.). My own experience in supervising California students abroad was that there was no uniformly positive or negative effect in their attitudes toward home and host cultures, but there was a great deal of fluctuation in these attitudes and a heightening of ambivalence toward both home and host countries—an observation consistent with du Bois's remark that study abroad generates "permanent ambivalences and re-evaluations" (1956, 73).

With respect to personal growth, the research appears to produce contrasting results (Kauffmann et al. 1994). Growth seems to be associated with students' level of maturity at the beginning of the experience, as well as the degree to which they immerse themselves in the host culture and interact with foreign nationals. The major change appears to be a reexamination of personal values arising from the confrontation of cultural differences (ibid.). My own experience with the nonrepresentative sample of almost three hundred students I supervised was that the vast majority of them profited from the experience developmentally, and among those many were able to initiate and clarify career decisions that had previously been in limbo. Two types of casualties were apparent for a small minority of students. (As one trained in psychoanalysis, I possessed the advantage of being sensitive to and responding to the "problems" that students developed, though I never pretended to assume the role of psychotherapist.) The first involved those few students who were simply overwhelmed with the newness and difference (or too fragile psychologically to contend with them) and fell into passivity and depression, thus wasting the experience. The second, also few in number, were those who experienced a crisis back home, such as their parents' divorce or the illness or death of a parent or sibling. Such events invariably produced a flood of guilt on the part of the student abroad. The usual psychological response was to want to withdraw from the program and return home in some kind of savior role. My role was to be supportive but to remind the student of the limits on what and whom they could reasonably save, and to suggest the alternative of a briefer home visit and finishing out the year with the program. The psychological dynamic involved in these episodes was that the natural and understandable shock of a crisis at home was augmented by an additional psychological force. That force was the special sense of privilege that the year abroad entailed and the guilt associated with experiencing that privilege. The response to others' suffering in that context was an impulse to desert that special—now painful—status of privilege and cast oneself in the role of sufferer.

The Sabbatical Leave

This institution is of relatively recent vintage in American higher education. Harvard University was the first to establish the practice, in 1880, during the presidency of Charles W. Eliot. Cornell, Wellesley, Amherst, Dartmouth, Stanford, and the Universities of California and Illinois followed suit (Eells and Hollis 1962). By now the sabbatical leave is a regular feature of research universities and liberal arts colleges, and has become a feature of other institutions of higher education (for example, state colleges and universities aspiring to gain visibility and prestige through research). The idea has been adapted to a limited extent in other settings, such as business corporations and the military (Axel 1992; Yardley et al. 2004).

As the designation *sabbatical* indicates, the practice includes a period of rest or respite from routine responsibilities, to be granted every seven years. Sabbaticals in some institutions still approximate this literal description, but variations abound. Some sabbaticals are automatically granted, others have to be applied for on a competitive basis; partial sabbaticals (i.e., for less than a year, or at less than full salary, or leave combined with diminished teaching) are also possible; the level of monitoring of work accomplished on sabbatical leaves varies from no accounting whatsoever to the submission of detailed statements of intention and final reports on work accomplished. In addition, since the advent of the age of sponsored research by private foundations and the federal government after World War II, the sabbatical proper has been supplemented by leaves of absence without pay, in which faculty members "buy out" of teaching and other university duties with funds granted by external agencies. When combined with continued expectations of sabbatical leave, the general upward trend in external consulting by academics, and the downward trend in teaching loads in research universities and other institutions, this practice has created problems for some academic departments in fulfilling teaching requirements and ensuring continuity in the supervision of graduate students. Leave policies have also generated concern on the part of academic administrators and state legislatures that universities are shirking their obligation to teach the undergraduates of their respective states. Many universities have established guidelines limiting time off, but enforcement varies. Excessive leave time has also become the object of derisive humor: "The definition of a university professor is a person who requests an additional semester off to supplement his sabbatical leave in order to prepare a course on the Puritan work ethic in American society."

The defining features of the sabbatical leave recapitulate many of the ingredients of an odyssey experience.

- It involves a process of destructuring. The faculty member is given relief from teaching responsibilities and committee and other service to his or her department and university.
- It is of fixed and known duration, typically an academic year or an academic term. This is the liminal period.

One is supposed to engage in some kind of creative activity during this period of freedom.

- It carries an expectation that the recipient will rejoin his or her faculty at the end of the sabbatical (restructuring). Most universities and colleges require that recipients teach in their home institutions for a period equal to the length of the leave, on pain of forfeiting their salary if they do not.

- It should be an experience of fulfillment and regeneration—an acceleration of one's own research, perhaps a tangible product such as a book or a series of articles, and a return to routine duties refreshed by the period of freedom. In 1959 a formal definition of the sabbatical offered in a dictionary of education mentioned "opportunity for self-improvement" (Good 1959, 424).

- The ordeal aspects of sabbatical leaves are almost completely subordinated to its rewarding aspects, but a general principle holds: the freedom generates expectations of performance, and responsibility for that performance lies more or less solely with the recipient. The expectation of proving one's scholarly worth through research and the unmooring from routine expectations constitute the arduous side of the experience.

Typically the sabbatical is a solo odyssey experience, though many scholars take the opportunity to collaborate with others or affiliate with colleagues in a laboratory or other team research setting. This means that the dimension of *communitas* is often lacking. This lack of collective involvement serves to augment the "unmooring" dimension of the sabbatical. A second special feature, closely related to the first, is the level of *personal discretion* involved. A faculty member on leave often has many ongoing opportunities and requests to attend conferences at home and abroad, to consult, to serve on special committees on or off the home campus, and to reengage in departmental affairs, especially if some crisis calls for his or her input or vote. If the recipient accedes to such opportunities and pressures, the isolated or "liminal" feature is correspondingly diluted.

In this connection, the issue of whether one takes sabbatical leave away from or in his or her place of residence is important. For personal reasons, I remained in Berkeley during my first sabbatical leave from the University of California and have regretted the decision ever since. First of all, that year did not have the magic that a year in New York or Europe would have had (and did have in subsequent leaves). That sabbatical seemed a continuation of normal life when it ought not to have been. Second, I learned that chairs, colleagues, and friends do not really believe that you are on sabbatical and do not hesitate to sound the call of obligation, even when one is not formally obliged. Furthermore, no matter how strong or determined, one cannot decline *all* these obligations without losing the goodwill of others. Being far away usually solves this problem.

I observed this principle years later when I was director of the Center at Stanford. We asked that fellows in residence at the center remain in residence and curtail their travel, and offered to assist them in declining invitations. That strategy did not always work, particularly for those scholars who believed that not to renew their professional contacts or to remain out of professional sight would in some way diminish their prestige. The problem was particularly acute for fellows whose home base was at Stanford University. They were forever under siege from their home institution and their networks of friends to continue to fulfill some of their obligations. As director I always countered their temptations by reminding them of the obligation of freedom that the fellowship entailed and remarking that the world's cemeteries were full of indispensable people. As often as not, these attempts to persuade proved futile. Subsequently, I have concluded that one motive for submitting to worldly temptations and obligations when in principle one should be happy to be rid of them lies in the anxiety involved in proving oneself once again while on leave. Remaining involved in ongoing routines offers a refuge from that anxiety by keeping the person busy in familiar ways.

In the end, then, for all the reasons developed, sabbatical leave must be regarded as an experience designed as an odyssey, but one that realizes itself as such only imperfectly.

Institutes for Advanced Study

An innovation in the twentieth century is the institute (or center) for advanced study, a setting for the gathering of scholars dedicated to pursuing their own research, usually for a year. Those who attend these institutions as visitors are often on sabbatical leave from their own universities or colleges, but typically they receive a supplementary stipend from the institute or center or they bring contracted research funds from other sources to support them for the period of residence. These institutes are thus in a sense collective sabbaticals. They have consolidated themselves as part of the infrastructural scene of higher education in the United States and Europe, with a few approximations in other parts of the world.

The first of these establishments was the Institute for Advanced Study in Princeton, founded in 1930. It was the brainchild of Abraham Flexner, a pioneer in American higher education. Flexner originally conceived it as a university without undergraduate students, in which professors and graduate students would be "left to pursue their own ends in their own ways . . . in tranquility" (quoted in Converse 2001, 1614). The institute, concentrating originally on mathematics and the physical sciences, gained great prestige almost immediately and was noted for the appointment of Albert Einstein to its faculty. The feature of a full-time, tenured, more or less obligation-free faculty—on permanent sabbatical, if you will, which conspired to defeat any odyssey principle—proved to be unique. Princeton later established a system of one-year visiting scholars as a supplement to the original ideal. Subsequently established institutes incorporated the principle of residential visitors but created no significant permanent faculty.

Notable among the later creations were the Center for Advanced Study in the Behavioral Sciences at Stanford (1954), the Netherlands Institute for Advanced Study in the Humanities and Social Sciences (1970), the National Humanities Center at Research Triangle, North Carolina (1978), the Wissenschaftskolleg in Berlin (1980), the Scandinavian Center for Advanced Study in the Social Sciences (SCASSS, 1985), the Collegium Budapest (1991), and the Radcliffe Institute for Advanced Study (1999). The visiting scholar program at the Russell Sage Foundation in New York and the Rockefeller Foundation's Study and Conference Center at Bellagio also resemble these centers in essentials. Other approximations have also appeared, often in the form of university research units. By and large, the major American institutions are supported by endowment and renewed funding, the European ones from state sources.

Keeping in mind the many local variations, the following more or less common characteristics emerge:

- Each is *residential* in that scholars come to a specific location to study and are expected to reside in the community where the institute is located. Some institutes provide housing directly; others arrange it in the local housing market.

- Each institution gives priority to *scholarly excellence* in selecting its resident scholars.

- Each is *interdisciplinary* in emphasis, usually by design. This feature is typically advertised as providing an opportunity for intellectual breadth and growth and constituting an advantage over the insularity of academic disciplines and departments in colleges and universities.

- Each provides at least partial *financial support* to its residential scholars, on the principle that their income during the residency should be more or less equal to their academic salaries.

- Each institute provides *additional services*—arrangements to supply books and journals from nearby university libraries, computers and technical advisors, clerical services, telephone and mail privileges, and in some instances, editorial services, health insurance arrangements, and parking.

- Each affords more or less complete *freedom* to carry out their work, with the proviso that they remain in residence. Most institutes require a statement of intended research in advance of selecting residential scholars, and a year-end report is typically requested.

- Residential scholars usually are formally *equal.* They have only one status—as fellows or scholars, without any qualifying rank such as senior or junior. This contrasts with highly stratified professorial ranking systems of colleges and universities. The one exception is the Princeton Institute, which has a two-class system of permanent faculty and visitors, a system that generates some envy and resentment. The Bellagio Center has residential fellows, who stay one month, and conference participants, who come for three or four days; similar tensions sometimes develop between three two groups.

- Any given cohort of resident scholars is excluded from *selecting* future cohorts of scholars. The administrative staff of the institute typically handles this process, with advice from a variety of sources.

- Though the primary emphasis is on individual study, opportunities exist for a *collective* experience. Most institutes have regularly scheduled presentations by resident scholars to the entire group. Some have special projects, arranged in advance and involving several scholars in formal collaboration. Some encourage and support spontaneously formed groups among residential scholars. Most have opportunities for collective meals. More generally, the concentration of scholars' studies in one or a few buildings encourages informal interaction.

- Some *attempts to isolate* residential scholars from outside contacts occur, though this is variable. Scholars are typically removed from their home colleges, universities, and communities. In some cases (e.g., Bellagio), the institute is remote. Most institutes, however, are located near major universities, mainly for convenience in obtaining library services and for the availability of a scholarly community, although they are not part of the university. Exceptions include the Radcliffe Institute, from the beginning a unit of Harvard University, and the center at Stanford, which merged formally with Stanford University in 2008, largely for budgetary stability. For a long period, the Center for Advanced Study at Stanford forbade telephones in fellows' individual study rooms, though this was opposed by many fellows. The prohibition became unenforceable with the advent of cellular telephones and was ultimately abandoned. More generally, the availability of continuous external electronic contact further compromises any effort to isolate the scholars.

• A sense of *special status* is endowed by participation in the institutes. This is conveyed mainly through extremely competitive selection procedures, which impart a feeling of belonging to an elite. Scholars who have been fellows at the institutes list them under "honors received" on their curriculum vitae, much as they would list receipt of a Guggenheim fellowship or election to office in a learned society. In the orientation session I conducted each year at the center at Stanford, I announced to the gathered fellows that this was going to be the best year of their lives (sometimes adding, "and next year is going to be the worst"). This sense of being special was augmented through interaction among the fellows throughout the

year. I was forever being asked how this class compared
with other classes, and fellows spent time inventing ingenious schemes that would ensure them a return year.

As far as I have been able to determine, no special organizational, social, or psychological theory—certainly no "odyssey" theory—was consciously applied in designing the defining
features of institutes for advanced study. The founding groups
may have been informed by general knowledge, but as a rule it
was the application of what they believed would constitute valuable and productive academic experiences in the context of the
larger higher-education establishment. Once a few institutes
became established, moreover, designers emulated ingredients
they regarded as workable and valuable. Despite the informal-
ity of design, the core ingredients combine to create settings
in which an odyssey is typically experienced. Many elements
of the odyssey are visible in characteristics listed above, but I
would now like to elucidate them more formally and comment
on the psychological experiences of residential scholars.

Certainly the element of destructuring is paramount. Residential scholars are taken from their home settings and removed
from all academic responsibilities. At the residential centers,
their lives are unstructured—they do not have to teach students
or serve on academic and administrative committees. Furthermore, almost all possible sources of contention are removed
from their experience during that year. Their remuneration is
fixed in advanced and not subject to negotiation; there are no
or insignificant status differences or opportunities for selective
advancement or promotion in the system; there are no curricula
to struggle over; there is no involvement in future appointments

to the institute; the range of services is clearly demarcated; and there is no competition over parking privileges. This pattern of liberation, in my estimation, is the most single important contributor to the intense solidarity, or *communitas*, that develops year after year at institutes.

The year itself, the liminal period, has all the characteristics of "betwixt and between" that characterize odyssey experiences. I mentioned the extreme solidarity. All the scholars are thrown together in the same place at the same time and for the same period of time. Under these conditions, new collaborative arrangements are forged and new friendships develop, many of which persist throughout scholars' lives. The scholars often characterize the experience as special and utopian; analogies such as Garden of Eden, Paradise, Shangri-la, and Magic Mountain recurred during my period as director of the center at Stanford. The year-end reports submitted by scholars are uniformly positive and enthusiastic, not only about the productivity the year afforded but also about social and emotional aspects of the experience. This uniform testimony is remarkable, because it is submitted by a subgroup of the population, academics, many of whom consider themselves members of the rational classes and immune or hostile to being swept up in nonrational or ritual experiences. Speaking for myself, in the three cases where I was a residential fellow—at the Russell Sage Foundation in 1989–90, at the Bellagio Center in 1992, and at the Library of Congress in 2006—I shared, in sobering textbook fashion, all the experiences of enthusiasm and euphoria (see chapter 2).

Yet the experience, like all odysseys, must come to an end. All scholars return to their home institutions or, in some cases, are recruited to new ones during their tenure at an institute. In any case it is an inevitable termination. Institutes stop issuing stipends at a given moment. They give residential scholars a final date at which they must depart, though some scholars protest, in half-jest, that they will not go unless physically removed. In all events, the end means a return to the routines of academic life. (This was the subtext of "next year will be the worst.")

A final word must be said about the underside of the basically positive, productive, and nostalgic elements of a year at an institute. That underside is, as should now be evident, closely linked with the features of freedom and being special. Freedom brings some disorientation. Fellows and their families have to adapt to a new community with new people, new schools, new places to shop, and new cultures. The freedom for research, along with the special status, is an extremely potent formula for producing guilt (why me and not others?), pressure to produce that next and perhaps more brilliant book or series of articles, and a residue of letdown and perhaps depression if a scholar perceives that he or she is falling short. This complex is similar to the "J.F. crisis" I described in the Harvard Society of Fellows. At one point, the center at Stanford appointed a psychiatrist to its staff, who was removed from administrative responsibility to be continuously available to fellows for any matter relating to health or general well-being. The psychiatrist never reported on his consultations to the director or other administrators of the center unless he deemed the welfare of the center to be involved. This arrangement was a piece of unconscious wisdom, in effect recognizing the fundamentally ambivalent character of all odyssey experiences. As far as I know, other institutes do not have such an arrangement, but when their directors have been told about it, they have thought it a brilliant idea.

THE PSYCHOTHERAPEUTIC PROCESS

A Note on Healing, Shamanism, and Conversion

The history of human healing is a vast and sprawling topic, and I will make no attempt to comprehend it in this book. To introduce the topic of psychotherapy, however, it is instructive to point to a few recurrent and comparable characteristics.

The field of medical anthropology has focused on worldwide patterns of explanation of illness and methods for curing and healing, all of which are embedded in cultural contexts. As a rule anthropologists stress the nondichotomous relations between non-Western and Western medicine (Strathern and Stewart 1999).

Shamanism and shamans have been topics of special attraction in the history of anthropology. Krippner defined shamanism formally as "socially sanctioned [practice] by those who claim to voluntarily regulate their attention in accessing information not ordinarily available and using it to facilitate healthy development and to alleviate stress and illness among members of their community and the community as a whole" (2000, 191). The essence of shamanism is that the stricken place themselves in the care of a healer who has access to special powers. The shaman and sometimes the stricken typically enter into trances or "altered states of consciousness," which are either self-induced (as in transcendental meditation) or brought on by use of substances such as alcohol, smoke and vapors, or drugs (Lewis 1989). The practices of shamans are often rooted in elaborate myths about the supernatural world, which serve as an ideational background for the healing process (Patai 1978). Shamanism is one form of folk healing, overlapping with exorcism, spirit possession, and some forms of witchcraft (Santino 1985). Healing through faith is also found in formal religions, such as Roman Catholicism (often an aspect of pilgrimage), Christian Science, Pentacostalism (Clements 1981; Kane 1974), and in more spontaneous forms (Strathern and Stewart 1999).

To bring the topic closer to the odyssey idea, it is notable that shamanistic beliefs often portray the shaman as having the capacity to "leave this world during a trance-like state, and engage in super-natural and mythical journeys" (Santino 1985). The experience of becoming a Tamang shaman, for example, involves "the withdrawal from society, nights spent running naked through the forest, hallucinations, conversations with spirits. . . . [T]he future shaman emerges from this 'sickness' with important insights: a new vision of the world, a vocation, and personality transformation" (Peters 1982, 38). Numerous scholars have pointed out continuities between modern psychotherapy and ancient mystical practices in Judaism (Bakan 1958), Christianity (Meier 1987), and the great non-Western religious traditions (Watts 1961; Olson and McBeath 2002). Explicit analogues between psychotherapy and shamanism have also been noted. Peters, for example, pointed to the common presence of a curer with special knowledge, and the practices of "remembering," "repeating," and "working through" as staples of shamanistic practices and psychotherapy (1982, 33).

Another cousin of modern psychotherapy is religious conversion. The evident point of contrast is that the latter is framed in the language and imagery of religion, while the former is primarily secular. Even this contrast is not a clean one, as the idea of "pastoral counseling" suggests. Many conversionist

movements and sects incorporate elements of secular psychotherapy into their repertoire. The similarities between conversion and therapy lie in the fundamental *process* at work: an
initial state of psychological/spiritual suffering or personal
disturbance; an effort to break down or destructure; a period
of liminality or remove, which is the conversion or therapeutic
journey itself; and an anticipated restructuring of the person in
a positive or regenerative way.

In pointing to these comparisons as I turn to the psychotherapeutic process itself, I should remind the reader that modern
psychotherapy is *not* identical to these kindred practices in all
respects—and for that reason, wholesale comparisons are not
warranted—but common vectors and dynamics embed them in
the family of odyssey experiences.

The Essentials of the Psychotherapeutic Process

While the dating of modern psychotherapy is somewhat arbitrary, its crystallization in the European medical tradition
under the influence of innovators such as Genet, Charcot,
Kraeplin, and above all Freud was decisive. Since that time it
has become consolidated as an established medical specialty,
psychiatry, and has spread far and wide, into nonmedical
clinical psychology, rehabilitative programs, secular curative groups, and religious and quasi-religious groups. More
recently, psychotherapy has come to supplement, sometimes
to compete with, pharmacological treatments of psychological
disorders. Though the sociology of the rise and consolidation
of psychotherapy is a complex subject, two factors certainly
have played a role—first, secularization, or the relative decline

of religious worldviews as defining and interpretative frameworks of the human condition and human suffering, and, second, the "developmental void" created by the relative decline of traditional ritualized transitions related to the life cycle (Stein and Stein 1987).

The search for the essentials of psychotherapy is complicated by the field's dizzying diversity. Here are the main ingredients:

- Theoretical frameworks, which include classical psychoanalysis and its many offshoots—gestalt psychology, behavioral psychology, cognitive psychology, group psychology, and biopharmacology—as well as many invented eclectic and syncretic perspectives.

- Defined clienteles, including the "mentally ill," generally unhappy people, alcoholics, drug-dependents, those with eating disorders, procrastinators, compulsive gamblers and spenders, families, unhappy couples, and disturbed children.

- Settings, including individual, couple, group, and institutional (clinics, hospitals, social movements, religious and quasi-religious organizations).

- Psychotherapeutic methods: directive and nondirective, affect-oriented, and behavior-oriented, as well as techniques such as free-association, hypnosis, meditation, and various kinds of "acting out."

- Frequency of psychotherapeutic sessions and envisioned length of the process.

- Types of change envisioned by the process—cure, new patterns of behavior, better adjustment, positive thinking, self-redefinition, satisfaction with life, self-love.

It is possible, however, to cut through this maze and identify the fundamental vectors, which are those of a psychological journey. I first examine examples from psychoanalysis because it is the most articulated version of the theory and technique of therapy. By way of a corrective and to demonstrate the generality of the process, I also make reference to a number of related cases—for example, grief and trauma management, encounter groups, and Scientology—which contrast with the psychoanalytic mode in explicit ways but reveal similar dynamics.

PRECONDITION: ILLNESS, SUFFERING, UNHAPPINESS

Without some experience of personal disequilibrium, the idea of psychotherapy is pointless, just as without some experience of sin, contamination, or evil, the impulse to religious conversion is absent. Of the list of preconditions for "all psychotherapy," Harper listed first "one or more persons (patients) with some awareness of neglected or mishandled life problems" (1958, 9). In classical psychoanalysis, the preconditions were characterized as the various neuroses (hysteria, obsessive-compulsive neurosis, neurasthenia). Horney defined neurosis as "a character disorder, a way of life in which a person is compulsively driven in an unhealthy direction by a variety of rigid and conflicting needs" (1999, 242). Psychiatric diagnostic systems, right up to the elaborate diagnostic and statistical manuals on mental disorders, revised and issued periodically by the American Psychiatric Association, are efforts to catalogue the range of sufferings amenable to therapeutic treatment. Other and sometimes esoteric sources of personal disorder are found in curative movements. For example, Scientology posits a "Bank" or reactive mind that forces one to act in "stimulus-response" ways and lose control over one's circumstances (Whitehead 1987). The Emin Society, a psychotherapeutic cult that arose in Israel in the 1970s (Beit-Hallahmi 1992), describes the operation of occult forces, such as electric charges. Psychiatrists and other practitioners frequently assert that psychotherapy is not effective with a person who has not acknowledged that the "presenting problem" is a matter of his or her internal suffering and personal failing, and point to the difficulty of treating, for example, psychopaths or hardened criminals who are ordered by courts into psychotherapy but do not see themselves as having personal problems. The same precondition of taking responsibility for suffering is also essential to the treatment of alcoholism in Alcoholics Anonymous, for instance. This observation points to a further parallel with religious conversion, the first precondition of which is the acknowledgment of personal sin.

Despite differences in characterizing the personal disequilibrium that is the precondition for psychotherapeutic treatment, the following axiom holds: *some* theory, ideology, or other intelligible framework must be available to characterize the disorder. Such a framework is a necessary condition for describing what is amiss in the world. A theory is also necessary for characterizing how and by what path the stricken individual moves from something worse to something better and for dictating what techniques should be employed to facilitate that journey. The framework also provides a basis for the therapist and patient/client to name and describe the disorder and to interpret what is going on and how he or she might change after treatment. To insist on this point is neither to say that all frameworks are equally productive of therapeutic change nor to deny that initial patient/client differences influence their relative efficacy. But the fact remains that treatment cannot proceed without some framework of intelligibility.

DISMANTLING AND DESTRUCTURING

Psychotherapy is based on the general premise that, if any kind of change or regeneration is to occur, there must first be a breakdown of existing dysfunctional structures (McHugh 1966). The destructuring process readies the patient/client for the therapeutic journey. Yet it is not a straightforward principle, because, according to the understanding gleaned from most theories on which psychotherapies are based, those structures, though dysfunctional, often constitute a valued personal modus operandi. They involve positive investments and even gratification on the part of the afflicted and, as a result, are difficult to change. In psychoanalytic terminology, mechanisms of defense become fixations, endowed with libido, and resist interpretation, understanding, and dismantling (Thompson and Cotlove 2005). In the psychoanalytic view, the defensive apparatus originates in the patient's struggles with unresolved childhood impulses and conflicts. Other therapeutic theories are not based on this version of onset but rest on the assumption that the patient or client is invested in debilitation in some systematic way, has dysfunctional patterns of affect and behavior, or has adopted a way of life that is counterproductive, even destructive to self and others.

One distinctive feature of the psychotherapeutic situation is that it constitutes a *socially* destructured situation that is presumably conducive to the process of *psychological* destructuring. Consider the features of classical psychoanalytic arrangements: they are based on a simplified contractual relation between analyst and therapist, with patient paying and analyst receiving payments, with the understanding that the patient can terminate the relationship at will but the analyst can terminate it only with cause (for example, uncontainable acting out, nonpayment, or "untreatability"). The patient is placed in a supine position, symbolizing passivity and dependency. The analyst sits behind and above, and can observe without being observed. There is also an asymmetry and simplification of the flow of information. Using free association (itself a mode of destructuring [freeing] thought and the communicative process), the patient says everything that comes to mind, and using the rule of abstinence, the analyst says little and resists being drawn into dramas of mutual acting out. The relationship is further simplified by a taboo on personal contact outside the analytic situation and the minimization of negotiation about location, scheduling, length of meetings, and amount and mode of payment. All these mechanisms act to destructure the situation and permit the uncontaminated flow of information from the patient and the development of as "pure" a transference relationship as possible.

Foulkes stresses the corresponding need for destructuring in group therapy:

> As a rule there is no contact apart from [group analytic sessions] either between patients or between any of them and the therapist . . . the members [patients, clients] have no previous relationship with one another. They are total strangers and should have as little contact outside the treatment situation as possible. They have no purpose for meeting other than treatment, no occupation, no programme of procedures. This . . . has the effect of bringing the personalities and their interrelationship into the open, the screen

of an occupation is removed and the way is open for an
analytic approach. Of particular significance is the nature
of communication and the use made of communication and
relationship. (1964, 39, 72–73)

Though other therapies do not generate these extreme conditions, it is generally acknowledged that the person who is seeking
help—even if referred to as a client rather than a patient—is in
a general sense dependent in that he or she is being put in the
hands of the therapist. Furthermore, it is generally believed that
the relationship should be a professional (i.e., uninvolved) one.
There are taboos on, even punishments for, affective (especially
sexual) involvement, and many of the scandals that have discredited extreme cults with a therapeutic component have arisen
from the exploitation of cult members by leaders (see chapter 6).

This process of destructuring is another source of danger,
because, if it does what it is supposed to do, it brings forth many
anxiety-provoking and threatening thoughts, fantasies, and
affects. As Menninger (1958) notes, analysis involves a period
of unsettling, regression, and frustration before the restor-
ative process begins. Another, more positive ingredient acts
as a counteractive force to the disruption: the therapist's cultivated attitude to be permissive, accepting, and nonblaming of
otherwise blameworthy thoughts and actions—the therapist's
"neutrality." More positively, Ralph (2005) refers to "support
and partnership," which is also connoted by the psychoanalytic
notion of a "therapeutic alliance." Hirschowitz notes the importance of a "we-feeling" (1974, 237), and Braatly (1954) refers to
the psychoanalyst's love as a means of "thawing" the patient.
Whatever the formulation, the supportive mode appears to be

an essential counterbalance to the disruptive and dangerous side of the therapeutic journey.

THE PROCESS ITSELF

What is the nature of that journey? The key concept emerging from Freud's writings on psychoanalysis is regression, or the emergence of "the initial, primitive, infantile part of mental life" (Freud 1963 [1917], 209–10), which is facilitated by the psychoanalytic situation. The clearest manifestation of this is transference, in which infantile feelings, attitudes, and fantasies toward parents, siblings, and others are projected on the analyst. According to Mendelsohn, these "regressive transference experiences" must be reached before "constructive growth can be realized" (1992, 142). The demonstration of the "unrealistic" and infantile nature of the transference is made possible because the analyst, revealing little or nothing about himself or herself, becomes a blank screen on which regressive feelings are projected, and—because of that blankness—they can be interpreted and exposed as "unrealistic" projections. Interpretation of the predominantly unconscious projections in the transference is the primary mechanism by which the patient works toward a redefinition of his or her infantile conflicts.

Whitehead acknowledges the centrality of the notion of regression but correctly regards it as a subclass of a more general phenomenon: "Depth psychotherapeutic methodologies . . . [activate and guide] a particular psychological process. The process has been recognized and partially comprehended under various theoretical rubrics: 'regression' in psychoanalytic theory, 'deautomization' in recent cognitive psychological studies of meditation, 'renunciation' in the older vocabulary of

Western mysticism. Cognitively, the process takes the form of (usually temporary) dedifferentiation of cognitive structures. It is this dimension of the experience that, manifested in extreme form, has won the label 'altered states of consciousness'" (1987, 25). Not all forms of therapy and rehabilitation give salience to renunciation. The treatment of schizophrenic patients by the "token economy" method, for example, is a therapy "very different from other methods of therapy" in that it rests on a "here-and-now" reinforcement of behaviors regarded as "adaptive, desirable, specifiable and reinforcible" by rewarding them with money, paper money, poker chips, stamps, or marks on pieces of paper. This method, strictly behavioral in derivation, presumably promotes "living successfully outside the hospital" and carrying on "a more responsible social role" (Maley 1974, 70–71). Nevertheless, the underlying dynamic is to eradicate dysfunctional behaviors through a process that renders patients passive, with the ultimate aim of regeneration.

The therapeutic process, though usually voluntary, does manifest ingredients of the ordeals examined in chapter 6. I mentioned the painful and threatening aspects of the destructuring process; Bion points out that the analyst's refusal to gratify the neurotic demands of the patient constitutes an "atmosphere of deprivation" (1963, 15). The "working-through" process is also painful, as interpretations on the part of the therapist are resisted by the patient, who has an emotional interest in preserving his or her defensive character armor, and who sheds this armor only after a period of persistent labor. The ordeal-like quality is also revealed by positive testimonials on how patients' lives have turned around, by those who believe they have profited from or even been saved by therapy. These testimonials resemble the positive narratives of those who have gone through a religious conversion (Austin-Broos 2003) and the nostalgic commentaries of those who have completed a painful "boot camp" or a related initiation (chapter 6).

By definition the aim of psychotherapy is to effect positive change in its recipients. In an early formalization based on his studies in hysteria, Freud formulated the results of analytic treatment as follows: "Each individual hysterical symptom immediately and permanently disappeared when we had succeeded in bringing clearly to light the memory of the event by which it was provoked and by arousing its accompanying affect, and when the patient had described that event in the greatest possible detail and had put the affect into words" (1955 [1893], 6, all italicized in the original). The operative phrase is "put the affect into words." Mastery has both emotional and cognitive restructuring dimensions. That version of the therapeutic underlies the work of Weiss and Sampson's (1986) "control-mastery" model. This process envisions not the dissolution or "cure" of neurotic conflict but rather realigning defenses and improving the capacity of the patient to cope with ongoing conflict. This appears to be the essence of insight therapy. The extension of this principle is that the solidified insights will work their way into new behavior patterns: "New experiences as a result of new responses and reactions" (Foulkes 1964, 292). The ideal end of the journey is, in a word, personal regeneration through understanding.

Cognitive and gestalt therapies stress insight but give less salience to the affective aspects. Behavior-modification therapies give salience to neither insight nor emotion but stress the direct restructuring of behavior through conditioning processes. Still other therapies emphasize acting out as a way of dealing with conflict and undesirable behavior. For example, Bach (1974) describes a method of "control aggression in groups," a catharsis in which limited expression of aggression through ritualized fighting enables patients to delineate conflict situations and work toward more rational solutions. Despite the diversity, the purpose of all these models is to make behavior more adaptive and positive and to enhance self-regard and self-esteem (Ralph 2005).

Some Less Traditional Illustrations

I have presented under the head of therapy a variety of more or less established methods, many deriving from classical psychoanalysis but some set in opposition to it. In conclusion, I sketch a number of very different therapies that, however, rely on similar dynamics.

OTHER SETTINGS

The twelve-step method of recovery designed by Alcoholics Anonymous entails personal acknowledgment of responsibility, followed by testimonial and storytelling sessions, along with close monitoring by former alcoholics to prevent backsliding. The method has been adapted to apply to other forms of substance abuse and to the treatment of families of abusers (Nowinski 1999; Brown and Lewis 1999). Turkovic, Hovens, and Gregurek (2004) describe a method of improving refugees' "desperate and passive attitude" by encouraging them to articulate traumatic experiences, reorganizing more active roles in caring for one another, and building a sense of community. The same ingredients appear in a model described by Elsass (1997) for the treatment of victims of torture and violence. Humphrey and Zimpfer (1996) describe a similar model for therapeutic management of bereavement and grief. The "halfway house" movement of the 1950s and 1960s developed a therapeutic process to rehabilitate the mentally ill, many of whom had been recently deinstitutionalized (Cook and Hoffschmidt 1993). And Cullen (1997) describes the application of therapeutic methods to prison settings, including establishing a supportive community, storytelling, and progressive involvement in positive social activities.

THE ENCOUNTER GROUP MOVEMENT

A new kind of therapy, a cousin of group therapy, came to flourish, almost as a social movement, in the fluid years of the 1960s and 1970s but, in the words of Yalom and Leszez (2005), is now "largely a thing of the past." That movement encompassed human relations groups, personal growth groups, marathon groups, potential groups, sensory awareness groups, and basic encounter groups. Usually composed of eight to twenty members, the groups stressed here-and-now interaction, exploration, confrontation, direct emotional expression, and acting out, which earned them the label "touchy-feely" from skeptics. Gatherings were usually of short duration and held in relative isolation. However diverse, the groups reveal some generic characteristics. The group goals are often vague; occasionally they stress merely the provision of an experience—joy, entertainment, being turned on—but more often they implicitly or explicitly strive for *change*—in behavior, in attitudes, in values, in lifestyle, in self-actualization, in one's relationship to others, to the environment, to one's own body. The participants are considered "seekers" and "normals," not "patients" or "clients," and the experience is considered not therapy but "growth" (ibid., 536). Described as such, encounter groups clearly constitute a journey that involves destructuring through group regression and personal regeneration.

More detailed evidence of this process is found in Holloman's case study of Esalen (1974). An institute housed in the beautiful environment of Big Sur, California, Esalen was founded in 1962 (a second branch opened in San Francisco in 1967). It was intended to synthesize several "esoteric traditions" (yoga, zen, and sufism) with the methods and technology of modern science. It is regarded by some as evidence of "California kookiness," but it has drawn the attention and participation of people from the military, education, and sports.

The collective meetings of Esalen involve a visible process of destructuring, almost "stripping" the person through self-disclosure to a group, concentrating on sense experiences, exercising, collective nude bathing, and massage (rolfing). Group leaders attempt to evoke and make coherent participants' emotional responses and offer support. Holloman describes the liminal phase using a framework derived from Turner—separation, status leveling, suspension or inversion of daily norms of conduct, "peak" experiences, and the joy of *communitas* (ibid., 272–3). The resulting regeneration is said to include a new sense of body and mind, increased self-awareness, a fusion of Eastern and Western values, increased personal responsibility, and personal growth. While very different in intention and design from traditional psychotherapeutic experiences, Esalen and other encounter experiments nevertheless express the essentials of an odyssey experience.

SCIENTOLOGY

Arising from the theory of dianetics enunciated by L. Ron Hubbard in the 1950s, Scientology took its place among the "new religions" (see chapters 3 and 6). The Church of Scientology in California was established in 1954 and has experienced widespread growth in the United States and abroad. The movement has a conspicuous psychotherapeutic component. Despite or perhaps because of its growth, some religious leaders, other therapeutic groups, and the public at large have viewed the movement as quackery. These sentiments are evident in the expressed hostility toward actor Tom Cruise and his positive statements about the movement.

For my purposes it is important to note that Scientology constitutes an unusual instance of the odyssey experience. Its therapeutic activities derive from a "theory of human nature" that renders them meaningful and coherent. The theory is syncretic, building on the work of Freud, the occult religions, Alfred Korzybski, Buddha, and Will Durant (Whitehead 1987, 27–28). As it has evolved, the framework includes the ideas that "one is a thetan, an immortal spirit with potentially limitless powers . . . that one has a Bank (Reactive Mind), which suppresses one's ability to be 'at cause' over Matter, Energy, Space and Time (either 'real' or 'mental'), which exercise 'force and the power of command over one's awareness' . . . and which causes one to act on a stimulus-response basis" (ibid., 194). The agent involved in eliminating the Bank and its associated counterproductive behaviors is an "auditor" (therapist), who asks questions and records the proceedings by the use of an E-meter. The intended effect of the repetitive question-and-answer process is to break down the dysfunctional behavior patterns and self-image of the believer and to "restore thetans to their original powerful state" (ibid.). The content of Scientology differs greatly from that of religious conversion and other psychotherapies but resembles them in social and psychological dynamics.

THE COMPARISON OF INCOMPARABLES

In this chapter and the foregoing, I have compared many distinct phenomena, both religious and secular, and have attempted to cut through their apparent differences and highlight their similarities. This has been in part an inductive process, but above all it involves a conceptual or even deductive operation—namely, the generation of concepts and categories that permit their inclusion in a larger class. Chapter 1, in which the generic characteristics of the odyssey experience were laid out, provided those concepts and categories. The analyses in chapters 3–6 apply these general categories to the multiple manifestations of odyssey experience.

An example from another area may clarify this process. If we wish to analyze comparatively the group or organization that operates as the administrative supplement to political leadership, the concept of civil service is not a very good one, because it refers to a relatively recent historical invention and does not cover the loyalty-based entourages that characterized monarchies and other traditional forms of administration. The term *bureaucracy* is better, because it includes it a wider range of cases than *civil service*, which is one subtype of bureaucracy. But bureaucracy is also historically and culturally limited as a comparative concept. Weber's concept of administrative staff is superior to both civil service and bureaucracy, because it allows for the inclusion of traditional and charismatic kinds of leaders and followers. In this case, the word is the thing. The right kinds of words are necessary to subsume and render comparable diverse structures.

If the diverse odyssey experiences considered—initiations, pilgrimages, conversions, travel, leaves of absence, psychotherapies—are analyzed in the language and symbolism specific to each, they are scarcely comparable. If a more generic language is chosen, the idiosyncrasies are diminished and the generalities highlighted. That is the deductive side of comparative analysis, which combines with but is seldom given as much attention as the inductive identification of common characteristics.

FIVE

Some Miscellaneous, More or Less Invented Experiences

By now the reader of these pages will have become aware of a pervasive difficulty I faced in organizing the chapter headings of this volume. Chapters 3 and 4 divided the world of odyssey experiences into religious and secular forms, but that division proved inexact. Chapter 3 included mainly religious illustrations, but I had to slide over into some mainly secularized cousins. Similarly, I include in chapter 6 what I call coercive illustrations, meaning the exploitation of odyssey experiences for political and social control. Yet many of the examples in earlier chapters—mainly rites of passage—have coercive or quasi-coercive elements as well, so the distinction between voluntary and coerced implied by the chapter headings is actually blurred. In constructing the table of contents, I struggled with alternative ways of organizing the chapters, but principles of inclusion and exclusion proved leaky, with empirical illustrations spilling over into chapters where they did not seem appropriate. I could have "solved" this problem only by including everything in one huge chapter, clearly an unacceptable alternative.

This chapter, which is meant to include both miscellaneous types (that is, not treated elsewhere) and invented experiences (in contrast to formalized or institutionalized forms) is also an unsatisfactory umbrella for its contents. Odyssey experiences that develop more or less spontaneously or adaptively have appeared in other chapters. For example, the odysseys of commercialized travel are invented cooperatively by commercial travel enterprises and willing tourists; the conversionist and socializing rituals of the new religious movements discussed in chapters 3 and 6 appear invented when compared with the rites of passage and conversion in the major traditional religions. So, in this chapter and others the reader will recognize—and I hope tolerate—a certain amount of unavoidable classificatory messiness.

AMBIVALENCES: THE UNIVERSALITY, VALUE, AND "GENUINENESS" OF RITUAL

The social scientific literature on ritual—of which some odyssey experiences are a subtype—is fraught with conflictual assessments. In a perceptive diagnosis, Scheff captures the situation: "Contemporary social science has two seemingly contradictory orientations toward ritual. The positive orientation views ritual, along with myth, as the foundation of all culture—the basis of human consciousness. The negative one sees it as an empty shell, a residue of beliefs and practices whose functions are lost in an irreversible past. Both of these traditions are deeply rooted in basic perspectives in anthropology, sociology, and psychology" (1977, 483). The contradiction shows up in the work of

Victor Turner. On the one hand he asserts that the dynamics found in myth, ritual, and drama have the status of "universals" (Turner 1990). On the other he discerns a fundamental difference between traditional and modern expressions—a difference found in his distinction between the "liminal" and the "liminoid." The liminal is the transitional spiritual state found in traditional religious rites of passage, which are dominant in tribal and early agrarian societies. The liminoid (implying something less pure than its liminal ancestors) is found in the leisure activities (dramas, sports, secular ceremonies) of advanced, differentiated societies. People work at the liminal, play at the liminoid. Clearly the liminoid is more recent, derived, and dispersed, and probably less authentic than the liminal.

For those who share the thesis of "decline of ritual" associated with the rise of modern societies, some welcome the development, some find it tragic. Following the assault on tradition associated with the Protestant Reformation, the French enlightenment, and more general trends toward secularization, ritual became associated with a backward past of religion and magic, to be replaced by the rational and a scientific organization of society (Muir 2005) (even though the French revolutionaries were scrupulous in inventing new rituals, such as liberty trees and election day festivals that replaced holy days).

This good riddance approach is countered by a nostalgic one, suggesting that the decline of received religious rituals has created a void if not a pathology. Stein and Stein, for example, observe that "modern society seems to lack a suitable ritual process for going though [the midlife transition]" (1987, 389). In a similar vein Kruckman (2000) argues that the salience of postpartum depression in the United States (and not elsewhere) can be traced in part to the absence of socially supportive rituals for new mothers. And Bernstein (1987) regrets the emptying out of masculine rites of passage, such as the Bar Mitzvah and military service, claiming that this has weakened masculine identity in modern times. Still others temper this regret by assuming or asserting that the void will be filled by functional alternatives to dead or dying rituals. Stein and Stein (1987) regard psychotherapy as easing midlife crises, and Mahdi assigns the same function to psychiatric services—to compensate for "the absence of socially sanctioned rites of passage" (1996, xviii). Stevens states the matter most forcefully: "[If] culture fails to provide [age-transition] symbols in institutional form then the Self . . . is forced to provide them *faute de mieux*" (1982, 164). A similar "universal" need for transitional rituals is expressed by Kimball, who asserts that "there is no evidence that a secularized urban world has lessened the need for ritualized experiences of an individual's transition from one status to another" (1960, xvii). However, some who argue that modern, invented forms are functional equivalents of older ones nevertheless see them as wanting: Muir, for example, regards "reinvented forms of religious worship," such as evangelical and revivalist movements, as resting on "far shakier theological grounds than anything rejected by the Reformation" (2005, 294).

I can see no way of evaluating these ambivalent and perhaps contradictory statements, because they seem to rest on global and unverifiable evaluations of the genuineness or artificiality of past and present civilizations (and their rituals). It does seem to be clear, however, that the decline of traditional rituals (including rites of passage) has not meant their disappearance. New forms and expressions appear and can be identified without assessing the degree to which they are genuine. It is also true that the great array of contemporary rites of passage and other rituals is more diversified and differentiated, frequently legalized, often privatized, and often transpiring without elaborate ceremony. Many of them, however, do reinvent the full array of ingredients of odyssey experiences.

ADOLESCENT RITES

Contemporary society reveals many moments of passage that mark young people's assumption of new responsibilities but pass without significant ritual or celebration—attaining the legal age to work for wages, to consent to sexual relations, to marry, to vote, to purchase alcoholic beverages, to be eligible for military service, and to secure a driver's license. Most of these pass quietly, though some have become more meaningful than others. High-school graduation is a widely celebrated ceremony symbolizing entry into a new world, though its near-universalization has subtracted from its specialness. In some educational systems, specific examinations, for example, the 11-plus in Britain and the Certificate of Primary Studies exam in France (Wylie 1957) have become highly loaded ritual ordeals for both pupils and families because they play such a significant role in the academic and occupational futures of those taking them. Getting a driver's license can be the occasion for a private family or peer celebration, the former sometimes tinged with regret and apprehension. Securing one's first home mortgage sometimes marks an important transition in adult life (Musgrove and Middleton 1981). Still other transitions, often informal, have an "invented" quality and resemble more traditional rites of passage.

Among the more formal of these are scattered courses and related programs in high schools that are self-consciously designed as facilitating the adolescent transition. Oldfield (1996) describes an invented program of his own, which he calls, interestingly enough, The Journey. It is self-consciously defined as an adventure into the unknown, using ceremonial masks, ordeals invented by the students themselves, a process of "finding a path" to the future, and a ceremony of passage. Kessler (1996) depicts a "Senior Passage" course involving games and artistic expression, quasi-therapeutic sessions of sitting in circles and "speaking from the heart," and a retreat into the wilderness for solitude and reflection—all designed to deal with the ambiguities and anxieties of the transition from high school to the "larger world." A "Walkabout Course" (Gibbon 1996) is a combination of academic concentration, life planning, and networking, self-consciously conceived as a rite of passage. A similar program designed for Native Americans goes under the name of VisionQuest (Burton and Rogers 1996). These and related experiments may be said to have been invented by teachers and administrators but within the constrained institutional context of the school.

Outside the institutional walls of the school, other adolescent rites have emerged. The most conspicuous example involves the rituals of urban gangs. In an analysis of selected gangs, Sanyika (1996) identifies the following elements of initiation: the presence of elders or knowers, the sacred place, symbolic death, trials and tribulations, revelation, resurrection and rebirth, and reincorporation into the community. Applied to the gang setting in particular, the elders are older, original gang members; the separation is from the other (family, community) involvements of the initiate; the sacred place is the neighborhood; symbolic death is getting "jumped" or fighting with members of other gangs; trials and tribulations are feats such as hijacking a car, shootings, even assassinations, all designed to show the "heart" of the initiate; revelations are the teachings of the history, rules, and spirit of the gang; resurrection or rebirth is a new name, a new uniform, new language, new signs, new ways of walking; and reincorporation is the new member's public representation of himself as a member of the gang.

Alves (1993) describes an interesting variant among nine- and ten-year-old urban Portuguese boys, a rampaging ceremony of peer-group invention and elaboration. Periodically groups of boys run wildly through neighborhoods, dumping waste cans, destroying objects, pillaging, and stealing. The behavior is semitolerated in the larger community as a "phase" of youth. The rampages are typically followed by narratives of exploits delivered by the boys to audiences of peer groups, in which their confrontations with and escapes from danger are touted as acts of bravery and heroism. Alves interprets the rampage and its narratives as a rite of passage from childhood into adolescence.

More innocent cousins of gang behavior can be seen in the ceremonial gatherings of youths, often on beaches, at specific moments of the school calendar year for episodes of drinking, rule-breaking, and sexual excesses. Florida beaches are frequent sites for such retreats among American adolescents. An interesting Australian variant, known as "Schoolies Week," is described by Winchester, McGuirk, and Everett (1999). At selected times in November–December (the summer holiday period that follows Australian school-leaving examinations), large numbers of youths gather on the beaches of the Australian Gold Coast for a period of revelry. Winchester, McGuirk, and Everett describe the episodes as having "pilgrimage dimensions"—a pilgrimage of unrestraint—"marked by the physical separation of these young adults from their parents and adult supervision, from the constraints and inhibitions associated with their home neighbourhoods and the confines of a daily life structured around attending high school" (65). The carnivalesque behavior includes lobby partying, discharging fire hoses and extinguishers, throwing broken bottles into swimming pools, balcony hopping, vomiting over balconies, writing obscenities, and trashing rooms. It is simultaneously a period of release tightly bounded by time and space and a rite of passage (leaving school). Local authorities maintain an uneasy balance between permissive toleration of the behavior within limits and cracking down on it when it transgresses those limits.

Similarly, Farnham depicts antebellum May Day ceremonies for young women in the South that were meant to mark the transition to "ladyhood" as defined in that region and that period: "The crowning of the May queen was [a] collective enactment of society's definition of femininity, whereby men offered women protection in return for deference. By placing them on a pedestal and paying homage to their beauty, purity, and virtue, men infused the realities of a patriarchal society with a romantic patina that made young women's position more palatable to them. The pageantry provided a glorious symbolic representation of the chivalry ideal forming the bedrock on which the image of the Southern belle was constructed" (1994, 68). Vida (1999) provides a journalistic account of a wide range of contemporary invented rites of passage, including debutante dips, gang drive-bys, and the Burning Man summer ceremony in Black Rock Desert, Nevada. The last is an annual convergence of thousands for art, revelry, alcohol and drug consumption, and heat exhaustion. The ceremony has evolved from a rite of passage for the young into a kind of bacchanalia for all ages (*San Francisco Chronicle*, September 3, 2007).

PROFESSIONALIZATION, COMMERCIALIZATION, AND POLITICAL STRUGGLE OVER ODYSSEYS: RECENT HISTORY OF BIRTHING AND DYING

Journeys from unborn to born and from living to dead are universally regarded as the most crucial transitions. All cultures, historical and present, have recognized their significance and have generated systems of belief, (mainly religious) rituals, and rich symbolism around them. My purpose is not to develop a comparative account of these transitions, but to use them as illustrations of the many vicissitudes that odysseys have undergone in the recent period of rapid social change in the United States.

Birth

Prior to the nineteenth century and surviving in diminished form in the twentieth, the established pattern of giving birth in the United States as elsewhere was in the home, with family and perhaps neighbors in attendance and with midwives serving as the principal agents of delivery. The main religious practices connected with birth were the rituals of baptism and circumcision, both marking the transition of the infant into the religious community. In the last century and a half, however, that mode and social organization of giving birth underwent a radical change as a result of interrelated developments:

- The increasing availability of technologies, including the use of improved forceps, the invention of chloroform in 1847, and the improvement of the Caesarian method in the 1860s. This technological march was to advance steadily through the twentieth century.

- The appearance of male professionals (obstetricians) who administered the new technologies, with corresponding claims that using them made birth safer and less painful. Almost all births remained in the home, however, until well into the twentieth century. Over time obstetrics became increasingly institutionalized and professionalized, developed extensive and demanding training programs, and came to enjoy a near-monopoly.

- The gradual defeminization of the control of birth, as midwifery declined in the face of competition from obstetrics. The emerging class of obstetricians often assaulted midwifery as crude, unscientific, and dangerous (Edwards and Waldorf 1984).

- The change in the locus of births from the home to the hospital. This was a slow development, reaching only 5 percent of the births in 1900, half by 1920, and almost all by the 1950s (Michaelson 1988).

- The gradual acceptance of hospital births as the preferred form in the larger population, largely on the basis of the presumed safety and freedom from pain they offered.

- A gradual loss of the control of mothers over all facets
  of the birth process, as obstetricians and their ancillary
  personnel assumed direction from beginning to end
  under the overarching rationale of the superiority of
  science-based medicine.

In a word, the development of the modern profession of obstetrics, fully consolidated by mid-twentieth century, manifested all the conditions necessary for the successful establishment of a profession: development of formal knowledge, elimination of competition, and public support for professionals' jurisdiction (Abbott 1988).

In the course of this march of professionalization, obstetricians, gynecologists, and their ancillary personnel developed—irregularly and with many variations—what might be called a planned and organized odyssey for the journey from pregnancy to the arrival of the newborn. The journey is a double rite of passage involving a transition from uterine to nonuterine life for the neonate, and the transition from nonpregnancy to parenthood for the mother and father (Davis-Floyd 2003). What were (and are) are some of the ideal-typical features of these transitions?

During pregnancy, normal procedures call for a sequence of examinations, tests, and precautionary or corrective treatments if problems develop. These are based on what is regarded as the necessary scientific applications of medical knowledge, but they also tend to take on the characteristics of ritual: they are not to be neglected; they should be performed at definite moments during the pregnancy; they are performed by "knowing elders" (gynecologists and obstetricians); and there is cause for anxiety and sometimes retribution if they are not performed. Orientation of the expectant mother includes formal preparation through pregnancy education classes and, frequently, informal bonding with other pregnant women and past mothers, which involves a focused commonality of interest and exchange of information about and experiences of the pregnancy experience (a kind of *communitas*).

In this tradition a certain ritual routine for the father also became solidified. He was isolated from the birth process in a waiting room (the "Heirport"), with stereotyped routines of waiting, pacing, and smoking. His receipt of the news ("It's a boy" or "It's a girl") was similarly routinized, as was the celebrative giving out of cigars to male friends in the days following the birth. The obstetric reasons developed for the father's separation from the process were modesty, the risk of contamination, the father's psychological vulnerability (losing control or passing out), and the need for efficiency in the birthing process (Reed 2005).

The routines of the birth experience are more detailed and fixed. According to the inventory of required procedures, Davis-Floyd (2003) mentions, among others, use of a wheelchair; the "prep," which includes donning a hospital gown; frequently, separation from the partner; shaving of pubic hair and administration of an enema; confinement to bed; fasting; administration of a sequence of drugs; cervical checks; transfer to the delivery room; sterilization procedures; episiotomy; delivery; determination of the Apgar score; washing the baby; prophylactic eye treatment, and a bonding period with the mother. Not all of these procedures are always undertaken, and many have been challenged by dissenters protesting mechanical application of this technological model. Again, although the diverse procedures evolved under the umbrella of a medical science rationale, they took on ritual ingredients of fixity of schedule, a preoccupation with "doing it right," anxiety and possible blame if not done right, and, above all, the control of unpredicatability through observance of proper procedures. The dominant symbolism of the model sequence stressed the passivity of the mother, control by the physicians and his or her assistants, and the mastery of the uncertainties of nature through standardized application of special knowledge.

From the mid-twentieth century to the present, this more or less established model of "technological birth" has been seriously challenged and some modifications have been adopted. A plausible beginning for this movement, best known as "natural childbirth," was the appearance of Dick-Read's *Natural Childbirth* (1933), followed with an even more influential book by Lamaze (1956) and a subsequent statement by Bradley (1965). These books emphasized the more active participation and empowerment of mothers in the birth process; minimization of pain-management medications; a new role for fathers as supporters, trainers, or coaches; and downplaying the ordeal aspects of birth with claims that "natural" modes were safe and less painful; and above all joy and self-realization for the mother. The ingredients were captured in Goodrich's formal definition of natural childbirth: "Intellectual, physical, and emotional preparation for childbirth, to the end that mothers realize their potentialities and enjoy the bringing forth of their babies" (1950, 2).

These statements were sometimes critical of the obstetric worldview, as in Dick-Read's assertion in his 1933 preface: "One of the most important factors in the production of complicated labor, and therefore of maternal and infant mortality, is the inability of obstetricians to stand by and allow the natural and uninterrupted course of labor" (1972, xix–xx).

The criticisms and claims developed into a kind of social movement and political struggle, mainly by middle-class groups, against the medical establishment. Friedan included the issue in her influential book, *The Feminine Mystique* (1963), incorporating the complaints of sadism in the delivery room that had appeared in a torrent of letters to the *Ladies' Home Journal* some years earlier. The natural childbirth movement was clearly a manifestation of the feminist impulse, but it preceded the massive and dramatic invigoration of the feminist movement in the late 1960s and 1970s. Needless to say, however, the "demedicalization of motherhood" movement and its offshoots were fully assimilated into and given greater strength by that surge (Michaelson 1988). Groups such as the American Society for Psychoprophylactics in Obstetrics, the Association for Childbirth Education, and La Leche League became consolidated as collective manifestations of the movement. Many concessions were made by obstetricians and hospitals with respect to women's preferences in the application of medications, as well as the presence and role of husbands in the birth process. Despite these modifications, technology and its presumed efficiency and safety prevailed in the end, and radical feminist statements still bemoaned the continuing control and dehumanization by obstetricians and hospitals and the failure to attain the "peace and protective calm" of truly natural childbirth (Arms 1975, 142).

Interestingly, like many movements that protest firmly established and ritualized arrangements, natural childbirth tended to develop its own set of alternative ritualized forms, including "mental indoctrination, physical reconditioning, breathing and relaxation techniques, emotional support and physical comfort, and intermittent and local obliteration of labor sensations" (Sandelowski 1984), to say nothing of the ritualization of the husband-father role in the birth process.

One final offshoot of the long political struggle over the control of birth was the emergence of a wider range of choices in every aspect of the pregnancy and birthing process: choices in pregnancy education, in the amount and kind of medication used, in alternatives to binding in the birth bed (such as squatting or water birth), and in the husband-father role. There was a salient call for "choices in childbirth" in the 1970s and 1980s (Michaelson 1988, 7). Among the most notable developments was a modest return to home birth (with the hospital often as backup) and the associated institutional reemergence of midwives, once an endangered profession, as part of the "rehumanization" of childbirth (Oakley and Houd 1990; Howell-White 1999). The net result of this diversification has been to provide contemporary birthing—though, once again, mainly in the middle classes—with many more choices available over a wide range of quasi-ritualized alternatives. Such arrangements produce many ingredients of personal choice: more freedom, less certainty, and possibly more anxiety than customary if not mandatory arrangements.

Death

The ritual recognition of death is universal. A century ago Frazer (1913) described the journey to the otherworld as probably humanity's oldest belief. Death holds a central place not only in the major world religions but also in local religious practices (Davies 2002). The formal and recognized journey is simultaneously a rite of passage from living to dead, an encouragement of life among the still living, and a reaffirmation of community despite loss (ibid.).

The recent history of death rituals offers many parallels with the corresponding rituals for birthing. Over the past two centuries, both the responsibility and the methods for "managing" dying and the disposal of the dead have undergone radical changes. Traditionally, death took place in the home, and the responsibility for laying out the dead resided with the family and community, women being central actors in the process. There has been a gradual movement from dying at home to dying in the hospital, which meant a "medicalization of death" assimilated to the medical treatment of illness. That movement eroded the role of family, community, and clergy in the "control of death" (ibid., 156). Dying in the hospital developed its own standardized procedures for bathing and turning the patient in bed and administering medications, as well as a division of responsibilities among physicians and nurses.

Changes in the disposal of the dead encouraged the gradual development of a new profession: the undertaker or funeral director. In colonial times the undertaker was mainly a carpenter or coffin-maker. With the gradual relocation of graveyards from church grounds to the periphery of towns, undertakers took on responsibility for moving the corpse to the graveyard. The transport of bodies to more remote places also generated the need for better preservation of the corpse, and beginning in the early nineteenth century, embalming was added to undertakers' responsibilities

(Metcalf and Huntington 1991). A further evolution resulted in the funeral director assuming more responsibilities, including ritualized activities such as removing the body, preserving it, arranging for viewing of the corpse, scheduling services, and consoling the bereaved in stylized ways (Bradbury 1999). The profession gained public recognition through the efforts of the Association of Funeral Directors, a powerful lobby. The drive toward full, respected professionalization has been muted, however, by an abiding ambivalence toward death and those who manage it. This ambivalence was given vivid expression in the comic figure of Digby O'Dell ("the friendly undertaker") in the *Life of Riley* radio and television shows in the 1950s, who entertained audiences with his occupational puns ("I've covered a lot of ground today"; "I'd better be shoveling off"). More recently, the television series *Six Feet Under* revealed the same ambivalences.

As in the case of childbearing, the increasing professional domination of death and disposal generated protest and the advocacy of alternatives. A critical event was the appearance of Mitford's *The American Way of Death* (1963), a savage attack on funeral directors' exploitative economic practices and the artificiality of many practices, such as the cosmetic treatment of corpses. This book has been widely cited as the impetus for the "death awareness movement," a putative corrective to the widely discussed denial of death in American culture. In all events, the protest and its ramifications have led to the development of a wider set of alternatives for disposal of the body, including low-cost, arranged-in-advance burial arrangements and informal scattering of ashes by families and friends.

With respect to dying, the main focus of protest was the dehumanization entailed in the medical management of death.

This complaint has resulted in the development of the hospice movement (Seale 1998). A revitalization of older religious practices, that movement has been oriented mainly toward providing an alternative to the depersonalization of dying in hospitals and nursing homes. It stresses preparing collectively for death in a nonmedical setting and restoring human feeling and dignity to dying (Davies 2002).

In the end, the modern vicissitudes of birth and death have their unique histories, but they follow a similar sequence: advancement of knowledge, appropriation, masculinization, professionalization, near-monopolization, commercialization, protest and political conflict, accommodation, and in the end, diversification and greater consumer choice—constrained, however, by economic and social status.

ODYSSEYS FOR THE TIMES: UFO SIGHTINGS AND THEIR ELABORATION

As a major change of pace, I conclude by discussing a modern adaptation of the odyssey idea, beginning in the context of a fascinating phenomenon of the second half of the twentieth century and continuing to the present. That phenomenon is the sighting of flying saucers and its development into a notable social movement known as "ufology" that includes thousands of individual sightings and testimonials; collectivization into clubs, research organizations, funding agencies, and some religious groups; and vigorous defensiveness and criticism directed toward scientific and governmental skeptics. As a social movement, ufology possesses a highly elaborated but not especially unified worldview that is a syncretic mix of religious, scientific, and quasi-scientific ingredients. From the many directions that ufology has taken, I will concentrate on its incorporation of the symbolism of the odyssey experience, especially in accounts by those who claim to have been abducted by aliens from space and by religious organizations that incorporate travel into space in their beliefs.

By including this account in a chapter with the word *invented* in its title, I do not mean to imply that odyssey sightings and related assertions are either real or imagined. By concentrating on the structure and dynamics of the symbolism of part of the ufological movement, I wish to sidestep that issue, which has dominated claims and counterclaims about flying objects and spacemen: whether they actually exist or are some kind of hallucination, projection, or other internally generated force, and therefore do not exist in reality. In this regard I am taking the some position as that of Carl J. Jung, the psychoanalyst, who, at the age of eighty-five, wrote a psychological/symbolic analysis of the flying-saucer phenomenon (1959). In that account he maintained that he was a "mere psychologist" who was not taking a stand on the truth claims of either sighters or doubters. However, because I concentrate on social-psychological symbolism, my remarks may be interpreted as leaning toward the skeptical side.

Many writers, including some ufologists, have traced sightings and explanations of objects in the skies to ancient origins (for example, Ezekiel's wheel in the Bible). Parallels in folklore have also been identified (Sanarov 1981). In modern times, a number of discrete "scares" have been identified:

- A wave of sightings of airships—known as "airship fever"—in the United States in 1896–97, a number of which included accounts of meeting pilots and crew members.

- Sightings of "Edison stars" in 1897, apparently triggered by the widespread knowledge that Thomas Edison was conducting wireless telegraphic experiments using balloons.

- A number of "Zeppelin scares" after Germany's invention of that craft in 1908, including sightings by thousands of New Zealanders (including fears of attack) and a rash of Zeppelin sightings in Great Britain in 1912–13, in the context of national unease about war with Germany.

- Many "phantom air raids" and sightings of "spy missions" in Canada, the United States, and South Africa in World War I.

- A rash of sightings of "rockets" over Sweden in 1946, following German rocket attacks on Britain toward the end of World War II and amid fears that the Soviet Union had confiscated a supply of those rockets. The sightings occurred in the midst of a period of heightened solar activity. They were subsequently discredited in an official Swedish government report (all incidents reported in Bartholomew and Howard 1998).

- One might add the closely related "War of the Worlds" radio broadcast of a Martian invasion in 1938, which triggered mass panic on the eastern seaboard of the United States (Cantril 2005 [1940]).

As indicated, the context of these episodes included factors such as anxiety about foreign aggression, traditional antagonisms between nations, and recent knowledge and lore about inventions. They are usually assigned to the category of "mass hysteria" by those who study them, based on the assumption that factors other than actual events account for them, because neither the events nor their attributed causes have been verified by independent investigation.

The contemporary flying-saucer era from the middle of the twentieth century is linked to a single event, according to the general consensus. On June 24, 1947, Kenneth Arnold, a businessman from Boise, Idaho, reported seeing saucer-shaped objects skipping over the Cascade Mountains in the state of Washington. The incident was reported in 150 newspapers, and two months later a national Gallup poll reported that 90 percent of respondents had heard of flying saucers, and that most believed that U.S. or Russian secret weapons were involved (Bartholomew and Howard 1998, 189–91). Many other sightings were reported in subsequent months.

The context of the 1947 scare is consistent with previous episodes. The V-2 rockets and devastating atomic attacks that ended World War II introduced the specter of unprecedented destructive weaponry into the public imagination. The cold war was beginning in earnest, generating a great deal of uncertainty and fear. In addition, the country was on the eve of the McCarthy hearings, which produced a dread of Soviet and Chinese communism. The federal government officially discredited the sightings, but with its own cold war preoccupations, initiated security investigations of those who claimed to have seen flying objects.

Unlike the largely one-shot episodes of the past, however, the flying saucer or unidentified flying object phenomenon was followed by waves of sightings of almost unending variety (Baker 1998). Reactions to these incidents gained a momentum of their

own and evolved into the complex and amorphous social movement of ufology. In July, one month after Arnold's sighting, the
crash of an unidentified flying object and a witnessing of aliens
were reported near Roswell, New Mexico. Debris was report-
edly found. Government discrediting of the event gave rise to
repeated accusations that these and other kinds of incidents
were being covered up by the government. Over time Roswell
assumed the status of a pilgrimage site, and in 1997 believers
and others gathered for a massive fiftieth-anniversary celebration (Curran 2001). Reports of meetings with aliens who had
landed on earth abounded, and the variety of reports on the
appearance and intentions of the aliens is dizzying. Public interest in the UFO phenomenon and extraterrestrial dramatics has
been sustained and even heightened by scores of books, films,
and television productions, the most notable of which were Stephen Spielberg's *Close Encounters of the Third Kind* (1979) and *ET*
(1982), *Independence Day* (1996), and television's *X-Files* series.
The ufology movement has produced a quasi-theological tradition of commentary and controversy over details of sightings,
landings, meetings, the nature and purposes of the aliens, and
the nature of extraterrestrial life. Psychological explanations of
UFO experiences—as folklore, wishful thinking, mispercep-
tion, and psychopathology—have also appeared in the literature (Saliba 2003b).

Two developments in UFO history are especially salient for
the study of the odyssey experience: reports of abduction into
space by aliens and the rise of "UFO religions," mainly apocalyptic and salvationist cults. Reports of abductions, like most
ingredients of the UFO phenomenon, stretch back into history.
However, the appearance of *Missing Time* by Budd Hopkins

(1981) stimulated an "almost exponential" increase in abduction reports (Partridge 2003, 26). These reports are diverse and highly elaborated, but certain themes recur. Abductees are carried mystically, by flotation or other means, into space. Some reported episodes are abductions for purposes of rape, torture, or murder, often by "reptilians" or "reptoids." Other repeated themes are abduction for purposes of impregnation (with offspring stolen by aliens) and the surgical extraction of ova and sperm for extraterrestrial breeding purposes (Bryan 1995).

Most abduction narratives, however, as surveyed by Partridge (2003) are more positive and manifest the ingredients of the odyssey. Abducting aliens are benign missionaries motivated by a desire to rescue humanity from sin or destruction. They are regarded as superior in culture to earthlings. Many abductees describe themselves as "chosen" agents to aid in the salvation of humanity. Most abductees regard the journeys as psychologically and physically regenerative experiences. Partridge describes the experience as a kind of externally imposed self-spirituality (ibid., 31–32). Many abduction narratives report that the experience occurs in a dream or a state of altered consciousness, recoverable through hypnosis (Devereux and Brookesmith 1997). Such accounts reveal ingredients of separation (from earth), a liminal period of travel and unusual experiences, and return to the Earth as part of a more encompassing plan of world improvement or transformation.

These themes appear even more clearly in the several UFO religious organizations that have emerged during the past half-century. Partridge (2003) and others interpret these cults as derivative of the theosophical tradition dating to the eighteenth century and given modern voice by George Adamski (an early sighter who had been exposed to theosophy). Examples of the extraterrestrial cults are the Raelian Church, Unarius, the Aetherius Society, and Heaven's Gate. All involve extraterrestrial beings (for example, Cosmic Masters, the god Elohim) who are engaged in missions of rescue and peace. The leaders receive revelations, and in some cases represent themselves as agents of the extraterrestrial powers. Several cults have millenarian and apocalyptic elements, and include a claim that believers will be rescued and transported into space at an appointed time. The most dramatic and tragic case is Heaven's Gate, thirty-nine members of which committed collective suicide in March 1997 in a mansion outside San Diego in anticipation of the world's destruction (on the day the Hale-Bopp comet came closest to the earth). On that day space beings would transport the faithful into space (Lewis 2003). In a more general survey of UFO groups, Wojcik delineated the major themes of apocalyptic and millenarian ideologies: world destruction and fantasy escape; the salvation of the chosen; technological angels; prevention of nuclear apocalypse; and the presence of benevolent agents committed to rescuing humanity—narratives, in short, that "warn of imminent worldly catastrophes but offer the promise of survival and transformation" (2003, 289).

My interpretation of the dominant themes of these abduction narratives and UFO religions is that they are invented, syncretic versions of the religious odyssey experience, adapted to current uncertainties and anxieties but in the end offering the comforting vision of a safe journey to salvation and regeneration in a menacing world. They gain plausibility by a double mechanism: first, by "updating," that is, incorporating, the language of contemporary science, technology, and world events;

and second, by combining these ingredients with long-standing and perhaps universal cultural beliefs regarding death and rebirth. This fusion of the contemporary with the eternal in a search for meaning is ubiquitous through history and should be expected to repeat itself in forever novel forms as long as civilization endures.

SIX

Some Coercive
Odyssey Experiences

At the outset I should confess an abiding ambivalence about including a chapter on coercive odysseys. Many of the outcomes (punishment, degradation, even torture) are usually regarded as negative or even evil, scarcely regenerative. Furthermore, at first glance, it seems a stretch to subsume processes as diverse as boot camp, prison correctional programs, tourism, and religious conversion under a common category. As I have considered the matter, however, I have concluded that the inclusion is a legitimate one, for three reasons: (1) the internal social and psychological characteristics of coercive experiences—and the processes by which these characteristics are ordered—are directly comparable to other types of odyssey; (2) the outcomes of many coercive ordeals are often regarded by those who impose them and sometimes by those who undergo them as regenerative or at the very least designed to change those who experience them; (3) experiences thought of as voluntary, such as taking a holiday trip or entering psychotherapy, often have quasi-coercive aspects because they are normatively regulated activities. Furthermore, once one has entered them, one may become "hooked" psychologically, and this constitutes an inner coercion. In all events, I am hopeful that the analyses undertaken in this chapter will build a plausible and legitimate case for folding coercive experiences into the broad framework that informs this book.

A GENERAL NOTE ON PAIN AND THE ORDEAL

Most of the coercive experiences considered in this chapter are, generally speaking, rites of transition, and most inflict suffering on those experiencing them. Anthropologists have noted that such rites are almost universally accompanied by the imposition of pain, sometimes extreme and sometimes resulting in mutilation. Therefore I must ask: why are these negative ingredients so common, when they are generally regarded as undesirable features of human existence? A partial answer is provided by Morinis. After addressing anthropologists' interpretations of adolescent initiation ordeals, he proposes the following functional interpretation: (1) Pain is the qualitative opposite of the virtues of social membership, and so fulfills a role as a structural component of the ritual's metamessage. (2) Pain and mutilation are symbolic of change and transformation. (3) The avoidance of pain and suffering is an instinctive human trait that is "culturized" in the rites of initiands. (4) Pain, as an intense, unforgettable experience, has an impact on the human system that is especially relevant to the transition from childhood consciousness to adult self-awareness (1985, 164).

One might mention other psychological possibilities that reinforce the connection: for example, infliction of pain gratifies ambivalent or sadistic impulses on the part of inflictors (who are often relatives or intimates of the victims), and experiencing pain provides a psychological rationale for the victims to inflict like pain on future generations of initiands. In all events, the principle is found in rationalized form in religious and folk homilies connecting suffering and salvation, pain and virtue: out of tragedy emerges strength and good, suffering builds character, unpleasant experiences are good medicine.

These theoretical musings do not establish the empirical validity of the association between pain and growth, but they do suggest why that association is built into so many ritual transitions.

FRATERNITY AND SORORITY INITIATIONS

The fraternity and sorority system has been a persistent if controversial adjunct of American higher education, even though its centrality to campus life varies. Fraternities and sororities serve as bases for residential living and social solidarity for selected undergraduates; as an organizer of social life and partying; as a mechanism for assortive dating and future marriage along class and ethnic lines (Scott 1965); as a basis for cultivating future business and professional contacts and friendships; as a way of segregating undergraduates, usually along social class lines; and as a basis for cultivating loyalty to the college or university and soliciting future donations from alumni. The controversial aspects of the system are a long but diminishing pattern of religious, ethnic, and racial discrimination; alcoholic excesses and rowdyism; cruel, harmful, and occasionally fatal practices in initiations; and insinuations of ghost-writing or securing already written term papers from commercial organizations.

In keeping with the general theme of this volume, I will focus on the initiation, including "rushing" and "hazing." Its closest cousins are religious and secular rites of passage, induction into secret societies, and programs of military socialization. The initiation into fraternities and sororities involves a sequence from voluntary to coercive. To apply to and rush for a society is a voluntary, indeed competitive, system in which applicants put themselves forward to be tested and are likely to fail. Once accepted, however, the initiation and all that accompanies it are mandatory, beyond the initiate's choice as to whether he or she wishes to become and remain a member.

From time to time college administrators and faculty members have written sympathetic accounts of fraternity and sorority life. Two themes emerge. The first is degradation, both in the initiation and during the first year, in which freshmen "should be kept in the background, should be required to do most of the 'dirty' work about the house, and should be denied many of the privileges which are open to other members" (Clark 1931, 41). In some cases there is extremely close scrutiny of members' behavior, including public sessions (called a "mutual admiration society" or "good and welfare") in which the "unfortunate and undesirable tendencies" of a member are publicly discussed and criticized, followed by public acknowledgment or even confession by the member (Musgrave 1923). The second is the "growth" or generative aspect. Degradation is intended to change and improve the member—to "develop character and manhood" (ibid., 75), to ensure that "their members are men rather than foolish, unruly boys" (Clark 1931, 3). Though fraternities and sororities exhibit wide variation among them and over time, these depictions communicate essential elements of an odyssey experience—specifically, stripping (destructuring), a liminal period of proving oneself through hardship, and a final restructuring phase of personal regeneration and assumption of full membership in an exclusive brotherhood or sisterhood.

The most detailed case study of fraternity life was conducted by Leemon (1972). His main intellectual inspiration is the theory of van Gennep. Accordingly, he organizes his analysis around the phases of separation, liminality, and incorporation. The process is marked by explicit incorporation into the fraternity or sorority and designation by a new status in a pledging ceremony that simultaneously makes the pledge a member, albeit temporarily as a second-class citizen. It is expected that the new member's social life will be concentrated in the fraternity or sorority, and that interaction with others in dorms, classrooms, and elsewhere will diminish correspondingly.

In the fraternity studied by Leemon, the pledge period was supervised by a whip, a secret figure, a kind of "magician-priest" (ibid., 49) who guided the activities of the pledges—training classes, menial chores, and rituals and ceremonials. The drill involved repeated degradation and humiliation, always accompanied by reminders of the pledge's inferior status and assurances that the seemingly "ridiculous, meaningless and unintelligible" activities demanded of the pledges were carefully designed by the members and aimed ultimately at elevating the pledges (ibid., 106).

Incorporation of the pledges at the end of the period was an elaborate ritual that marked full entry into the fraternity on a new and equal basis: "Ritual equality was augmented by an event in which the newly initiated acted out their new and equal positions as members of the fraternity by first throwing into the shower members who had been particularly active in enforcing the new initiates' prior position as pledges, and then throwing food and water on any member who happened to be present. . . . During the party in celebration of the initiation into membership, the new initiates dramatized their acquisition of membership status by destroying a symbol of their prior status as pledges. They burned their sacks" (ibid., 195).

MILITARY SOCIALIZATION: BASIC TRAINING, BOOT CAMP, AND SOME DERIVATIVES

Fundamental Components

Induction into military life includes an initiation involving routine, subordination, regimentation, and some physical hardship. The rationalizations for arduous socialization are many: to inculcate military culture and its codes of honor (Weitz 2003); to instill discipline, combat-readiness, and bravery in military fighters; to generate loyalty to the state; and to foster the ideals of masculinity—to make fighting men out of boys, to make men who are "fit, rough and nasty, not powderpuffs" (Hockey 2003, 16).

The readiest example of the extremities of military socialization is the subordination of first-year cadets ("plebes") at the U.S. Military Academy at West Point, other military academies, military schools, and basic training and boot-camp programs. The phenomenon has also received popular representation in films such as *The Right Stuff.* The process and its rationale was summarized by Janowitz:

> Training new recruits for combat has in the past been
> governed by a conception of shock treatment—of the need
> for a sudden and decisive break with civilian life and rapid

exposure to the rigors of military existence. The officer candidate had to receive a double dosage of shock treatment, since he had to be separated not only from civilian society but also from the enlisted ranks. The devices of shock range from the "beast barracks" of West Point for new cadets to the well-known Marine haircut. The sharp and sudden transition is often repulsive to the civilian orientation. But, in the military establishment, the assumption is that only a decisive break is effective in the long run and that the rigors of basic training are in effect natural techniques of selection (1965, 62).

Janowitz's summary reveals the characteristics of the odyssey experience:

- *Destructuring.* Military socialization aims to remove recruits from the normal features of civilian life and to subordinate them to a simplified, rank-based, regimented existence.

- *Isolation.* Recruits are, as a rule, put into camps isolated from relatives and friends (relieved by furloughs and leaves of absence), which is considered essential for their effective socialization. Some research reveals that recruits who attempted to maintain contact with their homes and families adjusted poorly to military training (Christie 1953).

- *Leveling.* Standardized clothing and sleeping arrangements, as well as subjection to identical routines and drills, symbolize the equal status of recruits and their common subordination to those in higher ranks.

- *Deprivation/degradation.* This is the signature of coercive odyssey experiences. It is what gives them their bite.

Degradation is achieved through long and arduous daily schedules and activities such as drill, circuit training, road runs, assault courses, and forced marches with heavy equipment. It extends to details such as how to sit at meals and mandatory language for addressing superiors. In a study of Philippine officer trainees, McCoy concludes that "ritual hazing of incoming plebes [including outright punishment] remains the defining moment of their lives" (1995, 696). The degradation is explicitly linked to "making men" of the recruits, and those who falter are called "sissies," "patsies," or "girls." In an interesting variant, Williams (1989) conducted a study of women recruits in the U.S. Marine Corps, reputedly the toughest and most "manly" of the services. Women in basic training were segregated from males except for religious services on Sundays, and even then men and women were prohibited from looking at or talking to one another. Women were required to remain "feminine" by wearing mandated makeup and were given courses on poise and etiquette. They carried the derogatory designation of "BAMS" or "bammies," derived from "broad-assed marines," and weathered psychological harassment as women at the hands of drill sergeants.

- *Regeneration.* The end of the line of military training is to mold effective fighting soldiers and to make men of boys—a persistent theme, however diluted by the increasing proportion of women in the military. Recognizing that not all will remain in the service, the armed services stress that military training fosters social mobility by equipping trainees with skills that will advance them in future civilian life. The stress on regeneration and self-realization is repeated in recruitment pitches on television commercials in the jingle "Be all that you can be in the Army."

Not specifically noted by Janowitz but equally conspicuous in military training programs are several additional features:

- *Indoctrination.* Recruits in basic training are constantly reminded that "this is the army," which usually means order and discipline. At West Point, students take courses in military history and leadership and are constantly indoctrinated into military culture in more informal ways. In the high days of Maoist domination in Communist China, trainees in the military academy were given ideological instruction in the thought of Marx, Lenin, and Mao Zedong, as well as military values. They were routinely subjected to question-answer sessions on their instruction (Heaton 1980). Indoctrination is one systematic restructuring device in coercive odyssey experiences.

- *Solidarity.* Cohesion is an explicit goal in military training. In a comparative study of military practices in the Soviet Union, the United States, North Vietnam, and Israel, Henderson (1985) found that a common element in training is "the creation of a cohesive unit" through resocialization. The process is a combination of routine, regimentation, and subordination that "totally consumes the soldier's attention and efforts for an extended period and from which he emerges with a new or adapted set of operating rules for his daily life" (18). Henderson went on to argue that in some cases, notably Israel, the effort to create cohesion is more effective because the military experience is more consuming and intense, whereas in the U.S. Army the process is weakened by high turnover, breaking up of units through individual reassignment, and the tendency to define military life more in occupational than "commitment" terms (ibid., 38, 50). A microscopic solidarity typically arises at the unit level in the formation of primary groups (Korpi 1964), which, repeated research has shown, is an important mechanism for sustaining loyalty and bravery (Grinker and Spiegel 1945). Needless to say, this kind of solidarity is an instance of *communitas* common to odyssey experiences.

• *Resentment and nostalgia.* In the U.S. military services, subordinated recruits' "griping" culture is legendary, no doubt reflecting the discontinuity between the dominant egalitarian values of the larger society and the emphasis on authority in the military. One of the most consistent findings in *The American Soldier* was chronic dissatisfaction and resentment toward the officer classes (Stouffer et al., 1949). Also prominent, however, is the tendency in later years to repress this negative side and stress the positive values of the military experience, especially solidarity with "buddies" and the maturing effects of military life.

So much for a recapitulation of an ideal-type odyssey of military socialization and, to some extent, military life in general. It is important to stress that this process varies by branch of service and by national military tradition. There is also evidence that in recent decades the pattern has weakened in the American military. Writing in the 1960s, Janowitz (1965) noted the move away from traditional emphases on mechanical and repetitive drill toward a "team" concept in training. Some officer training programs, especially the Officer Training School of the U.S. Air Force, have explicitly deviated from the model of harshness and heroism in training, replacing it with preparation of military "managers" (Wamsley 1972). And finally, the development of high-tech methods so evident in the two Iraq Wars and in the campaign in Afghanistan has no doubt elevated the technical-occupational components of military training at the expense of loyalty, national glorification, and ordeal, despite the persistent voice given to traditional military values and assertions about what makes a good military fighter.

Military-Style Corrective Programs

An interesting adaptation of the military socialization model is found in the prison system. The technique goes under the heading of correctional boot camp, but has been more benignly labeled "accountability programs" and "leadership camps." Origins of the system can be traced to the 1880s under the name of "shock incarceration," but the explicitly military model was introduced in prisons in Georgia and Oklahoma in the 1980s (Armstrong 2004) and given articulation in 1987 by a clinical psychologist in the Louisiana Department of Corrections (MacKenzie 2004a). It has been employed in some prisons as a mode of preparing inmates for release. Part of the popularity of the program is that it resonates with the "get tough on crime" theme in conservative law-and-order circles.

The philosophy of boot camp correctional programs has been described as "part punitive and part rehabilitative" (Armstrong 2004, 9), which reveals both the ordeal and the regenerative ingredients. The guiding idea is that if people are placed in a stress environment, they will be especially susceptible to influence. Though inmates usually volunteer for the program, a strict military regime is imposed once they do so: "Males are required to have their heads shaved (females may be permitted short haircuts), and they are informed on the strict program rules. At all times, inmates are required to address staff as 'sir' or 'ma'am,' or an associated military title such as 'Captain,' request permission to speak, and refer to themselves in the third person as 'this inmate' or 'this cadet.' The incoming group of inmates is called a 'platoon.' Platoons are kept together in all aspects of the program, including housing, meal times, physical training, and other activities" (ibid., 10). Other leveling and degrading devices include a daily routine beginning with reveille, fatigue uniforms for all, and ten to sixteen hours of scheduled duties. Correctional officers wear uniforms indicative of their superior rank. Inmates are rewarded for positive performance with privileges and responsibilities, symbolized by differently colored hats or badges. All of these elements illustrate the components of destructuring and humiliation in the coerced odyssey.

The restructuring aims of the program are to modify inmate attitudes, reduce recidivism, reduce community supervision, ameliorate prison crowding (inmates who complete the program successfully may be released earlier than scheduled), and create a positive environment conducive to change (ibid., 13). Proponents argue that the program instills personal discipline and responsibility and increases inmates' sense of self-esteem.

Also consistent with the military thinking behind the correctional camps, they are advertised as making "men out of boys" (MacKenzie 2004b).

Research on the effects of the program bears all the shortcomings of evaluation research in general. Results have not been decisive with respect to recidivism, but there is some evidence that those who go through the program develop more positive attitudes than those who do not (ibid.). Juveniles who participate in the program appear to find it a positive experience (MacKenzie, Wilson, Armstrong, and Gover 2004). Other comparative research found better "community adjustment" among successful boot-camp graduates than among boot-camp dropouts, parolees, and probationers (MacKenzie, Shaw, and Souryal 2004).

To conclude this section on coercive socialization and resocialization, we should remind ourselves of a few additional analogues. Traditional training of physicians in medical schools, internships, and residencies has its backbreaking aspects, including years of hard study, long hours of work, low pay, subordination to superiors, and only gradual and ritualized access to responsible, independent practice. The objective is to make a doctor—to imbue the trainee with the skills, attitudes, and worldview of a professional physician (for an illustration from obstetrics training, see Davis-Floyd 1987). That older physicians bemoan the recent relaxation of punitive aspects and believe that the new generation of physicians is coddled underlines the belief in the transformational power of punitive, ritualized training. The grind of the law school years is also legendary, the hardship and threat symbolized by the apocryphal law professor's admonition on the first day to each student to look at the person to the right and the person to the left, and to realize that one of the three will not be there at the end of the first year. In my own experience as an academic, I came to regard graduate study for the doctorate as having many ingredients of rites of passage, including demanding courses in theory and methods that graduate students come to regard as "hatchet courses," the orals examination as an often-degrading ritual, and the arduous years required to produce a dissertation. In all these illustrations, the ultimate goal is positive regeneration: the creation of a new self and the making of a better—in this case, more successful—person, the trademark of odyssey experiences.

SOME PROCESSES OF
PSYCHOLOGICAL COERCION

The notion that social and psychological isolation has deep and unsettling consequences for mental life is well established in knowledge and lore. We saw in chapter 3 that isolation of the initiate is a core feature of rites of passage. Eastern religions have stressed isolation and meditation as avenues to spiritual enlightenment and growth. One salient feature of the monastery is social isolation from the outside world and long periods of individual solace within its walls. The story of Robinson Crusoe describes the spiritual quest of an isolated man. The theme of isolation has a negative side as well. The essence of torture is systematic physical abuse combined with isolation. Solitary confinement in prisons punishes by depriving the prisoner of sensory stimulation and human contact. The wildness of the feral child derives from isolation from socializing agents. There are many anecdotal accounts of the psychologically debilitating influence of isolation on explorers, castaways, lifeboat survivors, submarine crews, and fighter pilots. One of the most vivid accounts is that of Admiral Richard Byrd (1938), who described the effects of his six-month isolation in a small hut buried in the snow in Antarctica. He experienced extreme anxiety, depression, hallucinatory symptoms, and a desperate longing for human company. At the same time he experienced moments of serenity and euphoria. Finally, the common language reflects the connection between loneliness and psychological suffering in phrases such as "stir crazy" and "cabin fever."

Around 1950, the connections among isolation, ordeal, and coerced change leaped into the consciousness of the public and scholars alike. This historical episode arose from the confluence of a number of powerful historical and cultural trends. In recent public memory were two phenomena in totalitarian countries: the perceived ingenious and omnipotent propaganda machine of Nazi Germany and the notorious extraction of confessions in the Soviet purge trials of the 1930s. Both had brought the idea of mental manipulation to salience. Arthur Koestler's *Darkness at Noon*, published in 1940, highlighted the Soviet trials. Scholarly interest in propaganda crystallized during World War II. In the more immediate past was the shocking and apparently forced confession of Cardinal József Mindszenty of Hungary in 1949, which again raised the imagery of a powerful Communist weapon. In the same year George Orwell's novel *Nineteen Eighty-four* appeared, depicting an all-powerful and manipulative party that dominated minds and rendered the population helpless. The method of Chinese thought control came into evidence after the Communist takeover of China in 1948. But the most powerful influence was a special Chinese method of interrogation (named "brainwashing" in 1953 by an American journalist) used on American prisoners in the Korean War. This convergence of events, occurring in the early anxious years of the cold war and the rise of the Soviet Union as a nuclear power, resulted in a great public preoccupation and even panic about the power and insidiousness of mind control.

In the paragraphs that follow I trace a number of manifestations of this preoccupation:

- the psychological literature on brainwashing
- the development of sensory deprivation research in psychology
- the reaction to some "new religions" as mind control.

My aim is to interpret these developments within the framework of the odyssey experience, although on the surface they are quite different from its other manifestations.

The Focus on Politically Motivated Brainwashing

The 1950s and 1960s saw an explosion of literature on the coercive manipulation of the mind, inspired mainly by the treatment of prisoners in the Korean War. Some of this work bordered on the sensational and alarmist, depicting mind control as an insidious weapon (e.g., Sargant 1957; Meerloo 1956). More scholarly treatments also appeared, the most notable of which were Lifton's (1961) analysis of thought-control methods by the Chinese Communist Party, a study of American prisoners of war by Schein (1961), and a synthetic work by Pear (1961).

The empirical cases that held most interest for the scholars were three:

- The Soviet mode of extracting confessions, in which the main elements were isolation of the individual, extreme coercion based on a "scientific" rationale, use of an individual interrogator, forced admission of ideological errors and crime, and typically execution ("extermination") of the prisoner.

- The tactics of the Chinese Communist Party during the period of thought reform, which relied more on persuasion than brutal coercion, involved an element of group support, forced the acknowledgment of errors, and ended with a publicly announced conversion to the communist belief system and way of life (Solomon 1983).

- The Chinese treatment of American prisoners of war, derived from the thought-control model.

The second and third modes commanded most of the investigators' attention, largely because they were regarded as more subtle and sophisticated (and perhaps for those reasons more threatening) and because, in the third case, Americans were the victims.

Lifton stressed two fundamental elements of the Chinese mode of thought control: *confession*, which involved renunciation of one's bourgeois background and errors as well as denunciation of the "old society"; and *re-education*, or the creation of a "new man" in the Communist image. The process was one of moral regeneration—an "uplifting, harmonizing, and scientifically therapeutic experience" (1961, 15). The imagery was of death and rebirth. The mechanisms involved an assault on the old identity of the subject, firm establishment of guilt about that identity, the offering of leniency and the opportunity for change, the extraction of a confession that renounced everything in the past, and the channeling of guilt into a commitment to work toward the perfection of the new society. The process has the elements of a radical, imposed odyssey experience—a destructuring (in this case attempted obliteration) of the old, a liminal period of change, and a more or less complete restructuring of individual beliefs and commitments in a new way of life.

Schein's psychological account of the tactics Chinese Communists used on American prisoners of war closely resembled Lifton's work on thought control (and, evidently, van Gennep's classic account of ritual change). For Schein, the process had three phases: a period of *unfreezing*, an assault on the existing patterns of beliefs and assumptions; *changing*, the renunciation of the old and systematic input of new and systematically controlled information, resulting in the subject's "seeing the light"; and *re-freezing*, or incorporation of the new beliefs into a new identity, accompanied by testimonials of enlightenment and pleasure. In the case of American prisoners, the renunciation involved a wholesale rejection of their own past lives, including a condemnation of American bourgeois capitalist society, and the conversion involved the enthusiastic embrace of communist ideals and society (Schein 1961, 19–20). Schein also stressed the exploitation of guilt, but above all the Chinese method involved a combination of implicit threats combined with friendly and lenient interrogators and an atmosphere of group support for the prisoners. These elements provided a stark contrast with the Soviet procedures and brought the process closer to a therapeutic model than brutal punishment. Parenthetically, they also made the Chinese process appear all the more insidious.

Schein explicitly compared the Chinese pattern of coercive persuasion to kindred "mortifications of the self" in religious orders, military training, hospitals, fraternities, and religious revival meetings, as well as the pattern of renunciation and reform in groups such as Alcoholics Anonymous, though he noted that voluntary elements are more conspicuous in most of these than in the distinctive Chinese pattern. He also pointed out some parallels with the mechanism of combined punishment and support—the "good cop–bad cop" technique—in prisons and mental hospitals (ibid., 271–75).

The public preoccupation with political brainwashing waned after the period of avid preoccupation, in part because the personality change appeared to be only short-term (Lifton 1961, 236–37), in part because of fading memories of the Korean War, and in part because of the waning and ultimate collapse of Soviet-style totalitarianism in later decades. *Brainwashing*, however, remains in the lexicon, typically employed to characterize efforts to persuade by exercising extreme pressure.

The Sensory Deprivation Line of Research and Practice

Anecdotal accounts of the relations between isolation and mental aberration have long been available. A few psychological studies linking boredom with inattention, alienation, and irritability reach back to the 1920s (Schultz 1965). But it was not until the early 1950s that interest burgeoned in the influence of radical reduction of stimuli on behavior. The trigger for this development was a series of experiments conducted at McGill University under the leadership of Donald O. Hebb, a distinguished neuropsychologist. Rooted in a long psychological interest in stimulus and arousal, the experiments themselves reflected a concern with mind manipulation and control. Hebb described that concern as follows: "The work that we have done at McGill University began actually with the problem of brain-washing. . . . [T]he chief impetus, of course, was the dismay at the kind of 'confessions' being produced at the Russian Communist trials. 'Brainwashing' was a term that came a little later, applied to Chinese procedures. We did not know what the . . . procedures were, but it seemed that they were producing some peculiar changes in attitude. How?" (1961, 40). The McGill experiments made no attempt to replicate the psychologically coercive interrogation of the Soviet political trials. Instead, researchers minimized the stimulation available to experimental subjects (hence the term *deprivation*) and observed the psychological consequences.

The model employed in the studies was relatively simple. Male college students were paid twenty dollars a day to lie for two days on a bed in a partially soundproof cubicle, wearing goggles, gloves, and cardboard cuffs and hearing only the low hum of a fan. Only meals and bathroom breaks broke the routine. In later experiments subjects were submersed in lukewarm water. The subjects reported pleasant feelings in the initial stage of the experiments, but as time went on, they became anxious, irritated, desirous of stimulation, and ultimately eager to quit the experiment. To the surprise of both experimenters and subjects alike, the deprivation brought on many forms of hallucination and a general deterioration of perceptual and intellectual abilities. These effects were diminished if subjects were given tasks to perform, and mental activity typically returned to normal after the experiment was over.

The impact of these studies on psychological research was dramatic. Research laboratories and experimental programs appeared in short order at more than a dozen leading American universities and several foreign centers, as well as the National Institute of Mental Health and the U.S. Army. Schultz reported an "incredible growth rate of the experimental literature" (1965, 4). In keeping with the methodological culture of experimental psychology, everything was varied—type of confinement, type of deprivation, contacts with experimenters, duration of isolation, measures of perceptual response, sex differences among subjects, and personality and cultural differences (Zuckerman 1969). Brownfield (1972) noted a proliferation of definitions and counted two dozen efforts to come up with a precise name for the phenomenon, including "restricted stimulation," "sensory isolation," and "social limitation."

It would serve little purpose in this volume to trace the great array of reported findings. However, in keeping with my theoretical interest in odyssey experiences, I will venture one theoretical observation about the tradition of sensory deprivation research and note the movement of the tradition in a therapeutic direction.

From the standpoint of the theoretical framework that informs this study, the sensory deprivation experiments themselves contain two of the three essential ingredients of the odyssey experience. The first is a radical destructuring of the sensory and perceptual environment of the experimental subjects. The experimental isolation itself constitutes a liminal period in which mental and affective productions are primitive and often beyond the perceptual and cognitive control of the subjects, and are "regressive" in terms of the level of mental functioning. What is missing from the standpoint of the odyssey experience is the third element, restructuring. The experiments ended with the expectation that the experimental effects would cease with the termination of the experiment and the accompanying assumption that the subjects would simply return to "normal." So, though stimulated by the confessional and brainwashing literatures, sensory deprivation experiments did not replicate the deliberate effort to create new and changed attitudes and loyalties. In that sense the experiments may be regarded as the creation of a partial or truncated odyssey experience.

Sensory deprivation research enjoyed a great boom during the decade after the McGill experiments, and the idea found its way into popular books and articles, including *The Mind Benders* (Kennaway 1963), which was later made into a movie. (A film with similar emphasis, *Holy Smoke*, appeared in 1999). The subsequent decade, the 1960s, was a period of exploration, refinement, and applications of the theory and method. Thereafter the topic experienced a precipitous decline in interest and funding, so that by 1980, Suedfeld could report that there were "relatively few programs of sustained research in the experimental sensory deprivation area" (1980, 29).

One spin-off of this chapter of theory and research should be noted, however: its adaptation as a mode of psychotherapy. Early in the McGill experiments, some members of the research team noticed particular psychological effects of sensory deprivation, which they described as a positive reorganization of psychic life. Mental patients seemed to benefit from the experience, and others showed a greater readiness to enter other types of therapy (Brownfield 1972). Out of these insights grew a number of efforts to turn the experience of stimulus deprivation into a therapeutic technique.

One aspect of these efforts was to press for a new name for sensory deprivation. The preferred term was Restricted Environmental Stimulus Technique (REST), a label advanced because, it was argued, it was more precise than sensory deprivation and avoided the misleading negative connotations of *deprivation* (Suedfeld 1980). Proponents of the technique pointed out the presence of restricted stimulation in mystical religions, rites of passage, psychoanalysis, other psychotherapies, and wilderness therapy. Therapists developed a specific REST method, which included not only restricted stimulation but also the presence of a friendly and supportive "monitor" who supplied "messages" to clients from time to time during the treatment (Borrie 1980). Proponents also presented evidence for the technique's success in modifying smoking behavior, alcohol consumption, obesity, phobias, and children's developmental problems.

The therapeutic applications of limiting sensory input did not develop into an institutionalized form, and the movement must be regarded as a footnote in the history of psychotherapy. It can be regarded, however, as an effort to bring the process closer to a full odyssey experience by adding a regenerative element to the destructuring and disorienting impulse of the sensory deprivation experiments.

The New Religions and "Brainwashing"

Citing the brainwashing literature, some commentators declared that new religious cults fell precisely into the same category. Singer and Ofshe (1990) enunciated the equivalence, and Clark et al. (1981) also used the brainwashing model to describe the strategies of these cults. The first phase was a deliberate strip-ping though personalized attention, extreme social pressures, rituals, and deprivation. The second was devoted to marathon activities—rehearsals, recitations, and behavioral repetitions. The third was the emergence of a "new self," a cult personal-ity, complete with a special language, patterned and controlled activities, and new social relationships. The logical stages of the model resemble conversion (and the odyssey experience in gen-eral), except that the process follows a coercive rather than a voluntary model.

In large part because of the public scare about brainwash-ing, a strong negative reaction developed to the new religious cults. Cult-watching groups sprang up as part of what came to be known as the "anticult movement" (Hexham and Poewe 1997). Its adherents included friends and relatives of converts, defectors, mental health counselors, and law enforcement offi-cials (Barker 2001). The American Family Foundation became actively concerned, and in several European countries the gov-ernment attempted to limit the spread of the cults through leg-islative action.

Reflecting the anticult impulse were two closely related devel-opments. The first was an interest in why people "deconvert," or leave cults, a process referred to as the "dynamics of defection" (Wright 1987). The major reasons cited were the failure of the cult sufficiently to insulate its recruits from the outside soci-ety, failure to meet the cognitive and affective needs of recruits, failure of leaders as role models, excessive discipline, and exces-sive regulation of converts' interpersonal relations. The second development was an active interest in "deprogramming" people who had been in cults, that is, restoring them to "normal life" through therapy, pastoral counseling, hospitalization, support groups, and return to their families (Langone 1993). The deprogramming process involved a semicoercive "reverse odyssey experience," in which the person who had been captured by the cult's coercive programming underwent a three-stage process of undoing and restoration (Collins 1991; Bromley and Richardson 1983).

The "brainwashing" interpretation of conversion, as well as the campaign to undo its effects, constituted a small moral panic accompanying the efflorescence of new religions. As that panic ran its course, cooler heads began to prevail. Zablocki's assessment makes the most sense: "Those who claim that cultic brainwashing does not exist and those who claim it is pandemic to cults are both wrong. Brainwashing is an administratively costly and not always effective procedure that some cults use on some of their members. A few cults rely heavily on brainwashing and put all their members through it. Other cults do not use the procedure at all" (2001, 204). Well before the end of the century, the flames of this controversy had flickered, and one reads little about it nowadays.

The title of this chapter might well have been "the social and political uses of the odyssey experience," because the episodes depicted—as well as various kinds of religious initiations described in chapter 3—capitalize on the ingredients of a generic and powerful experience and use that mechanism to effect changes in status, attitude, and personality. Regarded from the standpoint of an individualist value system that stresses human dignity and freedom, many of these practices are offensive because they manipulate and degrade. From the standpoint of the users, however, the practices are typically believed and advertised to be beneficial in their effects. Along with the other ingredients, this establishes the kinship of the coercive odyssey with episodes that are voluntary, benign, and acceptable.

SEVEN

Additional Theoretical Reflections

In this final chapter I will try to place the odyssey experience in a wider theoretical frame than I have done in the preceding chapters. I begin by noting that in pursuing theoretical questions one can discern two strategies that are opposite in some respects. The first is to lay out some general perspectives on human nature and society and then give meaning to, interpret, or explain an identified range of empirical phenomena consistent with those perspectives. The second is to start with empirical facts or regularities and tease out their broader theoretical significance.

I will proceed along the second path. In this volume I have identified a range of experiences, which—while varying in empirical settings, emphasis of ingredients, and degree of formality—appear to be linked to widespread if not universal features of the human condition. The essence of the odyssey experience is the temporary lifting or destructuring of routines, punctuated by a phase of less structured liminality and resulting in a restructuring (or an effort to restructure) and re-entry into the world of routine on a new and presumably regenerated basis. At the outset I laid out an ideal-type statement of its social and psychological ingredients, and then I identified in succeeding chapters many manifestations of this type, each expressing a general process and drawing on a different combination of ingredients. To review, I have covered initiation rites, religious pilgrimages, religious conversion, some idealistic social movements, travel and tourism, academic moratoria, psychotherapy and its cousins, some informally invented ritual forms, and some coercive and quasi-coercive variations designed to force attitudinal and personality changes. The aim in all these accounts has been to tease out common ingredients and dynamics.

One aspect of the pervasiveness of the odyssey experience is that it seems to be resistant to its own decline or disappearance. Despite inroads made on the world of ritual by the forces of secularization, modernization, and rationality (discussed in chapter 5; see also Smelser 1998a) and the weakening of rituals associated with traditional religions and stable communities, humans have shown an indestructible tendency to reinvent the ritual form in religious, secular, commercial, and informal guises. Odyssey-like ceremonies, rituals, transitions, stories, and fantasies continue to surface and resurface, often in private places, much as the development and redevelopment of family, friendship, and completely personal rituals continue to be a part of the social landscape.

The fundamental dynamic of the odyssey—destructuring, unstructuring, and restructuring—is a principle that permeates further into the general psychological and social processes of life. It is a dynamic typical of the socialization of the child, in which adaptations at early stages of development cease to be rewarded by parents or other socializing agents, occasioning some turbulence and resulting in the emergence of new and different adaptations, habits, styles, and traits. The old is not completely destroyed, as Freud's insistence on the importance of fixations reminds us, but the principle of restructuring as the road to maturation remains central to the process (Parsons and Bales, 1955). The dynamic may also be generalizable to many processes of political, social, and cultural change. Revolutions of all three types deliberately attempt to destroy the old in order to usher in a new world. More orderly processes of structural change—the building of communities, institutions, and nations—also involve the partial dismantling of older memberships, loyalties, and social arrangements as an integral part of the building process.

Without losing one's head in a generalizing frenzy, it is nevertheless reasonable to conclude that the experiences detailed in this book constitute a fundamental, ever-present, and indestructible feature of organized human life. If this is the case, some theoretical questions arise: Why should this be so? What are the elements in the human condition that find expression in the invention, institutionalization, and reinvention of the odyssey experience? This brief chapter explores these questions.

THE ODYSSEY EXPERIENCE AND THE EXISTENTIAL DIMENSIONS OF HUMAN LIFE

The Human Species as Developmental

The human being remains helpless and dependent for a longer period than other species. Moreover, its pathway to brain development, its adaptive skills, its social relationships, and its sense of self go further than other species. The odyssey experience, in all its manifestations, involves a recapitulation of the developmental process. The key elements are temporary withdrawal from one set of routines and structures, a period of fluidity, and then an immersion either in a new structure or with a different orientation to structure. Generation and regeneration are its essence. This principle holds, even though the process—especially in its coercive variants—often has punitive, cruel, and destructive aspects. These negative aspects are represented as essential parts of the process of change or improvement. Sometimes odyssey experiences are an integral part of the maturation process, notably in ritual passages from adolescence to adulthood. Sometimes they involve individuals who are already mature or well on their way to maturity—such as the religious pilgrimage, travel, and many moratoria for renewal—but all recapitulate the dynamics of developmental change. Even those that involve significant withdrawal from organized social life—for example, retirement rituals—are rich in the symbolism associated with entering a new and different phase of life, as the phrase "socialization to old age" connotes.

Many odyssey experiences, then, are contrivances for shaping the transitions of life. They involve a constant interplay between the principles of certainty and uncertainty in these transitions. The temporary dissolution of structure is a movement from the certainty and predictability of routines and understood human relations into a realm of the uncertain. Paradoxically, however, the uncertainty of liminality imposes a new kind of certainty, as new perils and threats, unanticipated affects, feelings of isolation, permissiveness, and perhaps license, and new ways of experiencing intimacy are given meaning and "normality" as an expected part of the journey. And emergence as a new or revitalized human being is a way of folding the whole experience into a new, different, and presumably better world.

I now turn to several subthemes that emerge as part of this master process of developing or recapitulating developmental process.

The Human Species as Variety-Seeking, Symbolizing, and Culture-Producing

The development of complex languages and the capacity for extensive and sustained abstract thought are perennially favorite candidates for the essential characteristics that distinguish human from nonhuman species, though research on primates has established that this, too, is a matter of degree. I break this assumption into two overlapping variants, one perceptual/experiential and the other cognitive/meaningful.

The first variant deals with the search for experiential variety. This principle constitutes the primary assumption that underlay the stimulus deprivation experiments and is the principle that affords stimulus restriction its potent effects. In introducing that particular line of experimentation, Suedfeld asserts: "Man thrives on variety. The most enjoyable dish palls when eaten for the fifth time in succession; the most awesome scenery rates only a glance when one has lived with it for a year; the most exciting work eventually becomes onerously routine; the most enchanting companion loses some of the enchantment after long intimacy" (1980, 1). Though this principle varies from individual to individual, it is evidently one that has general validity; it has worked itself into theories of human behavior, for example, in the principle of diminishing marginal utility, a basic guiding psychological assumption in the history of economics.

The odyssey experience thrives on this principle and generates a great deal of cultural play around it. By definition, the odyssey experience lifts a person or group from the world of stable structure and routines and generates an experience that is novel in relation to that world. In most cases it endows those who enter the experience with the feeling that they are experiencing the unusual and becoming special in doing so. The experience derives much of its power from this circumstance. Of course, ritual experiences—of which many odyssey experiences are a subtype—are themselves stylized, and routine repetition of those experiences would be expected to cloy. One does not repeat rituals endlessly unless one is a compulsive; one does not go incessantly from one pilgrimage to another, and few go continuously on one traveling vacation after another. Odyssey experiences "stick" because they are either one of a kind or periodic in their occurrence. This principle underlies a second, closely related one, the "you can't go home again" effect: one usually cannot repeat the same odyssey experience a second time with the same vividness of effect as the first. Furthermore, the rich symbolism that surrounds odyssey experiences adds to its variety and increases the opportunities for cultural play.

The second variant runs counter to the first in one important respect. Too much variation is also endangering, in that it renders the psychological and social environments of the individual too complex, even chaotic. Correspondingly, it is appreciated by psychologists and others that human adaptation is simultaneously a process of simplifying and making the inherently confusing flow of stimuli and events more predictable and manageable, in that way giving guidance to the organization of behavior. Habits and personal styles of behavior are the result of this process of cognitive and adaptive simplification. These principles underlie the universal human tendency to categorize experience, as well as often more reprehensible tendencies to stereotype others, to develop negative attitudes on the basis of those stereotypes (prejudice) and to act on those prejudices (discrimination). Some scholars (for example, Berger and Luckmann 1967) have argued that the principal functional significance of institutions in social life is that they render more predictable the fundamentally uncertain, confusing, and unmanageable flow of experiences. With special reference to rituals (and to odysseys in general, I would add), Brain argues: "Initiation rites . . . must be viewed as part of a general human concern with categorization, with order and disorder—with anxiety because of an inability to impose order and, arising out of this, the attribution of danger and/or power to persons and things that are not readily put into the categories of a particular culture" (2000, 192).

The odyssey experience is also a source of cognitive and experiential structuring in one of its many aspects. While fundamentally a break with routine realities, it is also a way of structuring behavior into new and meaningful sequences. This is especially true of those experiences that are ritualized or otherwise subject to normative shaping. One of the dictates of those experiences is that the participants should get it right— that is, think, behave, feel, and remember what one is supposed to in those special circumstances. So most odyssey experiences are a combination of or perhaps oscillation between variety and sameness, unpredictability and predictability, and, as we will also see, release and control. Most ingenious and enduring social forms do not serve a single human proclivity but provide for the activation and play of more than one, and this is certainly the significance of the odyssey experience with respect to the contrasting principles of variety and sameness.

The Human Species as Affect-Experiencing and Affect-Managing

An additional feature of the human species is that its psychic life involves a constant arousal of emotions and a constant interplay of these with perception, cognition, and the activation of behavior. Affects are many, both negative and positive—anxiety and fear, shame, guilt, disgust, despair, anger, pleasure, exhilaration, affection, and hope. Emotions keep human beings informed of the threatening, beckoning, and gratifying aspects of their external and internal environments. In some theories, emotions (especially anxiety and anger) are adaptive signals that constitute a step in the mobilization of perception and adaptive behavior, even if in some cases these emotions drive individuals to unreflective, mistaken, and counterproductive actions. In addition, emotions are frequently the most volatile and difficult to control features of the human psyche. As such they are the subject of constant internal monitoring and attempted though not successful regulation by the individual. Finally, emotions are the subject of constant social regulation as well, with normative expectations and sanctions serving to monitor how and when to feel and the appropriate occasions for expressing or not expressing feelings.

Odyssey experiences help regulate the flow of emotional life. As indicated at the outset (see chapter 1), they are the occasion for activating a wide range of affective experiences, with highly variable weighting and content, many of them powerful and "regressive" in character. In many cases, experiencing and expressing these emotions are taboo in more routine settings. At the same time, both experiencing and expressing are regulated in the odyssey experiences themselves. Being both temporary and exceptional episodes, they carry expectations that the expression of its accompanying affects is also temporary and exceptional, perhaps to be savored but not to be expressed in more ordinary rounds of life. This is perhaps what Scheff (1977) had in mind when he characterized ritual as a setting for the "distancing of emotion." The same general principle holds for odysseys. Those experiences are neither exclusive occasions for the special expression of affects nor exclusive occasions for controlling and moderating them; they are both. They are occasions for expression of many though not all of the contrasting affects of human life, and they are also occasions for insulating and moderating that expression. We must once again call on the principle of ambivalence, as well as the principles of oscillation and cultural play, in accounting for the broader human significance of those experiences.

The Human Species as Mortal

This wording is meant not to express the end of human life on earth but to underscore the existential fact that the individual lives of all human beings are finite, lasting a century or less except for rare exceptions, and that that finiteness is grasped by the living. This means that humanity must constantly renew and give continuity to itself from generation to generation, even though every member who lives in a given time period passes from the scene.

Death is no doubt the most fundamental of all human dilemmas. Its explanation and rationalization lies at the heart of religion and the religious mentality. Weber laid great stress on the problem of theodicy in religion, namely the problem of "how the extraordinary power of . . . a god may be reconciled with the imperfection of the world he has created and presides over" (1968, 2:519). The most profound imperfection is the death of human beings. Humans, as symbolizing creatures, can *imagine* immortality or life without death, and that imagined state finds its way into the belief systems of religions—eternal existence, life after death, life in another world, reincarnation. Despite this, the existential fact of death is universal and ultimately undeniable. Furthermore, death, even if universal, is unpredictable in its timing and in its reason for happening at a given time. This lies at the heart of the anxiety experienced by those who must die but on an unknown day, and lives in the hearts of those who survive and suffer grief at the death of a close one. Of course, feelings about death are always ambivalent—combining the dread of loss with release from a life that always involves suffering—and in some cases death is actually preferred to suffering, as in voluntary termination and suicide. On balance, however, death is unwanted and even dreaded by both those who will die and those who survive them. This combination of existential features tells us why the problem of death is never solved, despite all real and symbolic efforts.

We have seen that a dominant motif of many odyssey experiences is the appearance of immediate or remote symbols of death and rebirth. Symbolically, the movement from structure to liminality is a way of dying; liminality is a period of being removed or dead, and renewal and restructuring are ways of being reborn. Some odyssey episodes deal directly with death. Last rites and funeral services facilitate the passage of the dying to their new world, whether envisioned as a void or as a hereafter. Other episodes, such as the wake, are devices to ease the journey of survivors from a life with to a life without the dead. The symbolism of death and rebirth is often evident even when the event is not dying, as in the imagery of some initiations and rites of passage, pilgrimages, and religious conversions ("born again"). In still others, the symbolism of death and rebirth is subordinated to more manifest meanings and often lies beyond the immediate consciousness of those who participate in the experience. In all events, the theme of death and rebirth appears to be a master metaphor for the odyssey experience. Odyssey experiences provide symbolic recapitulations and answers to the dilemma of death and dying, but they are never completely satisfactory. Because the problem of death is so pervasive, recurrent, and insoluble, the supply of solutions is never enough for the demand. The solutions, including those provided by odyssey experiences, are always temporary. It is in this circumstance, perhaps, that we find the recurrence—one might even say the repetition compulsion—in the symbolic experiencing and reexperiencing of death and rebirth, and via that avenue, we arrive at one reason for the hardiness and survivability of those kinds of experiences.

FUSION OF THE EXISTENTIAL DIMENSIONS: THE OSCILLATION BETWEEN DEPENDENCE AND INDEPENDENCE

Running through all the existential dimensions reviewed is a central theme. It goes by many names: constraint and freedom, dependence and independence, control and autonomy. The process of socialization is an irregular movement from the former to the latter pole, though complete autonomy is never realized. All the dimensions are fused with perceptual, cognitive, and affective aspects. The search for variety in perception and stimuli is a break from repetitive routine, but when variety loses its novelty, it, too, becomes a constraining routine on experience. Elaboration, imagination, jokes, word games, fantasy, and other forms of creativity are all ways of breaking from the normative strictures of organized thought and seeking new ways and patterns. Experiencing otherwise forbidden or highly regulated affects is also a form of release, but once released, affects are never permitted to run completely free, as new efforts to corral or frame them inevitably arise.

There is reason to believe, moreover, that the oscillation between dependency and independence is never resolved. Independence is never achieved without nostalgia for dependency. Dependency forever excites the impulse to struggle against it. The result is a residue of thoroughgoing ambivalence toward both dependency and independence, a constant tug-of-war between the two principles but with the important proviso that that war is never won, only repeated as a permanently unsettling feature of life. We would do well to abandon any search for stable equilibria in this tension, but rather conceive of the relationship between dependency and independence as an enduring and unresolved tension, conflict, and flux (Smelser 1998a).

The varieties of odyssey experience are manifestations of this multidimensional and chronic feature of psychological and social existence. All odysseys involve a degree of release from the routine that participants leave behind when they experience them. In that respect they are declarations of independence, even though, especially in coercive experiences, a radically new structure is often abruptly imposed. This principle underlies Turner's characterization of the liminal phases of ritual and related experiences as "anti-structure," though we found reason to believe that this characterization overshoots the mark. Though unstructured, that phase of the process itself imposes a new structure, albeit simplified, in the form of the strictures of *communitas*, the regulation of behavior through ritual, and even the imposition of normative "ways of experiencing" events. The return, refreshed or renewed, to structure is yet another expression of the transition between dependency and independence. Yet that return, even if proclaimed as permanent rebirth, cannot be regarded as permanent or stable, because the impulse to seek release from it is still present. The odyssey experience, in a word, is a kind of repetition compulsion that offers temporary respite from an eternal tension, but its eternal nature provides the motive for repeating the cycle of release and restoration.

THE AXES OF TIME AND SPACE

In the initial search for descriptive terms of the odyssey experience, the terms *wandering, journey, voyage,* and *trip* appeared. All of these imply movement in time and space. Those dimensions are conspicuous in the classic adventures of Odysseus, who moved irregularly from Troy back to Ithaka over a period of ten years. In our journey through the world of odyssey experiences, we discovered that many of them—pilgrimages and travel, for example—are explicitly movements from place to place in geographic space and in time. Other odyssey experiences imply movement, but the representations of time and space are symbolic elaborations and are experienced in psychological, social, political, spiritual, and ritual time (Leach 1961) and space.

This time-space mode of representation falls into place as another piece in the puzzle of explaining the pervasiveness of odyssey experiences. They are represented in categories that are universally understood dimensions of psychological and social life. By this assertion I do not mean to claim that time and space are uniformly represented or measured. History and cultural variability have revealed a vast range of differences in representing, describing, and measuring both space (Levinson 2001) and time (Gell 1992). Beyond these differences, however, remains the principle that *some* confrontation with space and time is essential. Space is forever an obstacle to complete freedom of movement, however differently it is conceived linguistically and culturally. Some confrontation with the passage of time is also essential, and the imposition of diurnal, seasonal, annual, bodily process (e.g., menstruation), reproduction, generations, and life-cycle regularities impose this confrontation as part of the experience and indeed survival of the human species (Silverman 2001).

Being universal in that restricted sense, the categories of space and time constitute a universal basis for discourse. Representation of experiences in literal or symbolic time and space renders them intelligible. Odyssey experiences capitalize on this fundamental fact. They are cast in a language of familiarity, and a new language is not required to experience them. Odysseys occur in real or symbolic time and space, and the human experience of them relates to these categories.

A review of these theoretical reflections suggests that they are based on reasoning that is "functionalist" in the broadest sense of the term. What I have done in this volume is the following:

- Identify a range of phenomena that are evidently widespread or even universal features of human existence.

- Tease out the typical dynamics of these phenomena, respecting differences in content, setting, and level of profundity.

- Activate the assumption that, being general, repetitive, and indestructible as a genre of experience, they are evidently overdetermined—that is, they serve multiple psychological and social purposes for those who organize and experience them.

- Speculate, as I have done in this final chapter, in an effort to identify the many principles that odyssey experiences manifest or, put differently, to specify the masters they serve.

The final exercise is the functionalist one, but unlike much of the functionalist tradition, it does not regard structures as "fulfilling" a static set of needs or "functions." I have located the odyssey experience in the human struggle to deal with ambiguity, ambivalence, constant tension, and eternal flux. The essence and the dynamics of odyssey experiences cannot be fathomed without embedding them thus.

REFERENCES

Abbott, Andrew. 1988. *The system of professions: An essay on the division of expert labor.* Chicago: University of Chicago Press.

Abeles, Marc. 1988. Modern political ritual: Ethnography of an inauguration and a pilgrimage by President Mitterrand. *Current Anthropology* 29 (3): 391–404.

Alves, Julio. 1993. Transgression and transformation: Initiation rites among urban Portuguese boys. *American Anthropologist*, n.s., 95 (4): 894–928.

Arms, Suzanne. 1975. *Immaculate deception: A new look at women and childbirth in America.* Boston: Houghton Mifflin.

Armstrong, Gaylene S. 2004. Boot camps as a correctional option. In *Correctional boot camps: Military basic training or a model for corrections?* ed. Doris Layton MacKenzie and Gaylene Styve Armstrong, 7–15. Thousand Oaks, CA: Sage Publications.

Austin-Broos, Diane. 2003. The anthropology of conversion: An introduction. In *The anthropology of religious conversion*, ed. Andrew Buckser and Stephen D. Glazier, 1–12. Lanham, MD: Rowman & Littlefield.

Axel, Helen. 1992. *Redefining corporate sabbaticals for the 1990s.* New York: Conference Board.

Bach, George R. 1974. Constructive aggression in growth groups. In *The group as agent of change: Treatment, prevention, personal growth in the family, the school, the mental hospital, and the community*, ed. Alfred Jacobs and Wilford W. Spradlin, 116–47. New York: Behavioral Publications.

Bakan, David. 1958. *Sigmund Freud and the Jewish mystical tradition*. Princeton, NJ: Van Nostrand.

Baker, Alan. 1998. *Destination Earth: A history of alleged alien presence*. London: Cassell.

Barker, E. 2001. New religious movements. In *International encyclopedia of the social and behavioral sciences*, ed. Neil J. Smelser and Paul B. Baltes, 16: 10631–34. Oxford: Elsevier.

Bartholomew, Robert E., and George S. Howard. 1998. *UFOs and alien contact: Two centuries of mystery*. Amherst, NY: Prometheus Books.

Baumer, Iso. 1978. Gestalt und sinn der wallfahrt heute. In *Wallfahrt Heute*, ed. IsoBaumer and Walter Heim, 11–38. Freiburg: Kanislius Verlag.

Beck, Brenda E. F. 1978. The metaphor as mediator between semantic and analogic modes of thought. *Current Anthropology* 19 (1): 83–97.

Beckwith, Carol, and Angela Fisher. 1999. *African ceremonies*. Vol. 1. New York: Harry N. Abrams.

Beidelman, T. O. 1997. *The cool knife: Imagery of gender, sexuality, and moral rducation in Kaguru initiation ritual*. Washington, DC: Smithsonian Institution Press.

Beit-Hallahmi, Benjamin. 1992. *Despair and deliverance: Private salvation in contemporary Israel*. Albany: State University of New York Press.

Berardo, Felix M., and Hernan Vera. 1981. The groomal shower: A variation of the American bridal shower. *Family Relations* 30 (3): 395–401.

Berger, Peter, and Thomas Luckmann. 1967. *The social construction of reality*. Garden City, NY: Doubleday.

Bernstein, Jerome S. 1987. The decline of masculine rites of passage in our culture: The impact on masculine individuation. In *Betwixt and between: Patterns of masculine and feminine initiation*, ed. Louise

Carus Mahdi, Steven Foster, and Meredith Little, 136–58. La Salle, IL: Open Court.

Bettelheim, Bruno. 1962. *Symbolic wounds: Puberty rites and the envious male.* Rev. ed. New York: Collier Books.

Bion, W. R. 1963. *Elements of psychoanalysis.* New York: Basic Books.

Bonnemère, Pascale (ed.). 2004. *Women as unseen characters: Male ritual in Papua New Guinea.* Philadelphia: University of Pennsylvania Press.

Borrie, Roderick A. 1980. A practical guide to clinical REST. In *Restricted environmental stimulation: Research and clinical applications,* by Peter Suedfeld, with contributions by Henry B. Adams, Roderick A. Borrie, and Richard C. Tees, 365–81. New York: John Wiley & Sons.

Boyer, Neil A. 1966. Volunteers in the field: Great expectations. In *Annals of the American Academy of Political and Social Science: The Peace Corps,* ed. Thorsten Sellin, 365: 55–62. Philadelphia: American Academy of Political and Social Science.

Braatly, Trygve. 1954. *Fundamentals of analytic technique.* New York: John Wiley & Sons.

Bradbury, Mary. 1999. *Representations of death: A social psychological perspective.* London: Routledge.

Bradley, Robert A. 1965. *Husband-coached childbirth.* New York: Harper & Row.

Brain, James L. 2000. Sex, incest and death: Initiation rites reconsidered. *Current Anthropology* 18 (2): 191–208.

Bremer, Thomas S. 2000. Tourists and religion at Temple Square and Mission San Juan Capistrano. *Journal of American Folklore* 113 (450): 422–35.

Bromley, David G., and James T. Richardson. 1983. *The brainwashing/deprogramming controversy: Sociological, psychological, legal, and historical perspectives.* New York: Edwin Mellen Press.

Brown, David. 1996. Genuine fakes. In *The tourist image: Myths and myth making in tourism,* ed. Tom Selwyn, 33–47. Chichester: John Wiley and Sons.

Brown, Stephanie, and Virginia Lewis. 1999. *The alcoholic family in recovery: A developmental model.* New York: Guilford Press.

Brownfield, Charles A. 1972. *The brain benders: A study of the effects of isolation,* 2d ed. New York: Exposition Press.

Bryan, C. D. B. 1995. *Close encounters of the fourth kind: Alien abduction, UFOs, and the conference at M.I.T.* New York: Alfred A. Knopf.

Bryant, M. Darrol, and Christopher Lamb. 1999. Conversion: Contours of controversy and commitment in a plural world. In *Religious conversion: Contemporary practices and controversies,* ed. Christopher Lamb and M. Darrol Bryant, 1–19. London: Cassell.

Bryson, Bill. 1995. *Notes from a small island.* London: Black Swan.

Bulcroft, Kris, Linda Smeins, and Richard Bulcroft. 1999. *Romancing the honeymoon: Consummating marriage in modern society.* Thousand Oaks, CA: Sage Publications.

Burton, Bob, and Steve Rogers. 1996. 'VisionQuest.' In *Crossroads: The quest for contemporary rites of passage,* ed. Louse Carus Mahdi, Nancy Geyer Christopher, and Michael Meade, 199–211. Chicago: Open Court.

Butler, Richard W. 1992. Alternative tourism: The thin edge of the wedge. In *Tourism alternatives: Potentials and problems in the development of tourism,* ed. Valene L. Smith and William R. Eadington, 31–46. Philadelphia: University of Pennsylvania Press.

———. 2002. The development of tourism in frontier regions: Issues and approaches. In *Tourism in frontier areas,* ed. Shaul Krakover and Yehuda Gradus, 1–19. Lanham, MD: Lexington Books.

Byrd, Richard E. 1938. *Alone.* New York: E. P. Putnam's Sons.

Cantril, Hadley. 2005 [1940]. *The invasion from Mars: A study in the psychology of panic.* New Brunswick, NJ: Transaction Publishers.

Carlson, Jerry S., Barbara H. Burn, John Useem, and David Yachimowicz. 1990. *Study abroad: The experience of American undergraduates.* New York: Greenwood Press.

Chapple, Eliot Dismore, and Carleton Stevens Coon. 1978 [1942]. *Principles of anthropology.* Huntington, NY: Robert E. Krieger Publishing.

Chesser, Barbara Jo. 1980. Analysis of wedding rituals: An attempt to make weddings more meaningful. *Family Relations* 29 (2): 204–09.

Chidester, David. 1988. *Salvation and suicide: An interpretation of Jim Jones, the People's Temple, and Jonestown.* Bloomington: University of Indiana Press.

Christie, Richard. 1953. *An experimental study of modification of factors influencing recruits' adjustment to the Army.* Research Center for Human Relations, New York University, mimeographed.

Christopher, Nancy Geyer. 1996. Service as a rite of passage. In *Crossroads: The quest for contemporary rites of passage*, ed. Louise Carus Mahdi, Nancy Gayer Christopher, and Michael Meade, 125–32. Chicago: Open Court.

Clark, John, Michael D. Langone, Robert E. Schachter, and Roger C.G. Dalu. 1981. *Destructive cult conversion: Theory, research, and treatment.* Weston, MA: American Family Foundation.

Clark, Thomas Arkle. 1931. *The fraternity and the college: Being a series of papers dealing with fraternity problems.* Menasha, WI: George Banta Publishing.

Clements, William M. 1976. Conversion and communitas. *Western Folklore* 35 (1): 35–45.

———. 1981. Ritual expectation in Pentecostal healing experience. *Western Folklore* 40 (2): 139–48.

Cohen, Erik. 1989. Primitive and remote: Hill tribe trekking in Thailand. *Annals of Tourism Research* 16 (1): 30–61.

Coleman, S. 2001. Pilgrimage. In *International encyclopedia of the social and behavioral sciences*, ed. Neil J. Smelser and Paul B. Baltes, 17:1445–48. Oxford: Elsevier.

Collins, John J. 1991. *The cult experience: An overview of cults, their traditions, and why people join them.* Springfield, IL: Charles C. Thomas.

Colson, Elizabeth. 1977. The least common denominator. In *Secular ritual*, ed. Sally F. Moore and Barbara G. Meyerhoff, 189–98. Assen: Van Gorcum.

Converse, Philip E. 2001. Centers for advanced study: International/interdisciplinary. In *International encyclopedia of the social and behavioral sciences,* ed. Neil J. Smelser and Paul B. Baltes, 3:1613–15. Oxford: Elsevier.

Cook, Judith A. and Sara J. Hoffschmidt. 1993. Comprehensive models of psychosocial rehabilitation. In *Psychiatric rehabilitation in practice,* ed. Robert L. Flexer and Phyllis L. Solomon, 81–97. Boston: Andover Medical Publishers.

Cottle, Thomas J. 1976. "An analysis of the phases of development in self-analytic groups." In *Explorations in general theory in social science: Essays in honor of Talcott Parsons,* ed. Jan J. Loubser, Rainer C. Baum, Andrew Effrat, and Victor Meyer Lidz, 1: 328–53. New York: Free Press.

Cullen. Eric. 1997. Can a prison be a therapeutic community: The Grendon template. In *Therapeutic communities for offenders,* ed. Eric Cullen, Lawrence Jones and Roland Woodward, 743–99. New York: John Wiley & Sons.

Curran, Douglas. 2001. *In advance of the landing: Folk concepts of outer space.* New York: Abbeville Press.

Cusack, Carole M. 1998. *Conversion among the Germanic peoples.* London: Cassell.

Dann, Graham M.S. 1977. Anomie, ego-enhancement and tourism. *Annals of Tourism Research* 4 (4): 184–94

———. 1996. The people of tourist brochures. In *The tourist image: Myths and myth making in tourism,* ed. Tom Selwyn, 61–81. Chichester: John Wiley and Sons.

Davies, Douglas J. 2002. *Death, ritual and belief: The rhetoric of funerary rites.* 2d ed. London: Continuum.

Davis-Floyd, Robbie E. 1987. Obstetric training as a rite of passage. *Medical Anthropology Quarterly,* n.s., 1 (3): 288–318.

———. 2003. *Birth as an American rite of passage.* 2d ed. Berkeley: University of California Press.

Dawson, Lorne L. 1998. *Comprehending cults: The sociology of new religious movements.* Oxford: Oxford University Press.

Deutsch, Steven. 1970. *International education and exchange.* Cleveland: Press of Case Western Reserve University.

Devereux, Paul, and Peter Brookesmith. 1997. *UFOs and ufology: The first fifty years.* London: Cassell.

Dick-Read, Grantly. 1933. *Natural childbirth.* London: Heinemann.

———. 1972. *Childbirth without fear: The original approach to natural childbirth.* 4th ed., rev. and ed. Helen Wessel and Harlan F. Ellis. New York: Harper & Row.

Downton, James V, Jr. 1979. *Sacred journeys: The conversion of young Americans to Divine Light Mission.* New York: Columbia University Press.

Dubinsky, Karen. 1999. *The second greatest disappointment: Honeymooning and tourism at Niagara Falls.* New Brunswick, NJ: Rutgers University Press.

du Bois, Cora. 1956. *Foreign students and higher education in the United States.* Washington, DC: American Council on Education.

Dumazedier, Joffre. 1974. *Sociology of leisure.* Trans. Marea A. McKenzie. Amsterdam: Elsevier.

Durkheim, Émile. 1951 [1895]. *Suicide.* Glencoe, IL: Free Press.

———. 1954 [1913]. *The elementary forms of religious life.* Glencoe, IL: Free Press.

———. 1969 [1891]. *The division of labor in society.* Glencoe, IL: Free Press.

Eade, John. 1992. Pilgrimage and tourism at Lourdes, France. *Annals of Tourism Research* 19 (1): 18–32.

Edwards, Margot, and Mary Waldorf. 1984. *Reclaiming birth: History and heroines of American childbirth reform.* Trumansburg, NY: Crossing Press.

Eells, Walter Crosby, and Ernest V. Hollis. 1962. *Sabbatical leave in American higher education: Origin, early history, and current practices.* Washington, DC: Office of Education, Department of Health, Education, and Welfare.

Egan, James. 1973. Crusoe's monarchy and the Puritan concept of self. *Studies in English Literature 1500–1900* 13 (3): 451–460.

Eliade, Mircea. 1994 [1958]. *Rites and symbols of initiation: The mysteries of birth and rebirth.* Trans. William R. Trask. Dallas, TX: Spring Publications.

Elsass, Peter. 1997. *Treating victims of torture and violence: Theoretical, cross-cultural and clinical implications.* Trans. John Andersen and Harald Fuglsang. New York: New York University Press.

Engelhart, Monica. 1998. *Extending the tracks: A cross-reductionisti approach to Australian aboriginal male initiation rites.* Stockholm: Almqvist & Wiksell International.

Farnham, Christie Ann. 1994. *The education of the Southern belle: Higher education and student socialization in the antebellum South.* New York: New York University Press.

Fauset, Arthur Huff. 1971 [1944]. *Black gods of the metropolis: Negro religious cults of the urban north.* Philadelphia: University of Pennsylvania Press.

Fischer, J. I. 1963. The sociopsychological analysis of folktales. *Current Anthropology* 4 (3): 235–95.

Fishwick, Marshall W. 1952. The cowboy: America's contribution to the world's mythology. *Western Folklore* 11 (2): 77–92.

Foster, George M. 1986. South Seas cruise: A case study of a short-lived society. *Annals of Tourism Research* 13 (2): 215–38.

Foulkes, S. H. 1964. *Therapeutic group analysis.* New York: International Universities Press.

Frazer, James G. 1913. *The belief in immortality and the worship of the dead.* 3 vols. London: Macmillan.

Frederickson, Paula. 1986. Paul and Augustine: Conversion narratives, orthodox traditions, and the retrospective self. *Journal of Theological Studies* 37: 3–34.

Freud, Sigmund. 1955 [1893–95]. Studies in hysteria. In *The standard edition of the complete psychological works of Sigmund Freud,* ed. James Strachey, 1: 3–319. London: Hogarth Press.

———. 1955 [1921]. Group psychology and the analysis of the ego. In *The standard edition of the complete psychological works of Sigmund Freud,* ed. James Strachey, 18: 67–144. London: Hogarth Press.

———. 1961 [1930]. Civilization and its discontents. In *The standard edition of the complete psychological works of Sigmund Freud,* ed. James Strachey, 21: 64–145. London: Hogarth Press.

————. 1963 [1917]. Introductory lectures on psycho-analysis. In *The standard edition of the complete psychological works of Sigmund Freud,* ed. James Strachey, 16: 9–239. London: Hogarth Press, 1963.

Friedan, Betty. 1963. *The feminine mystique.* New York: Norton.

Furlough, Ellen. 1998. Making mass vacations: Tourism and consumer culture in France, 1930s to 1970. *Comparative Studies in Society and History* 40 (2): 247–86

Furnham, Adrian. 1984. Tourism and culture shock. *Annals of Tourism Research* 11 (1): 41–57.

Galanter, Marc. 1999. *Cults, faith, healing, and coercion.* 2d ed. New York: Oxford University Press.

Gell, Alfred. 1992. *The anthropology of time: Cultural construction of temporal maps and images.* Oxford: Berg.

Gersuny, Carl. 1970. The honeymoon industry: Rhetoric and bureaucratization of status passage. *The Family Coordinator* 19 (3): 260–66.

Gibbon, Maurice. 1996. "Walkabout in high school. In *Crossroads: The quest for contemporary rites of passage.* Louse Carus Mahdi, Nancy Geyer Christopher, and Michael Meade, 223–29. Chicago: Open Court.

Gilmore, John. 2000. *Manson: The unholy trail of Charlie and the Family.* Los Angeles: Arnok Books.

Glaser, Barney G., and Anselm Strauss. 1965. Temporal aspects of dying as a non-scheduled status passage. *American Journal of Sociology* 72 (1): 48–59.

Glazier, Stephen D. 2003. "Livin' wid Jah": Spiritual Baptists who become Rastafarians and then become spiritual Baptists again. In *The anthropology of religious conversion,* ed. Andrew Buckser and Stephen D. Glazier, 149–70. Lanham, MD: Rowman & Littlefield.

Gleason, William A. 1999. *The leisure ethic: Work and play in American literature, 1840–1940.* Stanford, CA: Stanford University Press.

Glock, Charles Y., and Robert N. Bellah (eds.). 1976. *The new religious consciousness.* Berkeley: University of California Press.

Goffman, Erving. 1962. *Asylums: Essays on the social situation of mental patients and other inmates.* Chicago: Aldine.

Good, Carter V. (ed.) 1959. *Dictionary of education.* Rev. ed. New York: McGraw-Hill.

Goodrich, Frederick W. 1950. *Natural childbirth: A manual for expectant mothers.* Englewood Cliffs, NJ: Prentice-Hall.

Graburn, Nelson H. H. 1976. *Ethnic and tourist arts: Cultural expression from the Fourth World.* Berkeley: University of California Press.

———. 1989. Tourism: The sacred journey. In *Hosts and guests: The anthropology of tourism,* ed. Valene L. Smith, 2d ed., 21–36. Philadelphia: University of Pennsylvania Press.

———. 1995. Tourism, modernity, and nostalgia. In *The future of anthropology: Its relevance to the contemporary world,* ed. Akbar Ahmed and Cris N. Shore, 158–78. London and Atlantic Highlands, NJ: Athlone Press.

Green, F. B. 1978. Recreational vehicles: A perspective. *Annals of Tourism Research* 5 (4): 429–43.

Grimes, Ronald L. 1985. *Research in ritual studies: A programmatic essay and bibliography.* Metuchen, NJ: Scarecrow Press.

———. 2000. *Deeply into the bone: Re-inventing rites of passage.* Berkeley: University of California Press.

Grinker, Roy R., and John P. Spiegel. 1945. *Men under stress.* Philadelphia: Blakiston.

Hagglund, Tor-Bjorn. 1978. *Dying: A psychoanalytic study with special reference to individual creativity and defensive organization.* New York: International Universities Press.

Harper, Marvin Henry. 1972. *Gurus, swamis, and avatars: Spiritual masters and their American disciples.* Philadelphia: Westminster Press.

Harper, Robert A. 1959. *Psychoanalysis and psychotherapy: Thirty-six systems.* Englewood Cliffs, NJ: Prentice-Hall.

Heath, Dwight B. 1966. The emerging volunteer subculture in Bolivia. In *Cultural frontiers of the Peace Corps,* ed. Robert B. Textor, 271–97. Cambridge, MA: MIT Press.

Heaton, William R., Jr. 1980. Professional military education in China: A visit to the military academy of the People's Liberation Army. *China Quarterly* 81: 122–28.

Hebb, Donald O. 1961. Sensory deprivation: Facts in search of a theory. *Journal of Nervous and Mental Diseases* 132: 40–43.

Heirich, Max. 1977. Change of heart: A test of some widely held theories about religious conversion. *American Journal of Sociology* 83 (3): 653–80.

Henderson, William Darryl. 1985. *Cohesion: The human element in combat: Leadership and societal influence in the armies of the Soviet Union, the United States, North Vietnam, and Israel.* Washington, DC: National Defense University Press.

Herdt, Gilbert H. 2003. *Secrecy and cultural reality: Utopian ideologies of the New Guinea men's house.* Ann Arbor: University of Michigan Press.

Hexham, Irving, and Karla Poewe. 1997. *New religions and global cultures: Making the human sacred.* Boulder, CO: Westview Press.

Hirschowitz, Ralph G. 1974. Small group methods in the promotion of change within interagency networks: Leadership models. In *The group as agent of change: Treatment, prevention, personal growth in the family, the school, the mental hospital and the community,* ed. Alfred Jacobs and Wilford W. Spradlin, 228–51. New York: Behavioral Publications.

Hitchcock, Michael. 2000. Introduction. In *Souvenirs: The material culture of tourism,* ed. Michael Hitchcock and Ken Teague, 1–28. Aldershot: Ashgate.

Hochschild, Arlie. 1979. Emotion work, feeling rules, and social structure. *American Journal of Sociology* 85 (3): 551–75.

Hockey, John. 2003. No more heroes: Masculinity in the infantry. In *Military masculinities: Identity and the state,* ed. Paul R. Higate, 15–25. Westport, CN: Praeger.

Hoffman, Elizabeth Cobbs. 1998. *All you need is love: The Peace Corps and the spirit of the 1960s.* Cambridge, MA: Harvard University Press.

Holloman, Regina B. 1974. Ritual opening and individual transformation: Rites of passage at Esalen. *American Anthropologist,* n.s., 76 (2): 265–80.

Holte, James Craig. 1992. *The conversion experience in America: A sourcebook on religious conversion autobiography*. New York: Greenwood Press.

Hoolihan, Michael. 2000. Souvenirs with soul: Eight hundred years of pilgrimage to Santiago de Compostela. In *Souvenirs: The material culture of tourism*, ed. Michael Hitchcock and Ken Teague, 18–24. Aldershot: Ashgate.

Hopkins, Budd. 1981. *Missing time: A documented study of the UFO abductions*. New York: R. Marek Publishers.

Horney, Karen. 1999. *The therapeutic process: Essays and lectures*. Ed. and with an introduction by Bernard J. Paris. New Haven, CN: Yale University Press.

Howell-White, Sandra. 1999. *Birth alternatives: How women select childbirth care*. Westport, CN: Greenwood Press.

Humphrey, Geraldine M., and David G. Zimpfer. 1996. *Counseling for grief and bereavement*. London: Sage Publications.

Hutt, Michael. 1996. Looking for Shangri-la: From Hilton to Lamichlane. In *The tourist image: Myths and myth making in tourism*, ed. Tom Selwyn, 49–60. Chichester: John Wiley and Sons.

James, William. 1963 [1902]. *The varieties of religious experience: A study in human nature*. New Hyde Park, NY: University Books.

Janowitz, Morris. 1965. *Sociology and the military establishment*. Rev. ed., in collaboration with Roger Little. New York: Russell Sage Foundation.

Janzen, Rod A. 2001. *The rise and fall of Synanon: A California utopia*. Baltimore, MD: Johns Hopkins University Press.

Jasper, James M. 2000. *Restless nation: Starting over in America*. Chicago: University of Chicago Press.

Jenkins, Philip. 2000. *Mystics and messiahs: Cults and new religions in American history*. Oxford: Oxford University Press.

Jules-Rosette, Bennetta. 1984. *The messages of tourist art: An African semiotic system in comparative perspective*. New York: Plenum Press.

Jung, Carl G. 1959. *Flying saucers: A modern myth of things seen in the skies*. Trans. R. F. C. Hull. New York: Signet Books.

————. 1971. *Four archetypes: Mother, rebirth, spirit, trickster.* Trans. R. F. C. Hull. Princeton, NJ: Princeton University Press.

Kane, Steven. 1974. Ritual possession in a southern Appalachian religious sect. *Journal of American Folklore* 87 (346): 293–302.

Kauffmann, Norman L, Judith N. Martin, Henry D. Weaver, with Judy Weaver. 1992. *Students abroad, strangers at home: Education for a global society.* Yarmouth, ME: Intercultural Press.

Kelly, Henry Ansgar. 1985. *The devil at baptism: Ritual, rheology, and drama.* Ithaca, NY: Cornell University Press.

Kemp, Louis Ward. 1983. Putting down routes: Folk and popular perceptions of the road. *Western Folklore* 42 (3): 157–78.

Kennaway, James. 1963. *The mind benders.* New York: Atheneum.

Kerr, Hugh T., and John M. Mulder. 1983. *Conversion: The Christian experience.* Grand Rapids, MI: William B. Erdmans Publishing.

Kessler, Shelley. 1996. The 'Senior Passage' course. In *Crossroads: The quest for contemporary rites of passage*, ed. Louse Carus Mahdi, Nancy Geyer Christopher, and Michael Meade, 185–97. Chicago: Open Court.

Kimball, Solon T. 1960. Introduction. In *The rites of passage*, by Arnold van Gennep, trans. Monika B. Vizedom and Gabrielle L. Caffee, v–xix. Chicago: University of Chicago Press.

Kohn, Tamara. 1997. Island involvement and the evolving tourist. In *Tourists and tourism: Identifying with people and places*, ed. Simone Abram, Jacqueline Waldren and Donald V. L. Macleod, 13–28. Oxford: Berg.

Korpi, Walter. 1964. *Social pressures and attitudes in military training.* Stockholm: Almqvist & Wicksell.

Krippner, Stanley. 2000. Altered states of consciousness and shamanic healing rituals. In *The nature and function of rituals: Fire from heaven*, ed. Ruth-Inge Heinze, 191–22. Westport, CN: Bergin & Garvey.

Kruckman, Lawrence. 2000. Rituals as prevention: The case of postpartum depression. In *The nature and function of rituals: Fire from heaven*, ed. Ruth-Inge Heinze, 213–28. Westport, CN: Bergin & Garvey.

Kyle, Richard G. 1993. *The religious fringe: A history of alternative religions in America*. Downers Grove, IL: InterVarsity Press.

Lacy, Roderic. 1990. Journeys of transformation: The discovery and disclosure of cosmic secrets in Melanesia. In *Cargo cults and millenarian movements: Transoceanic comparisons of new religious movements*, ed. G. W. Trompf, 181–207. Berlin: Mouton de Gruyter.

La Fontaine, J. S. 1986. *Initiation*. Manchester: Manchester University Press.

Lakoff, George, and Mark Johnson. 1980. *Metaphors we live by*. Chicago: University of Chicago Press.

Lamaze, Fernand. 1956. *Painless childbirth: The psychoprophylatctic method*. Chicago: Contemporary Books.

Lanfant, Marie-Françoise. 1995. Introduction. In *International tourism: Identity and change*, ed. Marie-Françoise Lanfant, John B. Allcock, and Edward M. Bruner, 1–23. London: Sage Publications.

Langone, Michael D. 1993. Introduction. In *Recovery from cults: Help for victims of psychological and spiritual abuse*, ed. Michael D. Langone, 1–21. New York: W. W. Norton.

Lanternari, Vittorio. 1963. *The religions of the oppressed: A study of modern messianic cults*. Trans. Lisa Sergio. New York: Knopf.

Leach, Edmund R. 1961. Two essays concerning the symbolic representation of time. In *Rethinking anthropology*, 124–36. London: Althone.

Leemon, Thomas A. 1972. *The rites of passage in a student culture: A study of the dynamics of transition*. New York: Teachers College Press.

Leone, Massimo. 2004. *Religious conversion and identity: The semiotic analysis of texts*. London: Routledge.

Lett, James W., Jr. 1983. Ludic and liminoid aspects of charter yacht tourism in the Caribbean. *Annals of Tourism Research* 10 (1): 35–56.

Levinson, S. C. 2001. Space: Linguistic expression. In *International encyclopedia of the social sciences*, ed. Neil J. Smelser and Paul B. Baltes, 22: 14749–52. Oxford: Elsevier.

Lewin, Bertram D. 1961. *The psychoanalysis of elation*. New York: Psychoanalytic Quarterly.

Lewis, J. M. 1989. *Ecstatic religion: A study of shamanism and spirit posses- sion.* 2d ed. London: Routledge.

Lewis, James L. 2003. Legitimizing suicide: Heaven's Gate and New Age ideology. In *UFO religions,* ed. Christopher Partridge, 103–28. London: Routledge.

Li, X. 2002. Perilous journeys and archetypical encounters: Critical observations on Chinese travel literature. *Neohelicon* 28 (1): 257–60.

Lifton, Robert Jay. 1961. *Thought reform and the psychology of totalism: A study of "brainwashing" in China.* New York: W. W. Norton.

Litrell, May Ann, Luella F. Anderson, and Pamela J. Brown. 1993. What makes a craft souvenir authentic? *Annals of Tourism Research* 20 (1): 197–215.

Lofland, John. 1977. *Doomsday cult: A study of conversion, proselytization, and maintenance of faith.* New York: Irvington Publishers.

Lofland, John, and Rodney Stark. 1965. Becoming a world-saver: A theory of religious conversion. *American Sociological Review* 30 (6): 862–74.

Luria, Keith P. 1996. The politics of Protestant conversion to Catholi- cism in seventeenth-century France. In *Conversion to modernities: The globalization of Christianity,* ed. Peter van der Veer, 23–46. Lon- don: Routledge.

MacCannell, Dean. 1976. *The tourist: A new theory of the leisure class.* New York: Schocken Books.

———. 1977. Tourism and the new community. *Annals of Tourism Research* 4 (4): 208–15.

MacKenzie, Doris Layton. 2004a. Introduction. In *Correctional boot camps: Military basic training or a model for corrections?* ed. Doris Layton MacKenzie and Gaylene Styve Armstrong, 1–3. Thousand Oaks, CA: Sage Publications.

———. 2004b. Inmates' attitude change during incarceration: A com- parison of boot camp with traditional prison. In *Correctional boot camps: Military basic training or a model for corrections?* ed. Doris Lay- ton MacKenzie and Gaylene Styve Armstrong, 152–70. Thousand Oaks, CA: Sage Publications.

MacKenzie, Doris Layton, James W. Shaw, and Claire Souryal. 2004. Characteristics associated with successful adjustment to supervision: A comparison of parolees, probationers, shock participants and shock dropouts. In *Correctional boot camps: Military basic training or a model for corrections?* ed. Doris Layton MacKenzie and Gaylene Styve Armstrong, 234–43. Thousand Oaks, CA: Sage Publications.

MacKenzie, Doris Layton, David B. Wilson, Gaylene Styve Armstrong, and Angela R. Gover. 2004. The impact of boot camps and traditional institutions on juvenile residents: Perceptions, adjustment and change. In *Correctional boot camps: Military basic training or a model for corrections?* ed. Doris Layton MacKenzie and Gaylene Styve Armstrong, 127–51. Thousand Oaks, CA: Sage Publications.

Mahdi, Louise Carus. 1996. Preface. In *Crossroads: The quest for contemporary rites of passage*, ed. Louise Carus Mahdi, Nancy Geyer Christopher, and Michael Meade, xiii–xix. Chicago: Open Court.

Maley, Roger F. 1974. Group methods and interpersonal learning on a token economy ward. In *The group as agent of change: Treatment, prevention, personal growth in the family, the school, the mental hospital and the community*, ed. Alfred Jacobs and Wilfred W. Spradlin, 63–86. New York: Behavioral Publications.

Marcus, Ivan G. 1996. *Rituals of childhood: Jewish culture and acculturation in the Middle Ages.* New Haven: Yale University Press.

McAdam, Doug. 1988. *Freedom Summer.* New York: Oxford University Press.

McCoy, Alfred W. 1995. "Some banana": Hazing and honor in the Philippine Military Academy. *Journal of Asian Studies* 54 (3): 689–726.

McHugh, Peter. 1966. Social disintegration as a requisite of resocialization. *Social Forces* 44 (3): 355–63.

Meerloo, Joost A. M. 1956. *The rape of the mind: The psychology of thought control, menticide, and brainwashing.* Cleveland: World Publishing.

Meier, C. A. 1987. Ancient incubation and modern psychotherapy. In *Betwixt and between: Patterns of masculine and feminine initiation*, ed.

Louise Carus Mahdi, Steven Foster, and Meredith Little, 415–27. La Salle, IL: Open Court.

Melczer, William. 1993. *The pilgrim's guide to Santiago de Compostela.* New York: Ithaca Press.

Melton, Gordon. 2004. Introduction to new religions. In *The Oxford Handbook of New Religious Movements*, ed. James R. Lewis, 16–35. Oxford: Oxford University Press.

Melton, J. Gordon, and Robert L. Moore. 1982. *The cult experience: Responding to the new religious pluralism.* New York: Pilgrim Press.

Mendelsohn, Roy M. 1992. *How can talking help? An introduction to the technique of analytic therapy.* Northvale, NJ: Jason Aronson.

Menninger, Karl. 1958. *Theory of psychoanalytic technique.* New York: Basic Books.

Merrill, William. 1993. Conversion and colonialism in Northern Mexico: The Tarahumara response to the Jesuit mission program, 1601–1767. In *Conversion to Christianity: Historical and anthropological perspectives on a great transformation*, edited by Robert W. Hefner, 129–63. Berkeley: University of California Press.

Messerschmidt, Donald A., and Jyoti Sharma. 1981. Hindu pilgrimage in the Nepal Himalayas. *Current Anthropology* 12 (5): 91–92.

Metcalf, Peter, and Richard Huntington. 1991. *Celebrations of death: The anthropology of mortuary ritual.* 2d ed., with a new introduction by Peter Metcalf. Cambridge: Cambridge University Press.

Meyer, Birgit. 1996. Modernity and enlightenment: The image of the devil in popular African Christianity. In *Conversion to modernities: The globalization of Christianity*, ed. Peter van der Veer, 199–220. London: Routledge.

Michaelson, Karen L. 1988. Childbirth in America: A brief history and contemporary issues. In *Childbirth in America: Anthropological perspectives*, by Karen L. Michaelson and contributors, 1–32. South Hadley, MA: Bergin and Garvey Publications.

Mitford, Jessica. 1963. *The American way of death.* New York: Simon & Schuster.

———. 1992. *The American way of birth.* New York: Dutton.

Mooney, James. 1896. The Ghost Dance religion and the Sioux outbreak of 1890. *United States Bureau of American Ethnology Annual Report* 14 (2).

Morinis, Alan. 1985. The ritual experience: Pain and the transformation of consciousness in the ordeals of initiation. *Ethics* 13 (2): 150–74.

Morrison, Karl F. 1992. *Understanding conversion.* Charlottesville: University Press of Virginia.

Mowat, Barbara A. 1994. The Tempest: A modern perspective. In *The Tempest by William Shakespeare*, ed. Barbara A. Mowat and Paul Werstine, 185–99. New York: Washington Square Press.

Muir, Edward. 2005. *Ritual in early modern Europe.* 2d ed. Cambridge: Cambridge University Press.

Musgrave, Wayne M. 1923. *College fraternities.* New York: Interfraternity Conference.

Musgrove, Frank, and Roger Middleton. 1981. Rites of passage and the meaning of age in three contrasted social groups: Professional footballers, teachers, and Methodist ministers. *British Journal of Sociology* 32 (1): 39–55.

Nash, Dennison. 1995. Prospects for tourism study in anthropology. In *The future of anthropology: Its relevance to the contemporary world*, ed. Akbar Ahmed and Cris N. Shore, 179–202. London and Atlantic Highlands, NJ: Athlone Press.

Nash, Dennison, and Valene L. Smith. 1991. Anthropology and tourism. *Annals of Tourism Research* 18 (2): 12–25.

Newport, Kenneth G. C. 2006. *The Branch Davidians of Waco: The history and beliefs of an apocalyptic cult.* New York: Oxford University Press.

Nock, A. D. 1998 [1933]. *Conversion: The old and the new in religion from Alexander the Great to Augustine of Hippo.* Baltimore, MD: Johns Hopkins University Press.

Nolan, Mary Lee, and Sidney Nolan. 1989. *Christian pilgrimage in modern western Europe.* Chapel Hill: University of North Carolina Press.

Nowinski, Joseph K. 1999. *Family recovery and substance abuse: A twelve-step guide to treatment.* Thousand Oaks, CA: Sage Publications.

Oakley, Ann, and Susanne Houd. 1990. *Helpers in childbirth: Midwifery today.* New York: Hemisphere Publishing.

Oddie, Geoffrey A. 1997. Introduction. In *Religious conversion movements in South Asia: Continuities and change,* ed. Geoffrey A. Oddie, 1–13. Richmond, Surrey: Curzon.

Oldfield, David. 1996. The journey: An experimental rite of passage for modern adolescents. In *Crossroads: The quest for contemporary rites of passage,* ed. Louse Carus Mahdi, Nancy Geyer Christopher, and Michael Meade, 147–65. Chicago: Open Court.

Olson, R. Paul, and Bruce McBeath. 2002. Convergence and divergence. In *Religious theories of personality and psychotherapy: East meets West,* ed. R. Paul Olson, 359–408. New York: Haworth Press.

Parsons, Talcott, Robert F. Bales, with the collaboration of James Olds, Morris Zelditch, Jr., and Philip R. Slater. 1955. *Family, socialization and interaction process.* Glencoe, IL: Free Press.

Partridge, Christopher. 2003. Understanding UFO religion and abduction spiritualities. In *UFO religions,* ed. Christopher Partridge, 1–47. London: Routledge.

Patai, Raphael. 1978. Exorcism and xenoglossia among the Sufed Kabbalists. *Journal of American Folklore* 91 (361): 823–33.

Paulson, Ronald. 1976. Life as journey and as theater: Two eighteenth-century narrative structures. *New Literary History* 8 (1): 43–58.

Peace Corps. 1995. *To touch the world: The Peace Corps experience.* Washington, DC: The Corps.

Pear, T.H. 1961. *The moulding of modern man: A psychologist's view of information, persuasion and mental coercion today.* London: George Allen & Unwin.

Pearce, Philip L. 1982. *The social psychology of tourist behaviour.* Oxford: Pergamon Press.

Peters, Larry G. 1982. Trance, initiation, and psychotherapy in Tamang Shamanism. *American Ethnologist* 9 (1): 21–46.

Porter, J.R. 1974. Muhammad's journey to heaven. *Numen* 21: 164–80.

Ralph, Ruth O. 2005. Verbal definitions and visual models of recovery: Focus on the recovery model. In *Recovery in mental illness:*

Broadening our understanding of wellness, ed. Ruth O. Ralph and Patrick W. Corrigan, 131–46. Washington, DC: American Psychiatiric Association.

Rambo, Lewis R. 1993. *Understanding religious conversion*. New Haven, CT: Yale University Press.

Rapoport, Robert, and Rhona Rapoport. 1964. New light on the honeymoon. *Human Relations* 17: 33–56.

Reader, Ian. 2000. *Religious violence in contemporary Japan: The case of the Aum Shinrikyo*. Honolulu: University of Hawaii Press.

Redmon, Coates. 1986. *Come as you are: The Peace Corps story*. New York: Harcourt Brace Jovanovich.

Reed, Richard K. 2005. *Birthing fathers: The transformation of men in American rites of birth*. New Brunswick, NJ: Rutgers University Press.

Reeves, T. Zane. 1988. *The politics of the Peace Corps and VISTA*. Tuscaloosa: University of Alabama Press.

Reik, Theodor. 1976 [1931]. *Ritual: Psychoanalytic studies*. Trans. Douglas Bryan, with a preface by Sigmund Freud. New York: International Universities Press.

Reimer, Gwen Dianne. 1991. Packaging dreams: Canadian tour operators at work. *Annals of Tourism Research* 17 (4): 501–12.

Rice, Gerard T. 1985. *The bold experiment: JFK's Peace Corps*. Notre Dame, IN: University of Notre Dame Press.

Rieff, Philip. 2007. *Charisma: The gift of grace, and how it has been taken away from us*. New York: Pantheon Books.

Riley-Smith, Jonathan. 1986. *The First Crusade and the idea of crusading*. London: Athlone.

Rinschede, Gisbert. 1992. Forms of religious tourism. *Annals of Tourism Research* 19 (1): 251–67.

Robbins, Thomas. 1988. *Cults, converts, and charisma: The sociology of new religious movements*. London: Sage Publications.

Rosenberg, David. 2006. *Abraham: The first historical biography*. New York: Basic Books.

Rybczynski, Witold. 1991. *Waiting for the weekend*. New York: Viking.

Sadler, P.G. and Archer, B.H. 1975. The economic impact of tourism in developing countries. *Annals of Tourism Research* 3 (5): 15–32.

Saliba, John A. 1995. UFO contactee phenomena from a sociopsychological perspective: A review. In *The gods have landed: New religions from outer worlds,* ed. James R. Lewis, 207–50. Albany: State University of New York Press.

———. 2003a. *Understanding new religious movements.* 2d ed. Walnut Creek, CA: AltaMira Press.

———. 2003b. The psychology of UFO phenomena. In *UFO religions,* ed. Christopher Partridge, 319–45. London: Routledge.

Sallnow, Michael J. 1987. *Pilgrims of the Andes: Regional cults in Cusco.* Washington, DC: Smithsonian Institution Press.

Sanarov, Valerii I. 1981. On the nature and origin of flying saucers and little green men. *Current Anthropology* 22 (2): 163–67.

Sandelowski, Margarete. 1984. *Pain, pleasure, and American childbirth: From the twilight sleep to the Read Method, 1914–1960.* Westport, CN: Greenwood Press.

San Francisco Chronicle. 2007. At desert bacchanalia 20-year-olds romp and hip seniors marvel at a different world. *San Francisco Chronicle,* September 3, E-1.

Santino, Jack. 1985. On the nature of healing as a folk event. *Western Folklore* 44 (3): 153–67

Sanyika, Dadisi. 1996. Gang rites and rituals of initiation. In *Crossroads: The quest for contemporary rites of passage,* ed. Louise Carus Mahdi, Nancy Geyer Christopher, and Michel Meade, 115–24. Chicago: Open Court.

Sargant, William. 1957. *Battle for the mind: A physiology of conversion and brain-washing.* London: Heinemann.

Scheff, Thomas J. 1977. The distancing of emotion in ritual. *Current Anthropology* 18 (3): 483–505.

Schein, Edgar H., with Inge Schneier and Curtis H. Barker. 1961. *Coercive persuasion: A socio-psychological analysis of the "brainwashing" of American civilian prisoners by the Chinese Communists.* New York: W.W. Norton.

Schultz, Duane P. 1965. *Sensory restriction: Effects on behavior.* New York: Academic Press.

Scott, John Finley. 1965. The American college sorority: Its role in class and ethnic endogamy. *American Sociological Review* 30 (4): 514–26.

Seale, Clive. 1998. *Constructing death: The sociology of dying and bereavement.* Cambridge: Cambridge University Press.

Shea, Donald R. 1966. The preparation of Peace Corps volunteers for overseas service: Challenge and response. *Annals of the American Academy of Political and Social Science: The Peace Corps,* ed. Thorsten Sellin, 365: 29–45. Philadelphia: American Academy of Political and Social Science.

Silverman, E. K. 2001. Time, anthropology of. In *International encyclopedia of the social and behavioral sciences,* ed. Neil J. Smelser and Paul B. Baltes, 23: 5682–86. Oxford: Elsevier.

Singer Margaret T., and Richard Ofshe. 1990. Thought reform programs and the production of psychiatric casualties. *Psychiatric Annals* 20: 188–93.

Slater, Philip. 1963. On social regression. *American Sociological Review* 28 (2): 339–63.

Slotkin, James S. 1956. *The peyote religion: A study in Indian-White relations.* Glencoe, IL: Free Press.

Smelser, Neil J. 1959. *Social change in the industrial revolution: An application of theory to the British cotton industry.* Chicago: University of Chicago Press.

———. 1962. *Theory of collective behavior.* New York: Free Press.

———. 1963. *The sociology of economic life.* Englewood Cliffs, NJ: Prentice-Hall.

———. 1976a. *The sociology of economic life.* 2d ed. Englewood Cliffs, NJ: Prentice-Hall.

———. 1976b. *Comparative methods in the social sciences.* Englewood Cliffs, NJ: Prentice-Hall.

———. 1991. *Social paralysis and social change: British working-class education in the nineteenth century.* Berkeley and New York: University of California Press and the Russell Sage Foundation.

———. 1993. *Effective committee service.* Newbury Park, CA: Sage Publications.

———. 1998a. The rational and the ambivalent in the social sciences. *American Sociological Review* 63 (1): 1–15.

———. 1998b. *The social edges of psychoanalysis.* Berkeley: University of California Press.

———. 2000a. Director's report. *Annual Report, Center for Advance Study in the Behavioral Sciences.* Stanford, CA.

———. 2000b. Sociological and interdisciplinary adventures: A personal odyssey. *American Sociologist* 31 (4): 5–33.

———. 2007. *The faces of terrorism: Behavioral and social dimensions.* Princeton, NJ: Princeton University Press.

Smith, Valene L. 1989. Introduction. In *Hosts and guests: The anthropology of tourism,* ed. Valene L. Smith, 2d ed., 1–17. Philadelphia: University of Pennsylvania Press.

———. 1992. The quest in guest. *Annals of Tourism Research* 19 (1): 1–17.

Smith, Valene L., and William R. Eadington (eds.). 1992. *Tourism alternatives: Potentials and problems in the development of tourism.* Philadelphia: University of Pennsylvania Press.

Snow, David A., and Richard Machalek. 1984. The sociology of conversion. *Annual Review of Sociology* 10: 167–90.

Solomon, Trudy. 1983. Programming and deprogramming the Moonies: Social psychology applied. In *The brainwashing/deprogramming controversy: Sociological, psychological, legal and historical perspectives,* ed. David G. Bromley and James T. Richardson, 163–82. New York: Edwin Mellen Press.

Starbuck, Edwin Diller. 1900. *The psychology of religion: An empirical study of the growth of religious consciousness.* London: Walter Scott Publishing.

Stark, Rodney, and William Sims Bainbridge. 1985. *The future of religion: Secularization, revival and cult formation.* Berkeley: University of California Press.

Stein, D. 1988. Lone Ranger. *Escape* (October), 13.

Stein, Jan O., and Murray Stein. 1987. Psychotherapy, initiation, and the midlife transition. In *Betwixt and between: Patterns of masculine and feminine transition*, ed. Louise Carus Mahdi, Steven Foster, and Meredith Little, 287–303. La Salle, IL: Open Court.

Stevens, Anthony. 1982. *Archetype: A natural history of the self.* London: Routledge and Kegan Paul.

Stouffer, Samuel A., Edward A. Suchman, Leland C. DeVinney, Shirley A. Star, and Robin M. Williams, Jr. 1949. *The American soldier: Adjustment during army life.* Vol. 1. Princeton, NJ: Princeton University Press.

Strathern, Andrew, and Pamela J. Stewart. 1999. *Curing and healing: Medical anthropology in global perspective.* Durham, NC: Carolina Academic Press.

Stromberg, Peter G. 1993. *Language and self-transformation: A study of the Christian conversion narrative.* Cambridge: Cambridge University Press.

Stuart, Susan. 1984. *On longing: Narratives of the miniature, the gigantic, the souvenir, the collection.* Durham, NC: Duke University Press.

Suedfeld, Peter. 1980. Introduction. In *Restricted environmental stimulation: Research and clinical applications,* by Peter Suedfeld, with contributions by Henry B. Adams, Roderick A. Borrie, and Richard C. Tees, 1–27. New York: John Wiley & Sons.

Tambiah, Stanley Jeyaraja. 1985. *Culture, thought, and social action: An anthropological perspective.* Cambridge: MA: Harvard University Press.

Taylor, Donald. 1999. Conversion: Inward, outward and awkward. In *Religious conversion: Contemporary practices and controversies,* ed. Christopher Lamb and M. Darrol Bryant, 35–50. London: Cassell.

Textor, Robert B. 1966. Introduction. In *Cultural frontiers of the Peace Corps,* ed. Robert B. Textor, 1–14. Cambridge, MA: MIT Press.

Thalmann, William G. 1992. *The Odyssey: An epic of return.* New York: Twayne Publishers.

Thompson, David. 1974. *Dante's epic journeys.* Baltimore, MD: Johns Hopkins University Press.

Thompson, J. Mark, and Candace Cotlove. 2005. *The therapeutic process: A clinical introduction to psychodynamic psychotherapy*. Lanham, MD: Jason Aronson.

Thompson, Joyce, and Phyllis Bridges. 1971. West Texas wedding cars. *Western Folklore* 30 (2): 123–26.

Tocqueville, Alexis de. 1968. *Alexis de Tocqueville: Journeys to England and Ireland*. Ed. J. P. Mayer. Garden City, NY: Doubleday.

Toner, J. P. 1995. *Leisure and ancient Rome*. Cambridge: Polity Press.

Tribe, John. 2005. *The economics of recreation, leisure and tourism*. 3d ed. Amsterdam: Elsevier.

Trow, Katherine Bernhardi. 1998. *Habits of mind: The experimental college program at Berkeley*. Berkeley, CA: Institute of Governmental Studies Press.

Turkovic, Silvana, Johannes E. Hovens, and Rudolf Gregurek. 2004. Strengthening psychological health in war victims and refugees. In *Broken spirits: The treatment of traumatized asylum seekers, refugees, war and torture victims*, ed. John P. Wilson and Boris Drozded, 221–42. New York: Brunner-Routledge.

Turner, Victor. 1969. *The ritual process: Structure and anti-structure*. Chicago: Aldine Publishing.

———. 1974. *Dramas, fields, and metaphors: Symbolic action in human society*. Ithaca, NY: Cornell University Press.

———. 1977. Death and dying in the pilgrimage process. In *Religious encounters with death: Insights from the history and anthropology of religions*, ed. Frank R. Reynolds and Earle H. Waugh, 24–39. University Park: Pennsylvania State University Press.

———. 1979. *Process, performance, and pilgrimage: A study of comparative symbology*. New Delhi: Concept Publishing Company.

———. 1982. *From ritual to theatre: The human seriousness of play*. New York: Performing Arts Journal Publications.

———. 1987. Betwixt and between: The liminal period in rites of passage. In *Betwixt and between: Patterns of masculine and feminine initiation*, ed. Carus Mahdi, Steven Foster, and Meredith Little, 3–19. La Salle, IL: Open Court.

———. 1990. Are there universals of performance in myth, ritual, and drama? In *By means of performance: Intercultural studies of theatre and ritual,* ed. Richard Schechner and Willa Appel, 8–18. Cambridge: Cambridge University Press.

———. 1992. *Blazing the trail: Way marks in the exploration of symbols.* Ed. Edith Turner. Tucson: University of Arizona Press.

Underwood, Alfred Clair. 1925. *Conversion: Christian and non-Christian: A comparative and psychological study.* London: George Allen & Unwin.

Utley, Francis Lee. 1974. Boccaccio, Chaucer, and the international popular tale. *Western Folklore* 33 (3): 181–201.

van der Veer, Peter (ed.). 1996. *Conversion to modernities: The globalization of Christianity.* London: Routledge.

van Gennep, Arnold. 1960 [1909]. *The rites of passage.* Trans. Monika B. Vizedom and Gabrielle L. Caffee, introduction by Solon T. Kimball. Chicago: University of Chicago Press.

Vida, Vendela. 1999. *Girls on the verge: Debutant dips, gang drive-bys, and other initiations.* New York: St. Martin's Press.

Vogel, Dan. 1974. A lexicon rhetoricae for "journey" literature. *College English* 36 (2): 185–89.

Wallace, Anthony F.C. 1966. *Religion: An anthropological view.* New York: Random House.

Walton, John R. 1981. The demand for working class seaside holidays in Victorian England. *The Economic History Review,* n.s., 34 (2): 349–65.

Wamsley, Gary L. 1972. Contrasting institutions of air force socialization: happenstance or bellwether? *American Journal of Sociology* 78 (2): 399–417.

Watts, Alan. 1961. *Psychotherapy, East and West.* New York: Pantheon Books.

Waugh, Earl. 1996. Persistent fragments: The trajectories of reincarnation in Islam. In *Concepts of transmigration: Perspectives on reincarnation,* ed. Steven J. Kaplan, 55–85. Lewiston, NY: Edwin Mellen Press.

Weber, Max. 1949. "Objectivity" in social science and social policy policy. In *The methodology of the social sciences,* ed. and trans. Edward

H. Shils and Henry A. Finch, with a foreword by Edward A. Shils, 49–112. New York: Free Press.

———. 1968. *Economy and society: An outline of interpretive sociology.* Ed. Guenther Roth and Claus Wittich, 3 vols. New York: Bedminster Press.

Webster, Hutton. 1968 [1908]. *Primitive secret societies: A study in early politics and religion.* New York: Octagon Books

Weiss, Joseph, and Harold Sampson. 1986. *The psychoanalytic process: Theory, clinical observation, and empirical research.* New York: Guilford Press.

Weitz, Mark A. 2003. "Shoot them all": Chivalry, honour and the Confederate Army Officer Corps. In *The chivalric ethos and the development of military professionalism,* ed. D.J.B. Trim, 321–47. Leiden: Brill.

Whitehead, Harriet. 1987. *Renunciation and reformulation: A study of conversion in an American sect.* Ithaca, NY: Cornell University Press.

Williams Christine L. 1989. *Gender differences at work: Women and men in nontraditional occupations.* Berkeley: University of California Press.

Williams, Clover Nolan. 1994. The bachelor's transgression: Identity and difference in the bachelor party. *Journal of American Folklore* 107 (2): 106–20.

Winchester, Hilary P.M , Pauline M. McGuirk, and Kathryn Everett. 1999. Schoolies week as a rite of passage: A study of celebration and control. In *Embodied geographies: Spaces, bodies and rites of passage,* ed. Elizabeth Kenworthy Teather, 59–77. London: Routledge.

Wojcik, Daniel. 2003. Apocalyptic and millenarian aspects of American UFOism. In *UFO religions,* ed. Christopher Partridge, 274–300. London: Routledge

Woodward, Robert H. 1957. The journey motif in Whitman and Tennyson. *Modern Language Notes* 72 (1): 26–27.

Worsley, Peter M. 1957. *The trumpet shall sound: A study of 'cargo' cults in Melanesia.* London: MacGibbon & Kee.

Wright, Stuart A. 1987. *Leaving cults: The dynamics of defection.* Washington, DC: Society for the Scientific Study of Religion.

Wylie, Laurence. 1957. Ordeal in Gordes. *French Review* 30 (4): 259–64.

Yalom, Irvin D, with Molyn Leszez. 2005. *The theory and practice of group psychotherapy.* 5th ed. New York: Basic Books.

Yardley, Roland J., Harry J. Thie, Kevin Brancato, and Megan Abbott. 2004. *An analysis of sabbatical leaves for navy surface warfare officers.* Santa Monica, CA: RAND, National Defense Research Institute.

Yarnold, Edward. 1994. *The awe-inspiring rites of initiation: The origins of the RICA.* Collegeville, MN: Liturgical Press.

Yiannakis, Andrew and Heather Gibson. 1992. Roles tourists play. *Annals of Tourism Research* 19 (2): 287–303.

Yoke, Carl B. 1987. Phoenix from the ashes rising: An introduction. In *Phoenix from the ashes: The literature of the remade world,* ed. Carl B. Yoke, 1–12. New York: Greenwood Press.

Yu, Anthony C. 1983. Two literary examples of religious pilgrimage: The "Commedia" and "The Journey to the West." *History of Religions* 22 (3): 202–30.

Zablocki, Benjamin. 2001. 'Towards a demystified and disinterested scientific theory of brainwashing. In *Misunderstanding cults: Searching for objectivity in a controversial field,* ed. Benjamin Zablocki and Thomas Robbins, 159–214. Toronto: University of Toronto Press.

Zamiatin, D.N. 2002. Travel images: Social interiorization of space. *Sotsiologicheskie Issledovaniya* 2: 12–20.

Zuckerman, Marvin. 1969. Variables affecting deprivation results. In *Sensory deprivation: Fifteen years of research,* ed. John P. Zubek, 47–84. New York: Appleton-Century-Crofts.

INDEX

Abraham's wanderings, in Bible, 3
academic world, 118–20; academic committees, xiii; alumni
solidarity, 18; author's experiences, 54–55; college as rite
of passage, 118–19; collegiate
myth, 118, 120; *communitas* of
collegiate years, 119; graduate school, 193; graduation
ceremonies, 120; institutes
for advanced study, 129–36;
liminality of collegiate years,
119; massification of higher
education, 119–20; undergraduate experiences, 24, 118–20. *See
also* education-abroad programs;
sabbatical leaves; *specific academic
institutions*
accountability programs. *See* military-style corrective programs
Adamski, George, 177–78
adolescents: alcohol at youth beach
gatherings, 161–62; ensuring

masculinity of young men, 158,
185, 192; religious conversions
of, 80. *See also* rites of passage,
of adolescent males
adventures: defined, 6; uncertainty
and danger associated with, 16
Adventures of Huckleberry Finn (M.
Twain), 4, 6
Aetherius Society, 178
Africa: colonial and missionary
pressures, 77; UFO sightings,
174
"airship fever," 173
alcohol and alcoholism: altered
states of consciousness, 137;
fraternity and sorority practices, 182; sensory deprivation
therapy, 202; sobriety as conversion journey, 84
Alcoholics Anonymous, 142,
149–50, 198
Alice in Wonderland (L. Carroll), 4
alien abductions, 173, 176–79

altered states of consciousness.
See trances
alumni, group solidarity and mutual
loyalty, 18
Alves, J., 160–61
ambition, limitations associated
with, 55
ambivalence: author's feelings of,
52; feelings about death, 215;
social destructuring and, 16;
toward dependency and independence, 217
American Family Foundation,
203–4
American Psychiatric Association,
diagnostic manuals, 141
American Society for Psychoprophylactics in Obstetrics, 168
American Soldier, 189
American Way of Death (J. Mitford),
171
Andes pilgrimages, 69
Annals of Tourism Research, 101
anticult movement, 203–4
"antistructure" concept, 12, 69–70,
218
Arnold, Kenneth, 175
ashes, scattering, 171
Association for Childbirth Education, 168
Association of Funeral Directors, 171
Aum Shinrikyo, sirin gas attack, 88
authenticity, tourist theme, 105,
106, 107

Bach, G. R., 149
Bainbridge, W. S., 81, 82
"BAMS" or "bammies," 187
Bank, Scientology principal,
141–42, 152–53

baptism: history of, 63–64, 77; sym-
bolism of, 64, 100–101, 163–64
bar mitzvahs, 62–63, 158
Baumer, I., 66–67
"beat generation," *communitas* values
of, 70
behavior-modification therapy,
148–49
Bellagio Study and Conference
Center, xii–xiii, 50–52, 130,
132–33, 135
bereavement and grief, 150, 171,
215
Berger, P., 212
Berkeley, California. *See* University
of California, Berkeley
Bernstein, J. S., 158
Bettelheim, B., 60
Bible, Old and New Testaments:
Abraham's wanderings, 3;
Christ's ascent into heaven, 3;
Christ's wanderings, 3; conversion experiences, 3, 76–77;
Ezekiel's wheel, 173; journey of
the magi, 3; Moses's flight from
Egypt, 3
Bion, W. R., 145
birth to death: finite nature of life,
10–11; metaphoric elaboration,
20. *See also* death and death ritu-
als; pregnancy and childbirth;
rebirth
black power/black separatist move-
ments, 94
boredom, effects of, 198
Boston Psychoanalytic Institute, 41
Braatly, T., 145
brainwashing. *See* indoctrination
Branch Davidian assault, 88
Bremer, T. S., 72

77–78, 81–82; to Christianity, 3, 75–89; death and rebirth symbolism, 216; defined, 7; deprogramming converts, 25, 203–4; essence, variations, and controversies, 75–78; examples, 77; genuineness of, 84–85; metaphors for, 20, 75; psychological preconditions for, 79–82, 141; psychological process of, 82–85; recent developments in thinking about, 85–88; religious transport, 22; to Scientology, 153; similarity to psychotherapy, 81, 83, 84, 88, 138–39, 147–48; sobriety as conversion journey, 84; social settings for, 78–79, 84, 89; voluntary vs. coerced, 85, 87–88

Cook's Tour, 99

correctional boot camp. *See* military-style corrective programs

Cosmic Masters, 178

Cottle, Thomas, 22

counseling. *See* psychotherapy

countercultural movements: of 1960s and 1970s, 87; black power/black separatist movements, 94; Freedom Summer and, 94; psychedelic drug culture, 7, 79. *See also* civil rights movement; new religions

country and western music, movement motifs, 5–6

cowboys, symbolism of, 5

Cruise, Tom, 152

Crusades, 5, 14, 67, 70–71. *See also* pilgrimages, religious

Cullen, E., 150

cults. *See* new religions

cultural and mythological traditions, of adolescent passage ceremonies, 61–62

cultural odyssey themes, 2

cultural values: of colonizers, 78–79; impact of mass tourism on natives, 110

danger. *See* uncertainty and danger

Dann, G.M.S., 104

darkness, rituals and rites associated with, 62

Darkness at Noon (A. Koestler), 194

Davis-Floyd, R.E., 166

Dawson, L.L., 88

death and death rituals, 169–72; adolescent rites of passage symbolism, 61–62; ambivalent feelings about death, 215; hospice movement, 172; medicalization of death, 170; odysseys that address death, 214–16; religious associations, 23, 65–66, 170, 172, 215; rituals associated with, 22, 24–25; scattering ashes, 65; similarity to birthing rituals, 170, 171; symbolism for death, 62, 102, 117, 215–16; undertakers and funeral directors, 170–72; as "unscheduled status passage," 11; urban gang member initiations and, 160–61; van Gennep's studies, 21. *See also* rebirth

death awareness movement, 171–72

deautomatization, psychotherapeutic process, 146

debutante dips, 162–63

Decameron (Boccaccio), 4

deconverts, defined, 203–4

degradation and humiliation:
Alcoholics Anonymous and, 198;
of fraternity/sorority initiations,
183–84; of military socialization,
185, 186–87, 197–98; of military-
style corrective programs,
191–92; of oral examinations,
193; by religious orders, 197–98
Delicate Arch (Utah), pilgrimages
to, 74
Deliverance, frontier myth, 104
dependence and independence,
odysseys as oscillation between,
216–18
deprogramming of cult members,
25, 203–4
destabilization of self, conversion
phase, 82–83
destructuring, social: colonialism
and, 78–79; conversion role,
82–83; on cruise ships, 106–7;
of education-abroad programs,
122–23; element of Chinese
thought control, 197; as encounter group strategy, 151; of
fraternity/sorority initiations,
184; of institutes for advanced
study, 132, 134–35; mass
tourism and, 111; of military
socialization, 186; of military-
style corrective programs, 191;
names for, 11; odyssey role,
11–12, 206–8; of pilgrimages,
68–69; in psychotherapy, 139,
143–46; of sabbatical leaves,
126; of sensory deprivation
experiments, 200; of Society
of Fellows, 38–39; as symbolic
death, 71; uncertainty and danger associated with, 14, 16

de Tocqueville, Alexis, 107–8
Deutsch, S., 121–22
devil. *See* evil and devil
discrimination: fraternity and
sorority practices as, 182;
psychological basis of, 212
disequilibrium (illness, suffering,
unhappiness): as precondition to conversion, 79–82; as
precondition to psychotherapy,
139, 141–43. *See also* ordeals;
uncertainty and danger
Downton, J. V., 80
Drake, Sir Frances, 5
dramatic performances, as rituals,
22, 157
driver's license, attaining as rite of
passage, 159
drugs and drug addiction: altered
states of consciousness, 137;
pharmacological treatments for
psychological disorders, 139;
psychedelic drugs, 7, 79
du Bois, C., 123
Durant, Will, 152
Durkheim, Émile, 21

Eade, J., 108
eclipse of sun or moon, rituals and
rites associated with, 62
"Edison stars," 174
Education Abroad Program,
author's involvement, 27, 47–48,
118, 121–24
education-abroad programs,
120–25; adaptation process,
121–22; destructuring, 122–23;
international perspective developed through, 123; liminality of, 121; personal growth,

destructuring, 69–70; to Solutré, 73; tourism and, 73–74, 96
pilgrimages, religious, 66–74;
death and rebirth symbolism,
71; examples, 4, 6; history
of, 66; to Mecca, 71–72; of
Mormons, 72–73; routinization
and commercialization of, 23,
67; as "structure-confirming"
events, 69–70; as tourism,
72–74, 100–101, 108; uncertainty and danger associated
with, 14, 70–71; van Gen-
nep's studies, 22, 101. *See also*
Crusades
Pilgrim's Progress (G. Bunyan), 4, 6
Portuguese boys, rites of passage,
161
postcatastrophic literature, 4–5
postliminal separation from routine
life, 22
postpartum depression, ritual processes for, 157–58
pregnancy and childbirth: father's
role, 166, 167–69; home
births, 164, 169; impregnation by extraterrestrials, 177;
natural childbirth movement,
167–69; postpartum depression, 157–58; rituals/rites
associated with, 21, 23, 24–25,
58, 165–67; similarity to death
rituals, 170, 171; technological
birth model, 163–69; uncertainty and danger associated
with, 165–66, 167–68; womb
symbolism, 62
prehistoric people, funeral rites, 65
preliminal separation from routine
life, 21–22

prison inmates: indoctrination
techniques, 198; military-style
corrective programs, 190–92;
resocialization, 25; solitary
confinement, 193; therapeutic
methods, 150
professional training roles, 25
Protestantism: Catholic conversions to/from, 77–78; conversions between denominations,
77–78, 81–82
protest movements: anti–Vietnam
War, 87, 94; black power / black
separatist movements, 94;
civil rights movement, 24,
57, 73, 87, 93–96; *communitas*
values of, 70; Gandhi's protest
marches, 73; Million Man
March, 73
psychedelic drug culture: predis-
position to cults and, 79; trip
terminology, 7
psychological and social space: of
coercive odyssey experiences,
25; of honeymoon experi-
ence, 113; impact of too much
variation on, 211–12; oscillation between dependence and
independence, 216–18; Peace
Corps experience, 93; preconditions for conversion, 79–82,
88; psychological features of
odysseys, 15–21; psychological
vs. social characteristics, 15–16;
social features of odysseys,
10–15; social ties and conversion, 84, 89; UFO sightings/
alien abductions, 173, 174–75,
176, 178; variation among tourist experiences, 102–9

psychotherapy: for advanced study participants, 136; author's experiences, 40–45; bereavement and grief, 150; clientele, 140; to compensate for transitional rituals, 157, 158; deprogramming of cult members, 25, 203–4; destructuring process, 139, 143–46; education-abroad students and, 123–24; encounter group movement, 150–52; finite nature of, 11, 42; goals of, 140; group therapy, 144–45; history of, 139; liminality, 139; mandatory participation, 142; methods, 140; nature of process, 146–48; negative elements, 42–43, 44; pastoral counseling, 138–39; pharmacological treatments, 139; preconditions for, 139, 141–43; regression process, 83; restructuring, 139, 148–49; Scientology as, 141–42, 152–53; sensory deprivation techniques, 201–2; settings, 140; similarity to religious conversion, 81, 83, 84, 88, 138–39, 147–48; similarity to shamanism, 138–39; theoretical frameworks, 140, 141–42, 146–47; therapist taboos, 145; uncertainty and danger associated with, 42, 145, 147; for victims of torture and violence, 150. *See also* healing and therapy journeys

purgatory, as liminal period, 65

quests, definition and examples, 6
Quine, Willard van Orman, 38

racial relations: black power/black separatist movements, 94; colonialism and, 2, 72, 78–79. *See also* civil rights movement

Radcliffe Institute for Advanced Study, 130, 133

Raelian Church, 178

Ralph, R. O., 145

rebirth: adolescent rites of passage symbolism, 61; alien abduction narratives, 179; baptism symbolism, 64–65; conversion symbolism, 76–77, 80; element of Chinese thought control, 196; movement from structure to liminality as, 215–16; pilgrimage symbolism, 71; regeneration journeys, 7; rites of passage symbolism, 61; rituals associated with, 22; stag party symbolism, 117; tourist symbolism, 100–101, 102; urban gang member initiations as, 160–61

re-education, element of Chinese thought control, 196

regeneration: alien abductions as, 177; conversions as, 7; defined, 193; element of Chinese thought control, 196; encounter groups as, 151; fraternity/sorority initiations as, 183; Freedom Summer as, 96; in human development, 209; military socialization as, 187–88; Peace Corps as, 91; as psychological journey, 7; tourism as, 100–101

regression, 83, 146

Reik, T., 61

reincorporation: following baptism, 64–65; tourist's reentry, 101,

rites of passage (*continued*):
98, 155; marriage rituals, 21,
111–12; for midlife transitions, 157, 158; pain associated
with, 181–82; Peace Corps, 91;
pregnancy and childbirth, 165;
as rituals, 58; Senior Passage
course, 160; sensory deprivation elements, 202; Southern
May Day ceremonies, 162; stage
parties, 117; of urban gangs,
160–61, 163; van Gennep's studies, 21–22, 113; VisionQuest,
160; Walkabout Course, 160;
youth beach gatherings, 161–62.
See also death and death rituals;
initiation rituals
rites of passage, of adolescent
males, 23; anthropology and
history of, 57–62; bar mitzvahs,
62–63, 158; consequences of
failure to undergo, 59; as death
and rebirth, 61; decline of,
158; mandatory participation,
58, 67; pain and mutilation
associated with, 60–61, 181–82;
Portuguese boys, 161; religious
worldview of people, 61–62;
sacred place for ceremony,
59–60; secrecy, 60; status transition features, 58–59; symbolism
of, 61–62; temporary license
elements, 60; tribal elders'
control of, 59
ritual possession, 23
rituals, 169; behavior regulated
by, 218; birth to death, 10–11,
22, 24–25; classifications of,
58; compared to tourism,
100–101; decline of traditional,

140, 157–58, 207; defined, 7;
distancing of emotions through,
214; Durkheim's theory of, 21;
Eliade's studies of, 22; homogenization of social relationships
through, 13; oral examinations
as, 193; pain associated with,
181–82; positive and negative
attitudes toward, 156; for pregnancy and childbirth, 21, 23–25,
58, 165–71; repetitions of, 211;
secular attitudes toward, 85;
traditional vs. modern expressions of, 157–59; universal value
of, 156–59; van Gennep's studies
of, 22. *See also* death and death
rituals; marriage rituals
ritual secrecy, 60
road images, 4, 5–6
Robinson Crusoe (D. Defoe), 4, 193
Rockefeller Foundation, Bellagio
Study and Conference Center,
xii–xiii, 50–52, 130, 132–33, 135
"rockets," UFO sightings, 174
Roswell, New Mexico, UFO sightings, 176
Roughing It (M. Twain), 4
"rushing." *See* fraternities and
sororities, initiation rituals
Russell Sage Foundation, 48–50,
130, 135
Russia. *See* Soviet Union and Russia
Rustique Olivette, 40

sabbatical leaves, 125–29; author's
experiences, 45–47, 49–50;
defined, 127; defining features,
126–27; destructuring, 11–12;
history of, 125; at institutes for
advanced study, 129–36; leave

shock treatment, military socialization as, 185–86

sin: Adam and Eve's primal sin, 64; alien abductions to rescue humanity from, 177; conversions to save believers from, 76–77, 80, 141; moral regeneration element of Chinese thought control, 196, 197. *See also* evil and devil

Singer, M.T., 202

Six Feet Under, 171

Slater, Philip, 22, 113

Smelser, Neil J.: Bellagio Study and Conference Center, xii–xiii, 50–52, 135; British Museum Library, 39; Center for Advanced Study in the Behavioral Sciences, 27, 48, 50, 118, 128–29; *communitas* experience, 107; early years, 29–30; Education Abroad directorship, 27, 47–48, 118, 121–24; at end of travel experience, 109; "getting away from it all" experience, 102–3; Harvard, 16–18, 30–31; Library of Congress, 52–54, 135; Oxford, 35–37; personal odysseys of, 28–56; psychoanalysis, 40–45; Russell Sage Foundation, 48–50, 135; sabbatical leave, 45–47; Salzburg Seminar in American Studies, 32–35; Society of Fellows, 16–18, 37–40, 136; University of California, Berkeley, 38

Smith, V.L., 98–99

Smith College, education-abroad program, 120–21

smoking cessation, sensory deprivation therapy, 202

Snow, D.A., 84, 85

social-intensifying rituals, 58

"social limitation" experiments. *See* sensory deprivation experiments

"social regression," of honeymoons, 113

social relationships: homogenization of, 13; influences on psychological processes, 15–16; social features of odysseys, 10–15; social ties and conversion, 84, 89. See also *communitas*; destructuring, social; psychological and social space

social science: experimental models, 26–27; sociology of habits and personal styles, 212; sociology of religion, 21

Society of Fellows: applicant emotions, 16–18, 136; author's experiences, 37–40

solidarity. *See communitas*

solitary confinement: in prisons, 193. *See also* isolation (social and psychological)

Solutré, pilgrimage to, 73

sororities. *See* fraternities and sororities

South Africa, UFO sightings, 174

souvenirs, tourism and, 105–6, 108

Soviet Union and Russia: cold war fear of, 175, 195; military socialization, 188–89; purge trails, 87, 194, 196, 197, 199; UFO sightings and, 174; Zamiatin's travel journeys, 4

space and time elements of odysseys, 218–20

space odysseys, 4

specialness of odyssey experience,
14–15; author's experiences, 52;
collegiate years, 119; diluted by
repeating experience, 52, 211;
education-abroad programs, 19;
institutes for advanced study,
133–35; Peace Corps, 91–92;
Society of Fellows, 39, 136
sports events, as rituals, 157
"spy mission" sightings, 174
stag parties. *See* bridal and bachelor
parties
Stanford University, Center for Advanced Study in the Behavioral
Sciences, 27, 48, 50, 128–30, 133
Stark, R., 81, 82
stereotyping, psychological basis
of, 212
Stevens, A., 158
stimulus deprivation experiments. *See*
sensory deprivation experiments
Stin, J.O. and M., 157, 158
structural changes in personality, 22
"structure-confirming" events,
pilgrimages as, 69–70
student activism: Freedom Summer, 24, 57, 93–96; free speech
movement, 94
Student Non-Violent Coordinating
Committee, 24, 57, 93–96
students. *See* academic world;
education-abroad programs
"success rates," of odyssey experience, 19–20
Suedfeld, P., 201, 210
suicide, 215
summer camps, finite nature of,
10–11
Summer Project. *See* Freedom
Summer

survivors of adventures or calamities,
group solidarity and mutual
loyalty, 18, 21
Synanon, 87

Tabernacle Choir, 73
Tambiah, S.J., 11
technological rituals, 58
"teeny-boppers," *communitas* values
of, 70
Tempest (W. Shakespeare), 4
Temple Square, Salt Lake City
(Utah), 72–73
Tennyson, Alfred Lord, 4
Thalmann, W.G., 8–9
theosophy, UFO religions and,
177–78
"therapeutic alliance," between
psychotherapist and client, 145
therapeutic rituals, 58
therapy. *See* healing and therapy
journeys; psychotherapy
time and space elements of odysseys, 218–20
Tohono O'odham Nation, "man in
the maze" motif, 2, 3
Tombstone, Arizona, frontier myth,
104
Tom Jones (H. Fielding), 4
torture and violence: Soviet purge
trails, 87, 194, 196, 197; treating
victims of, 150. *See also* ordeals
trances (altered states of consciousness): psychedelic drug
culture, 7; in psychotherapeutic process, 147; shamanistic
practices, 137–38; substance-
induced, 137
transference, psychotherapeutic
process, 146

Text:	10/15 Janson
Display:	Janson
Compositor:	Integrated Book Technology
Printer:	Integrated Book Technology